BuddyPress
FOR
DUMMIES®

BuddyPress FOR DUMMIES®

by Lisa Sabin-Wilson

Wiley Publishing, Inc.

BuddyPress For Dummies®

Published by
Wiley Publishing, Inc.
111 River Street
Hoboken, NJ 07030-5774

www.wiley.com

WILEY

About the Author

Lisa Sabin-Wilson is a creative designer and owner of E.Webscapes Design Studio (`www.ewebscapes.com`) and has worked hard at providing her clients with custom designed WordPress blogs and Web sites since 2003. Lisa is a frequent speaker at WordCamps and other national conferences, such as South by Southwest Interactive and meet ups local to her Southeastern Wisconsin home, like Milwaukee's Web development group, Web414. Lisa is highly regarded as a WordPress expert who specializes in helping users take full control over their Web publishing efforts through the use of the WordPress platform. She reaches thousands of people worldwide with her WordPress services, skills, and experience.

Lisa is the author of the popular *WordPress For Dummies*, first published in 2007. Her experience and knowledge of BuddyPress came from the rapidly emerging popularity of the platform; as more and more of her own clients started requesting BuddyPress integration on their Web sites, Lisa had no choice but to dig right in and figure out what it was all about! She's glad she did — it's a dynamic addition to any WordPress-powered Web site.

Lisa operates a few blogs online, all of which are powered by WordPress. Her personal blog (`lisasabin-wilson.com`) has been online since February of 2002 and her design business, E.Webscapes (`ewebscapes.com`), has been online since 1999. She also operates a successful Web hosting service, BlogsAbout Hosting (`blogsabout.com`), which caters to blogs and bloggers on a global scale, with an emphasis on WordPress users.

When she is not designing, or consulting with her clients, you can usually find her either at her favorite coffee shop sipping espresso, on a mountaintop somewhere hitting the slopes with her family, or 100 feet beneath the ocean waters, scuba diving with her husband and swimming with the fishes.

Lisa is actively involved in online social communities and you can find her on Twitter: @LisaSabinWilson or Facebook at `http://facebook.com/lisa-sabinwilson`.

Dedication

My family deserves all of the credit, for their love, support, and encouragement. My husband, Chris Wilson, gets an extra mention for being my rock and my reliable sounding board.

Author's Acknowledgments

When people use free and open software for community use, the people that spend countless hours and days developing the software sometimes get lost in the excitement. Because BuddyPress is incapable of running without the WordPress MU software, the first kudos go out to Matt Mullenweg, the founder of WordPress, and Donncha OCaoimh, the lead developer of the WordPress MU platform.

Andy Peatling is the lead developer of the BuddyPress project and has been the driving force behind development and community involvement. BuddyPress is truly a project driven by the community; Andy, and his team in the BuddyPress Forums (`http://buddypress.org/forums`), really does listen to user feedback, testers, and reports to improve existing features — and build new ones — for BuddyPress. Andy is also my technical editor for this book, so special thanks to him for keeping me on track.

To every WordPress and BuddyPress plugin developer and theme designer who donates his or her time, skills, and knowledge to provide the user community with invaluable tools that help us create dynamic Web sites, thank you a million times! And to the hundreds of volunteers and testers who destroy all those pesky pre-release bugs for each and every new version release — your time and efforts are so very appreciated.

Special thanks to Amy Fandrei, my acquisitions editor — an author could not ask for a better, or more supportive, publishing partner. Big thanks to Chris Morris, Brian Walls, and other editors from Wiley Publishing who were involved in this project for their support, assistance, and guidance.

To my family and friends, some of whom I have neglected during the process of writing this book, thank you for not abandoning me. Also, to my clients, many of whom showed incredible patience and encouragement during the months of writing these chapters.

Finally, thanks to my family — my husband, Chris; my son, Ben; my daughter, Melissa and my parents, Don and Penny Sabin — for their support for this book, and in life.

Publisher's Acknowledgments

We're proud of this book; please send us your comments at http://dummies.custhelp.com. For other comments, please contact our Customer Care Department within the U.S. at 877-762-2974, outside the U.S. at 317-572-3993, or fax 317-572-4002.

Some of the people who helped bring this book to market include the following:

Acquisitions and Editorial

Sr. Project Editor: Christopher Morris

Acquisitions Editor: Amy Fandrei

Copy Editor: Brian Walls

Technical Editor: Andy Peatling

Editorial Manager: Kevin Kirschner

Editorial Assistant: Amanda Graham

Sr. Editorial Assistant: Cherie Case

Cartoons: Rich Tennant
(www.the5thwave.com)

Composition Services

Project Coordinator: Kristie Rees

Layout and Graphics: Samantha K. Cherolis

Proofreader: ConText Editorial Services, Inc.

Indexer: BIM Indexing & Proofreading Services

Publishing and Editorial for Technology Dummies

    Richard Swadley, Vice President and Executive Group Publisher

    Andy Cummings, Vice President and Publisher

    Mary Bednarek, Executive Acquisitions Director

    Mary C. Corder, Editorial Director

Publishing for Consumer Dummies

    Diane Graves Steele, Vice President and Publisher

Composition Services

    Debbie Stailey, Director of Composition Services

Contents at a Glance

Introduction 1

Part I: Introducing BuddyPress................................ 9
Chapter 1: A New Friend Named BuddyPress 11
Chapter 2: Understanding WordPress Requirements 23
Chapter 3: Touring the WordPress Dashboard 45

Part II: Getting Up and Running with BuddyPress 63
Chapter 4: Setting Up Base Camp...65
Chapter 5: Configuring BuddyPress 81

Part III: Understanding BuddyPress Features 105
Chapter 6: Exploring Your New Community.....................................107
Chapter 7: Enabling Blogs..141
Chapter 8: Using the Groups Feature 153

Part IV: Customizing BuddyPress 165
Chapter 9: Default Theme and Widgets 167
Chapter 10: Finding and Installing Themes 185
Chapter 11: Understanding Themes and Templates..............................193
Chapter 12: Tweaking the Default Theme with CSS 203

Part V: Extending BuddyPress................................. 215
Chapter 13: Getting Plugged In with Plugins 217
Chapter 14: Integrating Popular Social Media................................231

Part VI: The Part of Tens 239
Chapter 15: Ten Useful BuddyPress Plugins 241
Chapter 16: Ten Free BuddyPress Themes 251
Chapter 17: Ten Real World Examples of BuddyPress 261

Appendix: Cutting Edge BuddyPress........................... 273

Index 289

Table of Contents

Introduction *1*

About This Book 3
Conventions Used in This Book 4
What You Are Not to Read 4
Foolish Assumptions 5
How This Book Is Organized 6
Icons Used in This Book 7
Where to Go From Here 8

Part 1: Introducing BuddyPress *9*

Chapter 1: A New Friend Named BuddyPress 11

Building a Social Community with BuddyPress 11
    Why build a social community? 13
    Types of people who build social communities 14
Discovering the Benefits of BuddyPress 15
    WordPress as the foundation 16
    BuddyPress is easy to use 18
    BuddyPress is flexible to your needs 18
    Extending BuddyPress capabilities 19
    Taking part in the BuddyPress community 21

Chapter 2: Understanding WordPress Requirements 23

Understanding Web Site Development Tools 24
    Understanding domain name extensions 25
    Considering the cost of a domain name 25
    Registering your domain name 26
Finding a Home for Your Blog 27
    Understanding PHP and MySQL 28
    Getting help with hosting WordPress 28
    Dealing with disk space and bandwidth 29
Transferring Files from Point A to Point B 31
Working with WordPress 32
    Setting up the WordPress MySQL database 33
    Uploading the WordPress files 35
    Web server configurations for WordPress MU 37
    Running the WordPress install script 39

Chapter 3: Touring the WordPress Dashboard **45**

Logging into WordPress 45
Getting Familiar with WordPress. 47
Navigating the WordPress dashboard 47
Configuring the Site Admin options. 48
Setting general site options 57

Part II: Getting Up and Running with BuddyPress 63

Chapter 4: Setting Up Base Camp **65**

Installing BuddyPress 66
Using the automatic installation method 66
Installing BuddyPress manually. 71
BuddyPress admin bar 73
Using Default BuddyPress Themes 74
Moving theme folders. 74
Activating themes 75
Finding the BuddyPress Menu 78

Chapter 5: Configuring BuddyPress **81**

Configuring the General Settings 81
Discovering BuddyPress Components 85
Activity Streams 86
Blog Tracking. 87
bbPress Forums 88
Friends. 88
Groups 90
Private Messaging. 90
Extended Profiles 91
Setting up bbPress Forums 93
Setting up a new bbPress installation 95
Using an existing bbPress installation 96
Building Profile Groups and Fields. 98
Adding new profile fields 98
Creating new profile groups 101

Part III: Understanding BuddyPress Features 105

Chapter 6: Exploring Your New Community **107**

Signing Up as a New Member. 108
New member registration 108
Activating a new member account 111

Navigating the Admin Bar...113
Exploring Your Profile..115
    Activity..116
    Profile...120
    Blogs..122
    Messages..123
    Friends...126
    Groups...127
    Settings..133
Discovering Site Wide Activity, Directories, and Searches.................134

Chapter 7: Enabling Blogs..141

Managing User Blogs in Your Community...............................141
    Enabling user blog creation...................................142
    Managing user blogs..144
Tracking Community Blog Activity....................................148
Publishing Blog Posts...151

Chapter 8: Using the Groups Feature.............................153

Enabling Groups and Forum Options.................................154
Participating in community groups..................................155
    Finding out about a community group.........................158
    Joining community groups......................................160
Joining the Discussion..160
Exploring the Groups Menu...163

Part IV: Customizing BuddyPress.............................. 165

Chapter 9: Default Theme and Widgets..........................167

Installing the Themes...167
Using BuddyPress Widgets..169
    Displaying site wide activity on the Classic theme..........172
    Using the Members widget......................................175
    Displaying community groups..................................177
    Creating a warm welcome message............................179
Blog versus Community Widgets.....................................182

Chapter 10: Finding and Installing Themes.....................185

Finding Free BuddyPress Themes....................................185
Downloading and Installing Themes.................................187
Activating a New Theme...189
    Enabling a theme in WordPress MU............................189
    Activating a new theme...190

Chapter 11: Understanding Themes and Templates **193**

Understanding Parent/Child Theme Relationships 193
Exploring the BuddyPress parent theme.......................................194
Exploring the child theme 195
Creating a child theme folder...196
Using a custom CSS file in the child theme 199
Using your own images in the child theme 199
Modifying Parent Template Files...200
Using a WordPress Theme with BuddyPress...201

Chapter 12: Tweaking the Default Theme with CSS **203**

Styling with CSS: The Basics 204
CSS selectors 204
Classes and IDs...205
CSS properties and values 207
Changing the Background Color...208
Using Your Own Logo in the Header...210
Changing Font Styles, Colors, and Sizes 212
Finding Additional CSS Resources..214

Part V: Extending BuddyPress **215**

Chapter 13: Getting Plugged In with Plugins **217**

Understanding What Plugins Are 217
Finding and Installing BuddyPress Plugins 218
Installing plugins using the Install Plugins interface..................219
Installing plugins manually...222
Managing Plugin Options...226
Uninstalling Plugins...227
Understanding Open Source Concepts..229

Chapter 14: Integrating Popular Social Media **231**

Discovering Popular Social Networks..231
Connecting BuddyPress and Facebook 232
Integrating Twitter...237

Part VI: The Part of Tens **239**

Chapter 15: Ten Useful BuddyPress Plugins **241**

BuddyPress Privacy Component...242
Featured Members Widget 242

Author Avatar List 243
BuddyPress Events Calendar 244
BuddyPress Geo 244
SEO (Search Engine Optimization) for BuddyPress 245
BuddyPress/Facebook Connect 246
BuddyPress-Kaltura Media Component 246
BuddyPress Stats 247
BuddyPress Welcome Pack 248

Chapter 16: Ten Free BuddyPress Themes **251**
Avenue K9 252
BuddyPress Corporate 253
Bruce 254
BuddyPress Fun 255
Shouty 256
BuddyPress Community 256
Purple & Black 257
MuddyPress 258
New Yorker 258
BuddyPress Default Theme 258
The Future of BuddyPress Themes 259

Chapter 17: Ten Real World Examples of BuddyPress **261**
BuddyPress 262
Nourish Network 263
WeEarth 264
We Heart This 265
GigaOM Pro 266
Flokka 268
Unstructure 269
Young People 270
VW TankWars 271
Tasty Kitchen 272

Appendix: Cutting Edge BuddyPress............................ 273
Staying in the Know 274
Subscribe to BuddyPress.Org 274
Browsing BuddyPress forums 276
Browsing and using BuddyPress Trac 279
Setting Up a Test Environment 280
Downloading and Using Nightly Builds 283
Upgrading BuddyPress 285

Index 289

Introduction

BuddyPress allows users to create their own social community on their Web site. BuddyPress entered the scene and began to gain attention in the blogging community during the summer of 2008, and brought a suite of plugins and add-ons to the very popular blogging platform, WordPress. Today, anyone can host a social community on their own Web site through the combined use of WordPress and BuddyPress. The really good news is that you can accomplish this on your own Web site for the cost of exactly nothing. BuddyPress is free, open-source software that you can download, install, and begin building your own social community on the Web today. Whoever said, "nothing in life is free" hasn't met the folks behind the BuddyPress and WordPress software development!

Social communities on the Web are all the rave today. They started with sites like MySpace (www.myspace.com) and Facebook (www.facebook.com), where people can go to the Web site, join, and immediately start connecting with other people who share similar interests, hobbies, ideas, and talents. These communities allow you to share photos, music, videos, news, information, and even personal anecdotes about you and your life. You're able to network with other people from around the world who share the same interests as you through searching for them, joining groups and discussion forums, and then creating friendships so that you can keep track of and stay in touch with the people you've met. Social communities are an event on the Internet in a room that's never empty and in which the party never ends.

BuddyPress isn't a stand-alone program; it requires the use of the WordPress software. This means that you have to be running WordPress on your Web site before you can add the BuddyPress component. WordPress is an insanely popular (and free) blogging platform that's open source, easy to install, and used to power the content management of your Web site. After you install WordPress, you can add BuddyPress and start building a community. As you'll find in the pages of this book, BuddyPress is easy to install and gets your site up and running in a very short amount of time.

Niche communities are popping up all over the Web. These communities encourage social groups that focus on specific topics, ideas, and talents to share information and enable community members to network with one another, regardless of geographical location. By using BuddyPress on a WordPress-powered site, the possibilities of social networking on the Internet are endless! Political groups, environmental groups, businesses large and small, knitting groups, bowling groups, sports groups . . . any special interest group of any kind can build a community space on the Web where people with the same interests can connect, discuss, and share.

BuddyPress, with WordPress, gives you several features that will make your community very attractive to visitors and members, including the following:

- **Extended Profiles:** Members can fill in bits of information that let other members of the community get to know them better.
- **Avatars:** Members can upload a photo of themselves to display on their profile and various areas of the community.
- **Friends:** Members can connect by sending and accepting friendship requests and creating a list of friends within your community.
- **Private Messages:** Members can send and receive private messages from their friends within your community.
- **Activity Streams:** A display of all your activity within the community, such as comments, blog posts, friendships, wire posts, and group activity.
- **Blog Tracking:** A display of blog posts that a member has made on his blog(s) within the community.
- **Forums:** Allows community members to create and manage their own discussion forums.
- **Community Blogs:** Using WordPress MU, users are able to create and manage their own blog within the community.

The really nice thing about the BuddyPress features is that you can use only the ones you want. You don't have to use all the available features — you can disable the ones you don't think you'll need and use only the ones you want. BuddyPress is flexible enough to help you create and customize your own social community.

This book presents an in-depth look at the BuddyPress platform and integrating BuddyPress into your existing WordPress-powered Web site. I cover the basics of setting up the WordPress software on your Web site as a foundation; however, if you need more comprehensive information on how to use Word Press, you might want to pick up a copy of my other book, *WordPress For Dummies*.

BuddyPress For Dummies, like all *For Dummies* books, focuses on you, the user — in this case it focuses on how you can build a social community on your Web site using the WordPress platform. This book does not cover PHP or MySQL programming, nor will it turn you into a WordPress or BuddyPress developer (for that, you might want to pick up *The WordPress Bible* by Aaron Brazell, published by Wiley). What this book will do is take you step-by-step through the process of installing, configuring, using, customizing, and maintaining a BuddyPress community on your Web site using all of the tools packaged within the BuddyPress and WordPress software.

About This Book

This book covers all the important aspects of using the BuddyPress platform to create a social community on your WordPress-powered Web site, including

- Registering a domain name, obtaining Web hosting, and exploring the basic tools needed to manage the WordPress and BuddyPress software on your Web server.
- Laying the foundation by installing and setting up the WordPress software on your Web server.
- Installing and configuring the BuddyPress software.
- Setting up BuddyPress and configuring such features as extended profiles, avatars, activity streams, blog tracking, friendships, groups, forums, and more!
- Discovering profile fields and individualizing them for your Web community.
- Integrating blogs by using WordPress and the blog-tracking component in BuddyPress.
- Displaying community activity and searchable directories for members, blogs, and groups within your community.
- Enabling and creating groups.
- Finding tips and advice on running and managing a large social community on your Web site, including advice on customer service and technical support.
- Finding and installing free BuddyPress themes.
- Customizing BuddyPress themes by tweaking existing free themes, or creating your own custom BuddyPress theme from scratch.
- Using BuddyPress widgets to add interactivity and community navigation options for your visitors.
- Understanding how to use BuddyPress plugins to extend the functionality of your BuddyPress community.
- Integrating popular social media memberships in your community, such as Twitter and Facebook.

✔ Finding out how to obtain BuddyPress support and assistance through community forums, groups, and Web site resources.

✔ Discovering real world examples of BuddyPress in action to see how BuddyPress looks and functions.

Conventions Used in This Book

Consistency is a good thing when you're taking on the task of learning new things. Throughout this book, you can count on a consistent set of typography conventions I've used to help guide you through the information presented:

✔ When I ask you to type something on your computer, you'll see the text I want you to type printed in **bold**.

✔ When I suggest a keyword or phrase that you may want to type in a search engine, the keyword or phrase is printed in *italics*.

✔ Text that appears in this `special font` is sure to be a URL (Web address), e-mail address, filename, folder name, or snippet of code.

✔ When I feel the need to define a word that I think you might not be familiar with, the word appears in *italic* text to let you know that I go on to define it next.

What You Are Not to Read

BuddyPress For Dummies is meant to assist and guide you through the mechanics of using and setting up BuddyPress and the various features of the BuddyPress platform on your Web site to build your successful social community. It isn't meant to be read from cover to cover. Rather, the information is organized in a logical order and presented in such a way that you can jump from one section to another to enable you to take what you need, and leave the rest for your neighbor.

Although this book doesn't contain extensive coverage of the WordPress platform, Wiley Publishing offers two books that comprehensively cover the use of WordPress. *WordPress For Dummies,* by (yours truly) Lisa Sabin-Wilson, focuses on the beginner-to-intermediate level WordPress user; and the *WordPress Bible,* by Aaron Brazell, goes in-depth on WordPress development, including plugin and theme development with the more advanced WordPress user in mind.

Visit the Table of Contents to discover the content covered in this book and flip to the pages that discuss the topic you need the most assistance with. For example, if you need the basics on setting up the WordPress foundation of your Web site, be sure to read Chapters 2 and 3, but if you already have WordPress set up on your Web server, you can skip Chapter 2.

If you need more of an introduction to the BuddyPress platform, be sure to read Chapter 1; then move on to Part II to discover the steps you take to set up the software and begin configuring the available options and features.

If you want to customize your BuddyPress-powered site with a really cool visual design and layout, then make sure you head to Part IV, "Customizing BuddyPress," in which you discover the default BuddyPress themes and information on how to customize the themes with HTML and CSS.

In a nutshell, you're safe to take what you need from this book and apply your new knowledge to your BuddyPress community. Then pass on your new found knowledge to your friends and wow them with your supreme geekiness!

Foolish Assumptions

I try not to make assumptions about people I've never met; however, for the purpose of this book, I have made a few assumptions about you:

- ✔ You have access to a computer — PC or Mac, this book covers both.
- ✔ Your computer has access to the Internet.
- ✔ You know how to type on a keyboard.
- ✔ You have a basic understanding of what blogs are and how they work.
- ✔ You know what WordPress is and have some basic experience with using the platform to run and maintain a blog or Web site on the Internet.

I've also assumed that you have a big interest in learning how you can create and maintain a social community on your Web site using the BuddyPress platform. If I'm right on that assumption, then you are definitely in the right place!

How This Book Is Organized

BuddyPress For Dummies is organized into 6 parts that encompass 17 chapters of information you need to know in order to use the BuddyPress platform.

✔ **Part I: Introducing BuddyPress** gives you an introduction of the BuddyPress platform and the advantages you will find in using it to build a social community of users on your Web site. In this part, you discover the tools you need to run BuddyPress on your Web site, including domain registration, obtaining a Web hosting provider, and using FTP (File Transfer Protocol) to transfer the necessary software files. Additionally, this part introduces you to the basics of the WordPress MU software requirements that need to be in place before you can install the BuddyPress platform on your Web site. This part also includes a basic run through of the WordPress dashboard and options, once you have WordPress installed and running on your Web server.

✔ **Part II: Getting Up and Running with BuddyPress** introduces you to the methods of installing BuddyPress on your WordPress-powered site: auto-installation with the WordPress plugin installer, or manual installation with BuddyPress by downloading the software and using FTP to upload it to your Web server. This part gives you a full understanding of the directory structure of the BuddyPress software files. In this part, you configure BuddyPress, set up the components you want to use within your social community, and set up the profile fields for your community members.

✔ **Part III: Understanding BuddyPress Features** takes you through all the exciting BuddyPress features that will make your social community a smashing success with your visitors. You explore how your users will benefit from such features as community registration, extended profiles and avatars, friendships, private messages, activity streams, community blogs, searchable directories, groups, and forums.

✔ **Part IV: Customizing BuddyPress** introduces you to BuddyPress themes and template tags that you can use to create a visual display that is individualized and unique to your community. Although BuddyPress comes bundled with nicely designed default themes to get you going right away, you'll find information on basic CSS and HTML that will help you tweak an existing free BuddyPress theme that you are using, or help you create your own custom theme. This part also takes you through the differences between the BuddyPress Home theme and the BuddyPress Member theme.

✔ **Part V: Extending BuddyPress** gives you the opportunity to explore how you can add different features to your BuddyPress community through third-party plugins developed by BuddyPress and WordPress community members. This part introduces you to the methods of finding, downloading, installing, and using BuddyPress plugins on your Web site. Additionally, this part also shows you how you can integrate other popular social network sites and communities (say Twitter, Facebook, and YouTube) in your own BuddyPress-powered community.

✔ **Part VI: The Part of Tens** is a staple in all *For Dummies* books. This Part of Tens explores real world examples of BuddyPress implementations on the Web so you can see how others are using the software to run successful communities. This part also explores some popular BuddyPress plugins and themes that will help you extend your BuddyPress site and create a community that will receive rave reviews from your members!

The Appendix covers some information for the true geeks out there! BuddyPress gives you the chance to use cutting-edge versions of their software before it releases to the public. This Appendix covers where to find a program called SVN (Subversion) to update your BuddyPress version to the latest cutting-edge (Beta) version.

Icons Used in This Book

Throughout this book, you can't miss the little icons that appear in the margins that spotlight certain points I want to emphasize. They highlight items you need to remember, warnings you need to be aware of, technical advice, and "how-tos" or tips that I think will really help you on your way. Here's what to expect when you see these icons throughout the pages of this book.

This icon appears next to information that I think you'll find very useful — advice and gems of information that I've discovered in my experiences with the BuddyPress software.

This icon looks like a little bomb for a reason! You definitely need to pay attention to these items because they contain information on things you should be doing — or not doing — when setting up and using the BuddyPress software.

This icon flags important points that I want you to remember while you set up and use your BuddyPress/WordPress-powered Web site. When I use this icon, I want you to read it two or three times and brand it into your brain forever and ever.

Let's face it, building Web sites, blogs, and social communities is kind of a geeky adventure. I use this icon to point out some technical mumbo jumbo — the sort of technical information that geeks love — that might be helpful while you set up your social community empire.

Where to Go From Here

I think I've gone on enough to give you a good understanding of what this book contains — it's time to get started! This book is a handy reference guide that contains information, tips, ideas, concepts, and tools that you need to start using BuddyPress. As I mention in the "What You Are Not to Read" section, thumb through the Index or the Table of Contents to find the sections that you feel will be most helpful to you. You can find this book's Cheat Sheet online at www.dummies.com/cheatsheet/buddypress.

Part I
Introducing BuddyPress

The 5th Wave   By Rich Tennant

"Basically, it's a car-chasing network, but it's also much more. We discuss mail carriers, UPS trucks, vacuum cleaners..."

In this part . . .

If you're ready to start building your own social community on the Web, you're in the right place! This part introduces you to the wonders of the BuddyPress platform and the WordPress blogging platform that you build your BuddyPress community on. I tell you all about social communities, why you want to include one on your Web site, how to lay the WordPress foundation required to begin the magic and give you a tour through the WordPress dashboard to make sure you can find your way around.

Chapter 1

A New Friend Named BuddyPress

In This Chapter

▶ Building a community-driven Web site with BuddyPress

▶ Creating communities for niche industries

▶ Discovering the benefits of BuddyPress

▶ Laying the WordPress foundation

▶ Exploring the BuddyPress community

*T*he popularity of social communities on the Web is undeniable. If you picked up this book, most likely, you're already familiar with WordPress. WordPress has created the world's most popular blogging platform (no kidding, the *world's!*), allowing millions of users all over the globe to freely publish content on the Internet and invite others to join the discussion. BuddyPress, introduced to the WordPress community in 2008, was the next logical step, enabling bloggers to expand their Web sites to include a social community for their visitors to participate in.

This chapter explores why you want to create a social community on your Web site and the benefits of using the BuddyPress platform to accomplish that goal. Because BuddyPress integrates with the WordPress blogging platform, you also discover some of the BuddyPress features that work in tandem with WordPress MU, such as member blogs and blog tracking features.

Building a Social Community with BuddyPress

Social communities are all over the Web today. One very popular example is Facebook (http://facebook.com). Facebook launched in 2004 and today is the largest and most popular social network on the Web, with more than 250 million users (and growing). Before getting into details of building your own social community with the BuddyPress platform, have a look at a few impressive statistics about Facebook (see Figure 1-1).

✔ More than 120 million users log in to Facebook at least once a day.

✔ The average Facebook user has 120 friends on the site.

✔ More than 1 billion photos are uploaded to Facebook each month.

✔ More than 10 million videos are shared on Facebook each month.

✔ More than 45 million active user groups exist on Facebook.

✔ The fastest growing demographic on Facebook are those 35 years old or older.

Those are some impressive statistics, no? You might be asking why I'm sharing Facebook stats (www.facebook.com/press/info.php?statistics) in a book about BuddyPress. The answer is simple: They illustrate the extreme popularity of social communities and the availability of a network where people can connect, share, and interact with others via a computer connected to the Internet.

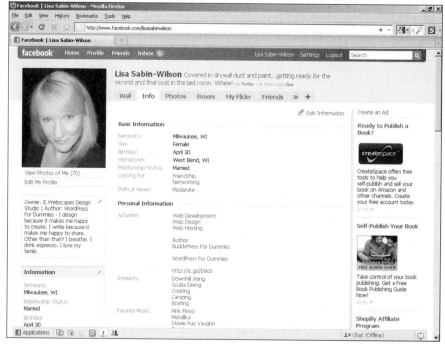

Figure 1-1: Facebook is the world's largest and most popular social community.

BuddyPress allows you to create a very similar type of social community on your own WordPress-powered Web site and helps you take your existing Web site to the next level by allowing your visitors to become members. A BuddyPress social community gives its members a handful of core features that are easy to set up and allows them to immediately connect with other members of the community. Members can have extensive profiles that contain personal biographical information that allows other members to find out more about them. Members share with other members any information they want, from personal information and news to Web site links, photos, videos, music, and more.

Why build a social community?

In March 2009, I attended a conference in Austin, Texas, called South by Southwest Interactive where geeks from all over the world gather for one weekend to network and discover the new, exciting, and innovative Internet trends and technologies. I attend this conference annually, and there is always a buzz about the major trend for that year. The buzz phrase at South by Southwest in 2009 was, "It's all about the conversation." The Web has become more than just a place to *obtain* information today; it has become a place to *share* information and connect with other people through ongoing conversations through different types of social media. Social communities give people the opportunity to *be* the media rather than just be consumers of the media.

One nice benefit to Facebook is its size — almost everyone I know has a Facebook account and I can find them there, add them as a friend, and connect with them easily (and probably more often than I would off the computer). A negative aspect of Facebook is that all the content shared on that site is stored on that site. Therefore, for people to find the source of the information they are seeking, they end up on the Facebook Web site, rather than your site; and the point of having a Web site is to build content that people want to read and consume.

Your Web site isn't generic, is it? Of course not! More than likely, your Web site is about something — a specific topic, product, or service. BuddyPress gives you the opportunity to open up your Web site for members to join your community and engage in discussions about topics that you're passionate about; so passionate that you started a Web site. You aren't the only one in the world with a passion for your particular topic — inviting others who share your passion to join your community will benefit you and your members by allowing the entire group to share advice, tips, and connections.

Types of people who build social communities

It's been said that there's a blog on the Internet for every possible topic that you can think of, and it's true! There are blogs about politics, education, media, technology, beauty, Hollywood, arts and crafts, designing, health and medicine, and news, just to name several. If you can think of a topic — I bet there's a blog about it.

These topical blogs function in the way you would suspect them to: The blog owner publishes articles and content that he or she thinks readers will find interesting; then visitors to the site are invited to participate in the discussion of the articles through blog comments.

Web site owners who want to take the interactivity on their site a few steps further can now build a social community where visitors to the Web site can create a membership and become part of the content and conversation. In addition to leaving comments on the articles, members can write their own articles, share more information, and participate in the site as a full contributor rather than just a visitor. Members can benefit from networking and connecting with other members within the community as well. Here are a few examples of the types of communities I'm talking about, all built with the BuddyPress/WordPress platform. (In Chapter 17, I give ten real-world examples of BuddyPress in action.)

- ✔ **Tasty Kitchen (`http://thepioneerwoman.com/tasty-kitchen`):** An active social community of members who like to cook.
- ✔ **Gigaom Pro (`http://pro.gigaom.com`):** A network of analysts providing technology-related research papers and notes.
- ✔ **VWTankWars (`http://tdi.vw.com`):** By Volkswagen, a network of VW TDI drivers working to make a world record mileage score.

Businesses large and small benefit from adding a social community component to their Web sites by gaining the ability to invite their customers, or potential customers, to participate in the discussion about their business.

Political movements are ripe for social community involvement because they encourage the sharing of ideas and news, and the involvement in causes. Some would say that the success of Barack Obama's campaign for President of the United States was aided tremendously by the very energetic and active social community of voters on the Internet. Barack Obama's campaign Web site was a social community of voters and potential voters, whose thoughts and ideas helped to shape a good portion of Obama's campaign. The success of that social movement on the Internet is undeniable, no matter which way your politics fall.

Other niche industries and communities can experience the same type of success when they gather people in one environment on the Internet — it's all about listening to the conversation that develops!

Discovering the Benefits of BuddyPress

Working with the BuddyPress software since July 2008, I can attest to the rapid (and wonderful) development that takes place to improve BuddyPress. BuddyPress is constantly improving the software and introducing exciting new and useful features with each new release. If you spend time on the official BuddyPress Web site at `http://buddypress.org` (see Figure 1-2), you'll find that the development of the platform is community-driven; that is, the community suggests ideas and wish lists for new features, and the developers of the BuddyPress software do their best to answer the call. Imagine a software company, say Microsoft, driving the development of its operating system in such a manner: The world would be a better place! It's exciting to be part of a development community that is so responsive to its users.

Figure 1-2:
The official
BuddyPress
Web site.

Aside from the exciting pace and quality of development, BuddyPress also offers the following advantages to users who wish to create a social community on their Web site:

- ✔ **WordPress MU:** BuddyPress plugs right into the WordPress MU platform. WordPress is very easy to set up and use, even for the novice Web site developer.

- ✔ **Ease of use:** BuddyPress is easy to install and set up; you don't need to be a major geek or programmer to accomplish these tasks.

- ✔ **Flexibility:** BuddyPress offers a suite of plugins for WordPress that you can choose from. You can choose to use all of them or just a few of them.

- ✔ **Extensibility:** Using plugins and themes, you can customize BuddyPress to suit your needs.

- ✔ **Community:** As I've already mentioned, the BuddyPress community is a very active adjunct to the already huge and active WordPress community. Finding assistance and camaraderie is just a mouse click away!

The following sections will quench your curiosity with more details on these features and point you to the various places in this book where you can find more detailed information.

WordPress as the foundation

You're probably aware of how easy the WordPress blogging platform (see Figure 1-3) makes creating a blog or Web site. Millions of users blog on WordPress (http://wordpress.org), a proven success in Web publishing and content management. Using such a solid and successful platform as WordPress for the foundation of your new social community (built with BuddyPress) is a formula for success because WordPress makes managing and maintaining a Web site very easy.

Three different versions of the WordPress software currently exist, as follows:

✔ **WordPress.com:** This is the hosted version.

✔ **WordPress.org:** This is the single user, self-hosted version.

✔ **WordPress MU:** This is the multi-user version.

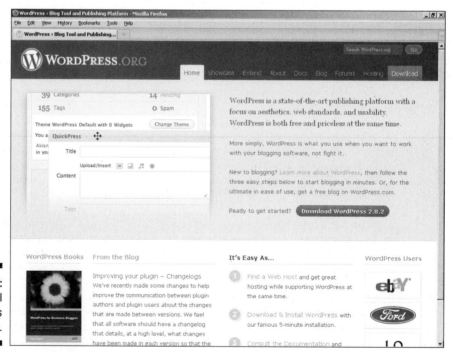

Figure 1-3: The official WordPress Web site.

Currently, the only version that is compatible with BuddyPress is the WordPress MU version. WordPress.com and WordPress.org do not have the ability to host the features of BuddyPress right now, although that may certainly change in the future. When I refer to WordPress in this book, I am referring to WordPress MU, the multiple user version of the software. You will find a great deal of information about WordPress MU in Chapters 2 and 3.

The WordPress platform gives you a great foundation for your social community with the following features:

- ✔ Multiple member blogs
- ✔ Articles organized by topic
- ✔ Content archived by month and year
- ✔ Categorized link lists
- ✔ Interactive comments
- ✔ Privacy controls
- ✔ Built-in RSS feed syndication
- ✔ Easy management of media files, such as photos, video, and music
- ✔ Hundreds of plugins and themes to extend your Web site

Once you have WordPress running on your site, you're more than halfway toward building a social community. Adding the BuddyPress suite of plugins gives you the ability to extend additional features to your visitors that allow them to join your site's community and create a full-featured member profile; create a blog on your site; and create groups, forums, photo albums, and more.

I mention in the Introduction that *BuddyPress For Dummies* is not a guide on using the WordPress software, but rather a book about adding the BuddyPress platform onto an existing WordPress-powered site. Although Chapters 2 and 3 of this book explore the basics of getting WordPress running on your site, this book assumes a certain level of existing familiarity with WordPress. You might also want to pick up my other book, *WordPress For Dummies* for more in-depth information on running WordPress on your Web site.

With WordPress, you already have a blog or Web site where you're publishing content and inviting visitors to join in the discussion by providing the opportunity for feedback on your content through comments. WordPress also gives you an extended Multi User option where you can invite visitors to join your site and create their own blog on your domain. You can choose to run only one blog (yours), or enable the options that allow your community members to create blogs of their own on your domain. A WordPress-powered blog with the multiple blog option enabled is typically referred to as a *blog network* because it creates a directory of different blogs written by different authors on a variety of topics, all hosted on your Web site.

One important thing to take away from this section is that BuddyPress requires the WordPress MU platform in order to work. That is, you cannot use BuddyPress if you aren't already using WordPress MU.

Be sure to read Chapters 2 and 3 for more information on the WordPress platform, including how to install WordPress on your Web server to lay the foundation for building your BuddyPress social community.

BuddyPress is easy to use

One of the most attractive features of the WordPress and BuddyPress platforms is the ease in which you can install, set up, and use the platform to manage and maintain your Web site. You don't need to be a certified geek or programmer to get BuddyPress up and running, as Chapters 2, 3, and 4 show you. Even someone new to WordPress and BuddyPress can have a full-featured Web site, blog, and social community up and running in a relatively short period.

WordPress has bragging rights to a 5-minute installation (see Chapter 2), and BuddyPress takes even less time to install. Setting up the options for the various BuddyPress features is transparent and easy — just use the WordPress dashboard to configure the feature options. Check out Chapter 3 for a guided tour through the WordPress dashboard to help familiarize yourself with the lay of the land.

Check out Chapter 4 for the steps to install BuddyPress and an exploration of the BuddyPress configuration options.

BuddyPress is flexible to your needs

BuddyPress is an extensive suite of plugins that allows you to create the following features within your social community:

- **Extended member profiles:** These include shared personal information about each member of your community.
- **Member avatars:** This feature allows your members to upload a unique personal photo.
- **Member and site activity streams:** A listing of member actions and activities throughout your community.
- **Activity wires:** A place where members can leave comments and messages for other members and groups in a public manner.
- **Member groups:** Community members can gather together in groups based on topics and interests.

✔ **Member forums:** Members can create and participate in topic-related discussions with other members.

✔ **Blog tracking:** A listing of blog activity throughout your community, including new blog posts and comments.

✔ **Searchable member, blog, and group directories:** Search through member lists, group lists, and blogs to find specific information you are looking for.

✔ **Member status updates:** Short but sweet updates members can share that answer the basic question: What am I doing right now?

You might find that you don't want or need to use all the features that BuddyPress has to offer, and that's okay. You don't have to use them just because they exist. BuddyPress allows you to use only what you need — you can even delete extraneous features completely if you don't want to use them — enabling you to tailor your BuddyPress community to your liking.

Chapters 5 through 8 provide an in-depth exploration of each BuddyPress feature to assist you in choosing the ones you want to use. Use them all, or use just one — the choice is completely yours.

Extending BuddyPress capabilities

As I mention at the beginning of this section, the BuddyPress development community is very active and constantly striving to improve the BuddyPress experience for both site owners and community members. Not only are development community members active and involved with the development of the BuddyPress software, but several members of the BuddyPress development crew also work to create BuddyPress plugins and themes.

BuddyPress plugins are additional pieces of software that, by themselves, would not work or do you any good. Combine them with BuddyPress and WordPress, however, and you can extend the functionality of your BuddyPress-powered social community to bring additional fun and exciting features to your users.

Using BuddyPress plugins, you can

✔ Integrate elements of popular social media sites, such as YouTube videos, into your community.

✔ Allow users to add Twitter feeds to their member profiles and activity wires.

✔ Integrate Facebook content into your BuddyPress community.

✔ Extend search engine optimization (SEO) enhancements to further improve the visibility of your BuddyPress social community in popular search engines, such as Google and Yahoo!.

These features aren't built into the BuddyPress platform, but you can add them by downloading and installing BuddyPress plugins. Chapters 13 and 14 provide you with the information needed to add these additional plugins and features to your site.

Another way to extend your BuddyPress social community is to customize the look and layout of your site with BuddyPress themes and templates. BuddyPress comes packaged with themes for you to use. Figure 1-4 shows the BuddyPress Default theme, but you can also use the BuddyPress Classic theme, which is shown in Figure 1-5.

The BuddyPress default themes include all the basic elements that you need when starting a new BuddyPress social community on your Web site. You can extend your community in several ways by using the plugins and themes released by members of the BuddyPress community, but these default themes are an easy way to get started.

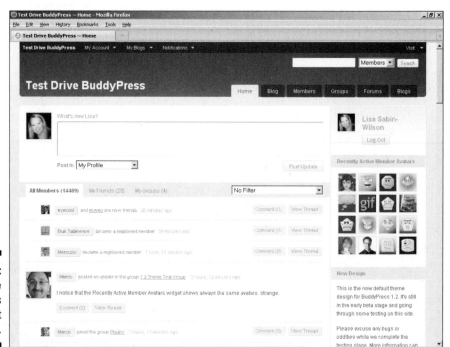

Figure 1-4: The BuddyPress Default theme.

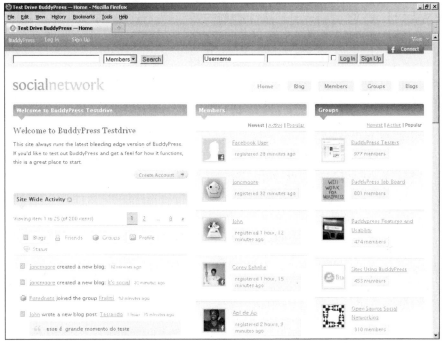

Figure 1-5:
The
BuddyPress
Classic
theme.

Chapters 9 through 12 provide you with information on how to customize your BuddyPress theme, including

✔ Finding, downloading, and installing free themes created by members of the BuddyPress development community

✔ Using HTML and CSS to customize the design and layout of your existing themes

✔ Using BuddyPress widgets to provide your site visitors with easy navigation features

✔ Creating a custom BuddyPress theme from scratch by understanding BuddyPress theme structure, template tags, and functions

Taking part in the BuddyPress community

The BuddyPress community was born from the larger WordPress community, which makes sense because BuddyPress is a component that you can add to the WordPress platform. WordPress is already a very large and active community of developers, designers, and users on the Web, full of people who are very passionate about the WordPress project. That excitement and passion has continued in the BuddyPress community — and the BuddyPress community is growing in numbers each day.

Why is this important information to know? As a user of the BuddyPress platform, it's nice to know that you have support out there when you need it. WordPress and BuddyPress are very much a "users helping users" community. Users from all over the world bring different levels of experience and knowledge to the community and freely share their experiences, tips, and advice with other users. This kind of grassroots involvement made WordPress the extreme success it is today.

You might be asking yourself, "Where do I find this passionate group of BuddyPress users?" Answer:

- ✔ `http://buddypress.org`: The official BuddyPress Web site where you can browse for news and information; click the Sign Up button at the top right of that site to become a member and start participating in the sharing and discussions that go on there.

- ✔ `http://buddypress.org/forums`: The support forums for BuddyPress where you find official BuddyPress developers and BuddyPress users and community members sharing their knowledge, information, and experiences with other BuddyPress users.

- ✔ `http://buddypress.org/developers`: The BuddyPress developers community — and you don't need to be a developer to join and participate. You find extremely helpful information and resources that help you on your way to building and maintaining a BuddyPress social community on your Web site.

- ✔ `http://twitter.com/buddypressdev`: Are you a Twitter user? Then follow @BuddyPressDev on Twitter; they always update their Twitter stream with information about new BuddyPress releases and features.

Chapter 2

Understanding WordPress Requirements

● ●

In This Chapter

▶ Discovering the WordPress MU platform

▶ Exploring the basic tools of Web site development

▶ Transferring the WordPress MU software to your Web site

▶ Setting up the WordPress MU database

▶ Installing WordPress MU on your Web site

▶ Familiarizing yourself with the WordPress MU dashboard

▶ Finding handy WordPress MU resources

● ●

*W*ith three distinctly different versions of the WordPress blogging platform — WordPress.com, the hosted version; WordPress.org, the self-hosted version; and WordPress MU, the multi-user version — it's easy to get confused about which one you need to use under certain circumstances. Because you intend to use the BuddyPress suite of plugins on a WordPress-powered Web site to build a social community, the version of WordPress that you must use is the WordPress MU platform, which can be found at http://mu.wordpress.org.

Before you can set up your social community with BuddyPress, you first lay the foundation of the WordPress MU software. MU stands for *multiple user*, which means the platform allows you to host multiple user blogs on your domain.

Two things to consider prior to downloading and installing WordPress: You need to register a domain name (your Web site's Web address) and you need to obtain Web hosting services (the place that houses your Web site data).

This chapter starts by taking you through the steps to register your domain name and obtain Web hosting services. When installing WordPress on your domain, you transfer the software files to your hosting account through a method called File Transfer Protocol (FTP), which I cover in the "Using File

Transfer Protocol" section. Finally, I show you how to install the WordPress platform and get it running on your own domain so that you can get going with BuddyPress.

When I refer to WordPress in this book (particularly in this chapter), I'm referring to the WordPress MU (multiple user) platform, unless otherwise noted. At some point in mid-2010, the WordPress developers plan to merge the code base of the regular WordPress.org (self-hosted) code with the existing WordPress MU code base — when that happens, only one version of WordPress will be available for download. Until then, in order to use BuddyPress, you must use the correct version: WordPress MU available at http://mu.wordpress.org.

Understanding Web Site Development Tools

The first things every Web site owner needs to do is to select and register a domain name. A *domain name* is the *unique* Web address that you type in a Web browser's address bar to visit a Web site. Some examples of domain names are WordPress.org and Google.com.

I emphasize the word *unique* because no two domain names can be the same. If someone has registered the domain name you want, you can't have it. With that in mind, finding an available domain name sometimes takes a bit of time. You have options, of course. You can contact the owner of the domain name to find out whether it's for sale and the cost. With this approach, however, chances are good that you'll pay *way* more for that domain name versus a domain name available through a domain registrar.

Domain names: Do you own or rent?

When you "buy" a domain name, you don't really own it. Rather, you purchase the right to use the domain name for a specified period. You can register a domain name for one year or up to ten years. Be aware, however, that if you don't renew the domain name when your registration period ends, you lose it — and most often, you lose it right away to someone who preys on abandoned or expired domain names. Some people keep a close watch on expiring domain names, and as soon as the buying window opens, they snap the names up and start using them for their own Web sites, with the hope of taking full advantage of the popularity that the previous owners worked so hard to attain for those domains.

Understanding domain name extensions

When registering a domain name, be aware of the *extension* that you want. The .com, .net, .org, .info, or .biz extension that you see tagged onto the end of any domain name is the *top-level domain extension.* When you register your domain name, you're asked to choose the extension you want for your domain (as long as it's available, that is).

A word to the wise here: Just because you register your domain as a .com doesn't mean that someone else doesn't, or can't, own the very same domain name with a .net. So if you register MyDogHasFleas.com, and it becomes a hugely popular site among readers with dogs that have fleas, someone else can come along and register MyDogHasFleas.net, and run a similar site to yours in the hope of riding the coattails of your Web site's popularity and readership.

You can register your domain name with all available extensions if you want to avert this problem. My business Web site, for example, has the domain name EWebscapes.com; however, I also own EWebscapes.net, EWebscapes. biz, and EWebscapes.info.

Considering the cost of a domain name

Registering a domain costs you anywhere from $3 to $30 per year, depending on what service you use and what options (such as privacy options and search-engine submission services) you apply to your domain name during the registration process.

When you pay the domain registration fee, you'll pay another registration fee when the renewal date comes up again in a year, or two, or five — however many years you chose to register your domain name for. (See the "Domain names: Do you own or rent?" sidebar.) Most registrars give you the option of signing up for an Auto Renew service. This service automatically renews your domain name and charges the credit card you set up on that account. The registrar sends you a reminder a few months in advance, telling you it's time to renew. If you don't set up Auto Renew, you'll need to log in to your registrar account before it expires and manually renew your domain name. The Auto Renew service does not cost extra; however, be aware that choosing this option means that the registrar will automatically bill your credit card for your domain renewal when the time comes.

Registering your domain name

The Internet Corporation for Assigned Names and Numbers (ICANN) certifies and approves domain registrars. Although hundreds of domain registrars exist, the ones in the following list are popular because of their longevity in the industry, competitive pricing, and variety of services they offer in addition to domain name registration (such as Web hosting and Web site traffic builders):

- **GoDaddy:** `http://GoDaddy.com`
- **Register.com:** `http://register.com`
- **Network Solutions:** `http://networksolutions.com`
- **NamesDirect:** `http://namesdirect.com`

No matter where you choose to register your domain name, here are the steps you take to accomplish this task:

1. **Decide on a domain name.**

   Do a little planning and forethought here. Many people think of a domain name as a *brand* — a way of identifying their Web sites or blogs. Think of potential names for your site, and then proceed with your plan to register and use the domain name you've chosen for your Web site.

2. **Verify the domain name's availability.**

   In your Web browser, enter the URL of the domain registrar of your choice. Look for the section on the registrar's Web site that lets you enter the domain name (typically, a short text field) to see whether it's available. If the domain name isn't available as a `.com`, try `.net` or `.info`.

3. **Purchase the domain name.**

   Follow the domain registrar's steps to purchase the name using your credit card. After you complete the checkout process, you receive an e-mail confirming your purchase, so be sure to use a valid e-mail address during the registration process.

The next step is obtaining a hosting account, which I cover in the next section.

Some of the domain registrars have hosting services that you can sign up for, but you don't have to use those services. Often, you can find hosting services for a lower cost than most domain registrars offer. It just takes a little research.

Finding a Home for Your Blog

When you have your domain registered, you need to find a place for it to live — a Web host. Web hosting is the second piece of the puzzle that you need to complete before you begin working with WordPress.

A *Web host* is a business, group, or individual that provides Web server space and bandwidth for file transfer to Web site owners who don't have it. Usually, Web hosting services charge a monthly or annual fee — unless you're fortunate enough to know someone who's willing to give you server space and bandwidth free. The cost varies from host to host, but you can obtain quality Web hosting services for $3 to $10 per month to start.

Web hosts consider WordPress to be a *third-party application.* What this means to you is that the host typically won't provide technical support on the use of WordPress (or any other software application) because support isn't included in your hosting package. Although most Web hosts attempt to assist you with the use of the software, ultimately the responsibility for running it on your server account is all yours. This condition is one of the big reasons why some folks opt to run a WordPress-powered blog on the hosted version at WordPress.com. If you choose to go the self-hosted route with the WordPress.org software, you can find WordPress help and support in the WordPress support forums located at `http://wordpress.org/support`.

Several Web hosting providers also have WordPress-related services available for additional fees. These services can include technical support, plugin installation and configuration, and theme design services.

Hosting services generally provide (at least) these services with your account:

- ✔ Hard drive space
- ✔ Bandwidth (transfer)
- ✔ Domain e-mail with Web mail access
- ✔ FTP access
- ✔ Comprehensive Web site statistics
- ✔ MySQL database(s)
- ✔ PHP

Because you intend to run WordPress on your Web server, you need to look for a host that provides the minimum requirements needed to run the software on your hosting account, which are

- ✔ PHP version 4.3 (or greater)
- ✔ MySQL version 4.0 (or greater)

Understanding PHP and MySQL

The WordPress software is a personal publishing system that uses a PHP and MySQL platform, which provides you with everything you need to create a blog without having to know any programming code. In short, all of your content is stored in a MySQL database on your hosting account.

PHP stands for PHP Hypertext Preprocessor, and it's a server-side scripting language for creating dynamic Web pages. When a visitor opens a page built in PHP, the server processes the PHP commands and then sends the results to the visitor's browser. MySQL is an open source relational database management system (RDBMS) that uses Structured Query Language (SQL), the most popular language for adding, accessing, and processing data in a database. If that all sounds Greek to you, just think of it as a big filing cabinet where all the content on you blog is stored.

Every time a visitor goes to your blog to read your content, he makes a request that's sent to your server. The PHP programming language receives that request, obtains the requested information from the MySQL database, and then presents the requested information to your visitor through his Web browser.

In using the term *content* as it applies to the data that's stored in the MySQL database, I'm referring to your blog posts, comments, and options that you set up in the WordPress Administration panel.

 The easiest way to find out whether a host meets the minimum requirement is to check the Frequently Asked Questions (FAQ) section of the host's Web site if it has one. If not, find the contact information for the hosting company and fire off an e-mail requesting information on exactly what it supports. Any Web host worth dealing with will answer your e-mail within a reasonable amount of time (12–24 hours is a good barometer).

Getting help with hosting WordPress

The popularity of WordPress has given birth to services on the Web that emphasize the use of the software. These services include WordPress designers, WordPress consultants, and — yes — Web hosts that specialize in using WordPress.

Many of these hosts offer a full array of WordPress features, such as an automatic WordPress installation included with your account, a library of WordPress themes, and a staff of support technicians who are very experienced in using WordPress.

Here is a list of some of those providers:

- ✔ **Blogs About Hosting:** `http://blogs-about.com`
- ✔ **Laughing Squid:** `http://laughingsquid.net`
- ✔ **AN Hosting:** `http://anhosting.com`
- ✔ **DreamHost:** `http://dreamhost.com`

A word about Web hosts and domain registration: A few Web hosting providers offer free domain name registration when you sign up for their hosting services. Research this topic and dig through those hosting providers' terms of service because that free domain name sometimes comes with a few conditions.

Many of my clients have gone this route only to find out a few months later (when they're unhappy with the unreliable hosting service and want to change to another host) that the Web hosting provider has full control of the domain name. That is, they can't move the domain off the host's servers for a set period (usually, a year or two) if ever. I feel that it's always best to have the control in *your* hands, not someone else's, so I recommend registering your domain name yourself with an independent domain registrar, such as GoDaddy.

Dealing with disk space and bandwidth

Web hosting services provide two very important things with your account:

- ✔ Disk space
- ✔ Bandwidth transfer

Think of your Web host as a garage that you pay to park your car in. The garage gives you the place to store your car (disk space). It even gives you the driveway so that you, and others, can get to and from your car (bandwidth). It won't, however, fix your rockin' stereo system (WordPress or any other third-party software application) that you've installed — unless you're willing to pay a few extra bucks for that service.

Managing disk space

Disk space is no more complicated than the hard drive on your computer. Each hard drive has the capacity, or space, for a certain amount of files. An 80GB (gigabyte) hard drive can hold 80GB of data — no more. Your hosting account provides you a limited amount of disk space, and the same concept applies. If your Web host provides you 10GB of disk space, that's the limit on the file size that you're allowed to have. If you want more disk space, you need to upgrade your space limitations. Most Web hosts have a mechanism in place for you to upgrade your allotment.

Starting with a WordPress blog doesn't take much disk space at all. A good starting point for disk space is between 3–5GB of storage space. If you find that you need additional space, contact your hosting provider for an upgrade.

Time for a public-service announcement: A good Web host has a system in place that sends you a warning (via e-mail) when you reach at least 80 percent of your total disk space capacity. This warning helps you manage the space in your hosting account. With this warning, you can plan on either doing some account maintenance of your own and clearing out some unnecessary files that may be taking up space, or getting in contact with your Web host to upgrade your account.

Choosing the size of your bandwidth pipe

Bandwidth refers to the amount of data that is carried from point A to point B within a specific period (usually, only a second or two). I live out in the country — pretty much the middle of nowhere. The water that comes to my house is provided by a private well that lies buried in the backyard somewhere. Between my house and the well are pipes that bring the water to my house. The pipes provide a free flow of water to our home so that everyone can enjoy their long hot showers while I labor over dishes and laundry, all at the same time. Lucky me!

The very same concept applies to the bandwidth available with your hosting account. Every Web hosting provider offers a variety of bandwidth limits on the accounts it offers. When I want to view your Web site in my browser window, the bandwidth is essentially the pipe that lets your data flow from your "well" to my computer and monitor. Similar to the pipe connected to my well — it can hold only a certain amount of water before it reaches maximum capacity — your bandwidth limit is determined by how much bandwidth your Web host allows for your account — the larger the number, the bigger the pipe. A 50MB (megabyte) bandwidth limit makes for a smaller pipe than does a 100MB limit.

Web hosts are pretty generous with the amount of bandwidth they provide in their packages. Like disk space, bandwidth is measured in gigabytes (GB). Think about what you're planning to do with your Web site. Running a social community with BuddyPress can require a lot more bandwidth and disk space than just running a blog without a social community because you now have members who are trafficking your site, connecting with friends, and sharing information. I recommend a hosting service that provides you, initially, with 50 to 100GB of bandwidth per month with disk space allowances of up to 500MB of space. Those recommendations are for starters; most Web hosting providers give you the opportunity to upgrade your bandwidth and disk space, as needed.

Web sites that run large files — such as video, audio, or photo files — generally benefit from higher disk space compared with sites that don't involve large files. Additionally, Web sites running WordPress MU and BuddyPress, by nature, will use more bandwidth than a regular (single user) WordPress Web site because of the amount of traffic your community members create on your site. Keep this point in mind when you sign up for your hosting account. Planning now for sufficient hard disk space and bandwidth transfer allowances will save you a few headaches down the road.

Transferring Files from Point A to Point B

This section introduces you to the basic elements of FTP. The ability to use FTP with your hosting account is a given for almost every Web host on the market today. FTP is the method you use to move files from one place to another — for example, from your computer to your Web hosting account. This method is referred to as *uploading.*

Using FTP to transfer files requires an FTP client. Many FTP clients are available for download. Following are some good (and free) ones:

- **WS_FTP:** www.ipswitch.com/_download/wsftphome.asp
- **SmartFTP:** www.smartftp.com/download
- **FileZilla:** http://sourceforge.net/projects/filezilla
- **FTP Explorer:** www.ftpx.com

Earlier in this chapter, in the section "Finding a Home for Your Blog," you find out how to obtain a Web hosting account. Your Web host gives you a username and password for your account, including an FTP IP address. (Usually, the FTP address is the same as your domain name, but check with your Web host, as addresses may vary.) You insert this information — the username, password, and FTP IP address — into the FTP program to connect it to your hosting account.

Figure 2-1 shows my FTP client (FileZilla) connected to my hosting account. The directory on the left is the listing of files on my computer; the directory on the right shows the listing of files on my hosting account.

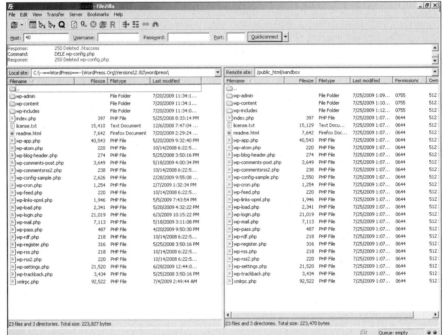

Figure 2-1:
FileZilla is a popular FTP client that makes file transfers easy.

FTP clients such as FileZilla make it easy to transfer files from your computer to your hosting account by using a drag-and-drop method. You simply click the file on your computer that you want to transfer, drag it to the side that lists the directory on your hosting account, and then drop it. Depending on the FTP client you've chosen to work with, you can refer to its user manuals or support documentation for detailed information on how to use the program.

Working with WordPress

By the time you're finally ready to install WordPress, you should have done the following things:

✔ Purchased the domain name registration for your account

✔ Obtained a hosting service on a Web server for your blog

     ✔ Established your hosting account username, password, and FTP address

     ✔ Acquired an FTP client for transferring files to your hosting account

If you've missed any of the items listed, you can go back to the beginning of this chapter to reread the portions you need.

Without further ado, go get the WordPress MU software at `http://mu.wordpress.org/download`.

WordPress gives you two compression formats for the software: Zip and Tar.gz. I recommend getting the Zip file because it's the most common format for compressed files, and you can use a program like WinZip (`http://winzip.com`) to decompress the files on a PC. Macs will automatically decompress a Zip file when you open it.

The first step in the WordPress installation process is to download the WordPress software to your computer and *decompress* (or *unpack*, or *unzip*) it to a folder on your computer's hard drive. Having the WordPress software on your own computer isn't enough, however; you also need to *upload* (transfer) it to your Web server account (the one you obtain in the section, "Finding a Home for Your Blog," earlier in this chapter). Before installing WordPress on your Web server, you need to make sure that you have a MySQL database set up and ready to accept the WordPress installation. The next section tells you what you need to know about MySQL.

Setting up the WordPress MySQL database

The WordPress software is a personal publishing system that uses a PHP-and-MySQL platform, which provides everything you need to create your own blog and publish your own content dynamically without having to know how to program those pages yourself. In short, all your content (options, posts, comments, and other pertinent data) is stored in a MySQL database in your hosting account.

Every time visitors go to your blog to read your content, they make a request that's sent to your server. The PHP programming language receives that request, obtains the requested information from the MySQL database, and then presents the requested information to your visitors through their Web browsers.

Every Web host is different in how it gives you access to set up and manage your MySQL database(s) for your account. A popular account administration interface is cPanel (shown in Figure 2-2), which I use in the example in this section. If your host provides a different interface, the same basic steps apply, but the setup in the interface that your Web host provides might be different.

Figure 2-2:
cPanel is a
Web
hosting
account
manager
provided
by several
Web hosting
companies.

To set up the MySQL database for your WordPress blog with cPanel, follow these steps:

1. **Log in to the administration interface with the username and password assigned to you by your Web host.**

   I'm using the cPanel administration interface, but your host might provide NetAdmin or Plesk, for example.

2. **Locate the MySQL Database Administration section.**

   In cPanel, click the MySQL Databases icon.

3. **Choose a name for your database and enter it in the Name text box.**

   Be sure to make note of the database name because you'll need it during the installation of WordPress later.

   For security reasons, make sure that your password isn't something that sneaky hackers can easily guess. Usually, I give my database a name that I will easily recognize later. This practice is especially helpful if you're running more than one MySQL database in your account. If I name this database something like *WordPress* or *wpblog,* I can be reasonably certain — a year from now, when I want to access my database to make some configuration changes — that I know exactly which one I need to deal with.

4. **Click the Create Database button.**

   You get a message confirming that the database has been created.

5. **Click the Go Back link or the Back button on your browser toolbar.**

6. **Choose a username and password for your database, enter them in the Add New User text boxes, and then click the Create User button.**

   You get a confirmation message that the username was created with the password you specified.

   Make sure that you note the database name, username, and password that you set up during this process. You *will* need them in the next section before officially installing WordPress on your Web server. Jot them down on a piece of paper, or copy and paste them into a text-editor window; either way, just make sure that you have them immediately handy.

7. **Click the Go Back link or the Back button on your browser toolbar.**

8. **In the Add Users to Database section, choose the user you just set up from the User drop-down menu; then choose the new database from the Database drop-down menu.**

   The MySQL Account Maintenance, Manage User Privileges page appears in cPanel.

9. **Assign user privileges by selecting the All Privileges check box.**

   Because you're the administrator (owner) of this database, you need to make sure that you assign all privileges to the new user you just created.

10. **Click the Make Changes button.**

    A page opens with a confirmation message that you added your selected user to the selected database.

11. **Click the Go Back link.**

    You go back to the MySQL Databases page.

Uploading the WordPress files

To upload the WordPress files to your host, return to the folder on your computer where you unpacked the WordPress software that you downloaded earlier. You'll find all the files you need (shown on the left side in Figure 2-1) in a folder called /wordpress-mu.

Using your FTP client, connect to your Web server, and upload all these files into the root directory of your hosting account.

If you don't know what your root directory is, contact your hosting provider and ask, "What is my root directory for my account?" Every hosting provider's setup is different. On my Web server, my root directory is the `public_html` folder; some of my clients have a root directory in a folder called `httpdocs`. The answer really depends on what type of setup your hosting provider has. When in doubt, ask!

Here are a few things to keep in mind when you upload your files:

- ✔ **Upload the *contents* of the /wordpress-mu folder to your Web server — not the folder itself.** Most FTP client software lets you select all the files and drag and drop them to your Web server. Other programs have you highlight the files and click a Transfer button.

- ✔ **Choose the correct transfer mode.** File transfers via FTP have two forms: ASCII and binary. Most FTP clients are configured to autodetect the transfer mode. Understanding the difference as it pertains to the WordPress installation is important, so that you can troubleshoot any problems you have later:

  - *Binary transfer mode* is how images (such as `.jpg`, `.gif`, `.bmp`, and `.png` files) are transferred via FTP.

  - *ASCII transfer mode* is for everything else (text files, PHP files, JavaScript, and so on).

  For the most part, it's a safe bet to make sure that the transfer mode of your FTP client is set to autodetect. But if you experience issues with how those files load on your site, retransfer the files using the appropriate transfer mode.

- ✔ **You can choose a different folder from the root.** You aren't required to transfer the files to the root directory of your Web server. You can make the choice to run WordPress on a subdomain or in a different folder on your account. For example, if you want your blog address to be `http://yourdomain.com/blog`, you would transfer the WordPress files into a folder named `/blog`.

- ✔ **Choose the right file permissions.** You need to pay attention to file permissions when you're transferring files to your Web server. *File permissions* tell the Web server how these files can be handled on your server; that is, whether they're files that can be written to. Generally, PHP files need to have permission (`chmod`) of 666, whereas file folders need a permission of 755. Almost all FTP clients let you check and change the permissions on the files if you need to. Typically, you can find where to change file permissions within the menu options of your FTP client.

Some hosting providers run their PHP software in a more secure format called *safe mode*. If this is the case with your host, you need to set the PHP files to 644. If you're unsure, ask your hosting provider what permissions you need to set for PHP files.

Web server configurations for WordPress MU

This section gives you important information about the configurations of your Web server. These configurations need to be in place to run WordPress MU successfully. If you can perform the configurations in this section yourself (and if you have access to the Apache configuration files), this section is for you. If you don't know how, are uncomfortable with adjusting these settings, or do not have access to change the configurations in your Web server software, you'll need to ask your hosting provider or hire a consultant to perform the configurations for you.

These configurations are essential, so make sure they're in place before you try to run WordPress MU.

Apache

Apache (http://httpd.apache.org) is Web server software that's loaded and running on your Web server. Not everyone has access to Apache configuration files, however. Usually, the only person who has access to those files is the Web server administrator (this is usually your Web host). Depending on your own Web server account and configuration, you may or may not have access to the Apache software files.

mod re_write

The Apache module that's necessary for WordPress MU to create nice permalink URLs is mod_rewrite. This module must be configured so that it is installed and activated on your server.

You or your Web host can make sure that mod_rewrite is activated on your server; open the httpd.conf file and verify that the following line is included within:

```
LoadModule rewrite_module /libexec/mod_rewrite.so
```

If it isn't, type that line on its own line and save the file. You will probably need to restart Apache before the change takes effect.

Virtual Host (or vhost)

In the same httpd.conf file that I discuss in the previous section, you need to adjust the <VirtualHost> section. Follow these steps:

1. **Find the <VirtualHost> section in the httpd.conf file.**

   This line of the httpd.conf file provides directives, or configurations, that apply to your Web site.

2. **Find the line in the `<VirtualHost>` section of the `httpd.conf` file that looks like** `AllowOverride None`.

3. **Replace that line with** `AllowOverride FileInfo Options`.

4. **On a new line, type** ServerAlias *.*yourdomain.com*.

   Replace *yourdomain.com* with whatever your domain is. This line defines the host name for your WordPress MU site and is essential for the virtual host to work correctly.

DNS (domain name server)

WordPress MU gives you two ways to run a network of blogs on your domain. You can use the subdomain option or the subdirectory option. The most popular option (and recommended structure) sets up subdomains for the blogs created by your WordPress MU community. With this subdomain option, the URL of each blog looks cleaner, and the username of the blog appears first. Also, if you intend to take advantage of plugins that are available for WordPress MU, you'll find that most of the plugin structures are written with a subdomain set up in mind.

You can see the differences in the URLs of these two options by comparing the following examples:

- ✔ A **subdomain** looks like this: `http://username.yourdomain.com`
- ✔ A **subdirectory** looks like this: `http://yourdomain.com/username`

In the subdomain example, see how the username appears first? That's the most desired method of setting up a WordPress MU network of community blogs.

If you want to use a subdomain for each blog in your WordPress MU community, you must add a wildcard record to your DNS records on your Web server. If you are unsure of what a wildcard record is, or how to set one up for your domain — just ask your Web hosting provider. You also need to add a hostname record pointing at your Web server in the DNS configuration tool available in your Web server administration software (like WebHost Manager, a popular Web host administration tool). The hostname record looks like this: `*.yourdomain.com` (where *yourdomain.com* is replaced with your actual domain name).

PHP (PHP Hypertext Processor)

In this section, you edit the PHP configuration on your Web server. To run WordPress MU, PHP needs to have the following configurations in place in the `php.ini` file on your Web server:

- ✔ Set your PHP so that it doesn't display error messages in the visitor's browser window. (This is usually turned off by default; just double-check to be sure.)

✔ Find out whether your PHP is compiled with memory limit checks. You can find this out by looking for `memory_limit` in the `php.ini` file. Usually, the default limit is 8MB. Increase the memory limit to at least 32MB, or even 64MB, to avoid PHP memory errors when running WordPress MU.

✔ Global variables should be set to Off. Usually, the default setting does have global variables turned off, but double-check to be sure. An easy way to configure this is to open the `.htaccess` file (found on your Web server in the same directory you install the WordPress MU files) and add the following lines to the very top:

```
php_flag register_globals 0

php_flag display_errors 0
```

Running the WordPress install script

The final step in the installation procedure for WordPress is connecting the WordPress software you uploaded to the MySQL database. Follow these steps:

1. **Type this URL in the address window of your browser, replacing *your domain.com* with your own domain name:**

   `http://yourdomain.com/wp-admin/install.php`

   If you chose to install WordPress in a different folder from the root directory of your account, make sure you indicate this fact in the URL for the install script. If you transferred the WordPress software files to a `/blog` folder, for example, you would point your browser to the following URL to run the installation: `http://yourdomain.com/blog/wp-admin/install.php`.

   Assuming that you did everything correctly (see Table 2-1 for help with common installation problems), you see the message shown in Figure 2-3.

2. **Click the Create a Configuration File button.**

   The next page that opens displays a Welcome to WordPress MU message and gives you the information you need to proceed with the installation, including the initial settings and database configurations that you need to fill in. Read through the What Do I Need? section on this page and confirm that you have the necessary items:

   • Access to your Web server via FTP

   • A valid e-mail address

   • An empty MySQL database

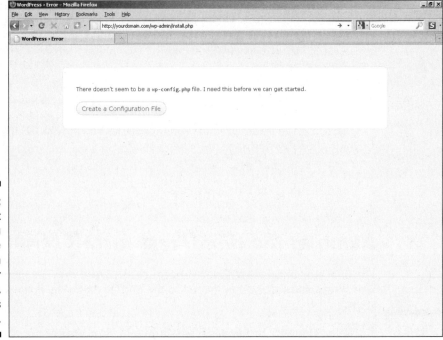

Figure 2-3:
The first
time you
run the
installation
script for
WordPress,
you see this
message.

3. **In the Blog Addresses section, select either the Sub-domains or the Sub-directories radio button.**

   You need to choose how you would like to set up your network of community blogs. If you aren't sure which option to choose, review the earlier "DNS (domain name server)" section.

You can't go back and change the options from Step 3 later — so be sure you check the right option for your setup in this step.

4. **Type the name of your database, the database username, the password, and the database host in their respective text boxes, as shown in Figure 2-4.**

   • *Database Name:* Type the database name you used when you created the MySQL database before this installation. Because hosts differ in configurations, you need to enter either the database name or the database name with your hosting account username appended.

If you named your database *wordpress,* for example, you would enter that in this text box. Or if your host requires you to append the database name with your hosting account username, you would enter ***username*_wordpress**, substituting your hosting user-name for *username.* If my username were *lisasabin,* I would enter **lisasabin_wordpress**.

- *User Name:* Type the username you used when you created the MySQL database before this installation. Depending on what your host requires, you might need to append this username to your hosting account username.

- *Password:* Type the password you used when you set up the MySQL database. You don't need to append the password to your hosting account username here.

- *Database Host:* Ninety-nine percent of the time, you'll leave this field set to *localhost.* Some hosts, depending on their configura-tions, have different hosts set for the MySQL database server. If *localhost* doesn't work, you need to contact your hosting provider to find out the MySQL database host.

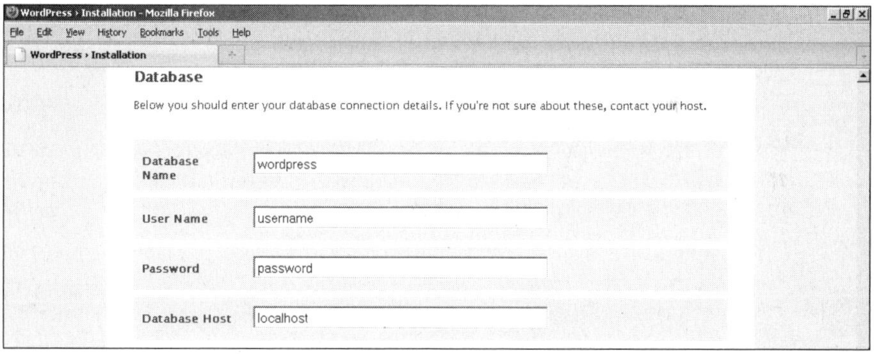

Figure 2-4: At this step of the WordPress installation phase, you need to enter the database name, user-name, and password.

5. **Type your domain name in the Server Address text box.**

   This should be the shortest version of your domain name. For example, type *yourdomain.com*, not *www.yourdomain.com* (where *your domain.com* is your actual domain name). Don't include the http:// portion of the domain name here either.

6. Type the title of your Web site in the Site Title text box.

The title is what you would like to call your WordPress-powered community site. You can edit this later if you change your mind.

7. Type your e-mail address in the Email text box.

This is the e-mail address where you want to receive all site-related information (such as contact information, notifications, and so on). Consider it the site administrator's contact e-mail address.

8. Click the Submit button.

This puts the WordPress MU installation script to work, and you see a page with the message, "Installation Finished!" This page also has the login information you need (username and password) to log in to the WordPress administration panel, where you will administer, manage, and maintain your Web site (see Figure 2-5). Make note of this login information and store it in a safe place.

After you click the Install WordPress button, you receive an e-mail with the login information and login URL. This information is handy if you're called away during this part of the installation process. So go ahead and let the dog out, answer the phone, brew a cup of coffee, or take a 15-minute power nap. If you're somehow distracted away from this page, the e-mail sent to you contains the information you need to log in to your WordPress blog successfully.

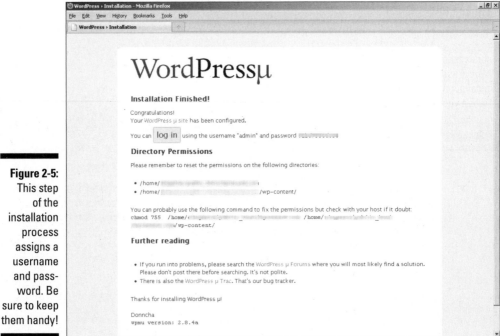

Figure 2-5:
This step of the installation process assigns a username and password. Be sure to keep them handy!

If you happen to lose this page before proceeding to the next step, you can always find your way to the login page by entering your domain followed by the call to the login file (for example, `http://yourdomain.com/wp-login.php`).

9. **Click the Log In button to log in to WordPress.**

You know that you're finished with the installation process when you see the login page, as shown in Figure 2-6. Check out Table 2-1 if you experience any problems during this installation process; it covers some of the common problems users run into.

Figure 2-6:
You know you've run a successful WordPress installation when you see the login page.

The good news is — you're done! You have all the vital information you need to get WordPress running on your Web site. And let me be the first to congratulate you on your newly installed WordPress blog. Were you expecting a marching band? WordPress isn't that fancy . . . yet. Give them time, though. If anyone can produce it, the folks at WordPress can.

Table 2-1	Common WordPress Installation Problems	
Error Message	*Common Cause*	*Solution*
Error Connecting to the Database	The database name, username, password, or host was entered incorrectly.	Revisit your MySQL database to obtain the database name, username, and password; and reenter that information.
Headers Already Sent Error Messages	A syntax error occurred in the `wp-config.php` file.	Open the `wp-config.php` file in a text editor. The first line should contain only `<?php`. The very last line should contain only `?>`. Make sure that those lines contain nothing else — not even white space. Save the file changes.
500: Internal Server Error	Permissions on PHP files are set incorrectly.	Try setting the permissions (`chmod`) on the PHP files to 666. If that change doesn't work, set them to 644. Each Web server has different settings for how it lets PHP execute on its servers.
404: Page Not Found	The URL for the login page is incorrect.	Double-check that the URL you're using to get to the login page is the same as the location of your WordPress installation (such as `http://yourdomain.com/wp-login.php`).
403: Forbidden Access	An `index.html` or `index.htm` file exists in the WordPress installation directory.	WordPress is a PHP application, so the default home page is `index.php`. Look in the WordPress installation folder on your Web server. If there is an `index.html` or `index.htm` file in there, delete it.

Chapter 3

Touring the WordPress Dashboard

In This Chapter

▶ Logging into WordPress MU

▶ Exploring the WordPress dashboard

▶ Discovering the Site Admin options

▶ Performing general site management duties

*W*ith the WordPress software successfully installed, you can begin to explore the software. In this chapter, you discover the WordPress MU dashboard, how to set administration configurations, and how to manage your network of users.

Some of you might be intimately familiar with how to use the WordPress dashboard to administer your Web site. If so, you can breeze through this chapter or skip it entirely. This chapter is geared toward the reader who's unfamiliar with the back-end of WordPress, its vital settings, and the tools you need to manage and maintain your site and community.

Feeling comfortable with the dashboard sets you up for successful entrance into the world of WordPress. For a great depth of information on WordPress, try my other book, *WordPress For Dummies*.

Logging into WordPress

When you log in to WordPress, you see the dashboard first. Follow these steps to log in to WordPress and view the dashboard:

1. **Open your Web browser and type the WordPress login page URL (Web address) into the address box.**

   The login page address looks like `http://yourdomain.com/wp-login.php`.

If you installed WordPress into its own folder, be sure to include that folder in the address you type when you log in. For example, if you installed WordPress into a `wordpress` folder, the login URL would look like `http://yourdomain.com/wordpress/wp-login.php`.

2. **Type your username into the Username text box and your password into the Password text box.**

   I hope you kept your username and password in a safe place. Enter that information in the text boxes provided on the login page, as shown in Figure 3-1.

Figure 3-1:
The WordPress login page.

3. **Select the Remember Me check box if you want WordPress to place a cookie in your browser.**

   The cookie tells WordPress to remember your login credentials the next time you load the login page in your browser window. The cookie set by WordPress is harmless and stores your WordPress login on your computer. Because of the cookie, your username and password will be remembered the next time you visit.

4. **Click the Log In button.**

   This loads the WordPress dashboard, which I cover in the next section.

Getting Familiar with WordPress

You need to be familiar with the WordPress interface because that's where you find all the BuddyPress goodies after you install BuddyPress. Additionally, you will tweak your settings several times throughout the life of your Web site. In this section, I give you a very basic idea of what the dashboard looks like and how you navigate the menus to find the settings and options that you need.

Navigating the WordPress dashboard

Following a successful WordPress install and login, the WordPress dashboard appears, as shown in Figure 3-2.

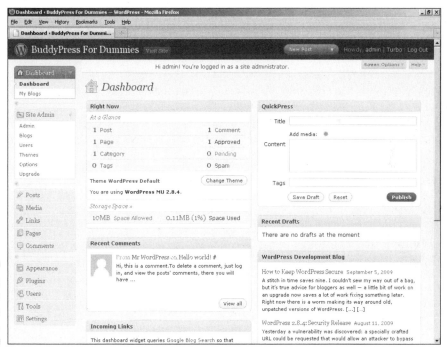

Figure 3-2: The WordPress dashboard.

The dashboard is where you find and configure all the settings and options for running a WordPress-powered Web site. In Chapter 5, I show you where you can find all the BuddyPress configurations. (For information on installing BuddyPress, see Chapter 4.)

The WordPress dashboard gives you some quick, at-a-glance information about your WordPress installation. Here you find statistics about your WordPress site, such as

- How many posts, pages, and comments you have.
- The number of categories and tags you've created.
- The name of the theme and number of WordPress widgets you are using.
- The five most recent comments visitors have left on your blog.
- The five most recent drafts you've saved to publish later.
- Information and links to recent WordPress news and plugins.

The dashboard is a portal to the other sections of your WordPress interface. In the navigation menu on the left side of the page, you can configure and manage your WordPress blog or Web site. With a WordPress MU Web site, you can manage your Web site two ways:

- **As site administrator:** This role manages the overall settings and community aspects of your site. Within this role, you manage your user base, community blogs (if you have them set up), available themes, member registration options, and overall site-wide community settings.
- **As site publisher:** This role publishes content to your site, whether it's posts to a blog; static pages for your site; or categories, link lists, and media files you create and maintain.

How you use the WordPress dashboard completely depends on which role you're fulfilling at that moment.

Configuring the Site Admin options

The Site Admin menu is directly beneath the dashboard menu in the navigation on the left side of the page. When you hover your cursor on Site Admin, a drop-down arrow appears to the right. (Each menu in this area has a drop-down arrow that functions in this manner.) If you click the drop-down arrow, the Site Admin options appear. This section covers all six options shown in Figure 3-3.

Admin

The first item on the Site Admin menu is Admin. Click Admin and the WordPress MU Admin page appears where you can search for users and blogs within your community. Obviously, you won't perform this search if you don't have any users or blogs yet. However, this function is extremely useful when you have a community of users and blogs within your network.

Figure 3-3:
The
WordPress
dashboard
menus
expand to
reveal menu
items.

The Search Users feature allows you to search usernames and user e-mail addresses. If you search for the user *Lisa,* for instance, your results will include any user whose username or e-mail address contains *Lisa* — so you can receive multiple returns when using just one search word or phrase. The Search Blogs feature returns any blog content within your community that contains your search term, too.

The WordPress MU Admin page has two links near the top of the page that are very useful:

- ✔ **Create a New Blog:** Click this link to create a new blog within your community. Once clicked, the Blogs page appears where you can add a new blog. I cover how to do this in the upcoming "Blogs" section.

- ✔ **Create a New User:** Click this link to create a new user account within your community. Once clicked, the Users page appears where you can add a new user to your community. I cover how to do this in the upcoming "Users" section.

Additionally, the WordPress MU Admin page gives you a real time count of how many blogs and users you have in your community, which is nice-to-know information for any community site owner.

Blogs

The second item on the Site Admin menu is Blogs. The Blogs page is where you find several options for managing your community blogs.

At the top of the Blogs page is a search box that allows you to search through your community's blogs by name, ID, or IP address. This is especially helpful if you have a large community and a user contacts you with a question about his blog. You can visit the Blogs page and pull up that particular blog pretty quickly with the search feature.

The Blogs page also lists all the blogs within your community. The listing shows the following statistics about each community blog:

- ✔ **ID:** The blog's ID number assigned when it was created
- ✔ **Blog Domain:** The domain URL (Web address) of the blog
- ✔ **Last Updated:** The date the blog was last updated (or published to)
- ✔ **Registered:** The date the blog was registered in your community
- ✔ **Users:** The username and e-mail address associated with the user(s) of that blog

Underneath the listing of existing blogs in your community is the handy "Add a Blog" area, in which you can add a new blog easily by following these few steps:

1. **Type the address in the Blog Address text box.**

   The Blog Address is also the URL (Web address) of the blog you are creating. For example, if you typed in the word *newblog*, then the resulting URL of the blog will be `http://newblog.yourdomain.com` (if you are using subdomains) or `http://yourdomain.com/newblog` (if you are using subdirectories in your community), where *yourdomain.com* is the domain name of your community).

2. **Type the title in the Blog Title text box.**

   This is the title of the new blog you are creating. An example of a title: My New Blog — unlike the Blog Address, which cannot be changed, this title can be changed at any time within the WordPress dashboard settings.

3. **Type the e-mail address of the blog owner in the Admin Email text box.**

   This is the e-mail address of the person who is the owner of this blog. If the user is not already a member of your community, WordPress will create a new user and send that user an e-mail with his username and password for his new blog.

4. **Click the Add Blog button.**

   This action creates the blog in your network, and the Blogs page refreshes; you now see the newly created blog in the listing of blogs within your community.

For detailed information about using and managing community blogs, see Chapter 7.

Users

The third item on the Site Admin menu is Users. The Users page lists all your users and provides the following information about each one:

✔ **Username:** This is the login name the member uses when she logs in to her account in your community.

✔ **Name:** This is the user's real name, taken from her profile. If the user has not provided her name in her profile, this column will be blank.

✔ **E-mail:** This is the e-mail address the user entered when she registered on your site.

✔ **Registered:** This is the date when the user registered.

✔ **Blogs:** If you enable blogs within your WordPress community, this lists any blogs the user is a member of.

When you hover on a username with your mouse, an Edit link appears that you can click to edit that user's profile if you need to.

Also on the Users page, you can add new users with the interface near the bottom of the page, as shown in Figure 3-4.

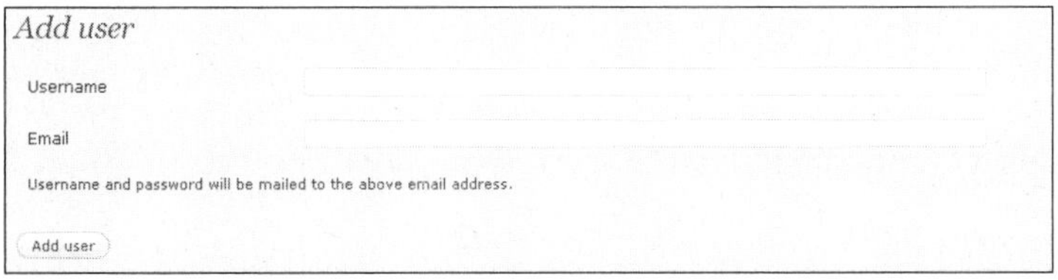

Figure 3-4:
Add a new
user on the
Users page.

Add user

Username

Email

Username and password will be mailed to the above email address.

(Add user)

Maybe you have a reluctant friend who's been dragging her feet about joining your community. You've been begging and pleading with her to join, and she keeps promising she will, yet days go by, and her user registration doesn't come through your e-mail. (Mom, are you paying attention?) Well, fix her up with an account on your site right this very minute! Here's how to add a new user to your community:

1. **Type the desired username in the Username text box.**

2. **Type the user's e-mail address in the Email text box.**

3. **Click the Add User button.**

   The page reloads with an Options Saved message at the top. You now see the new user in the list of users on the Users page.

The new user you created receives a confirmation e-mail. You've graciously helped your friend along, but she still has to confirm the registration. Nevertheless, you're one step closer to having your friend on board in your community!

Themes

The fourth item on the Site Admin menu is Themes. The Site Themes page lists available themes that you can use within your community, and is where you enable or disable installed themes for use on your site. Additionally, if you integrate community member blogs within your WordPress/BuddyPress web site (see Chapter 7), you can enable several themes for the bloggers to choose from.

You enable the BuddyPress theme that you want to use on your own main site on the Site Themes page. For more information about enabling and using the default BuddyPress themes, see Chapter 4.

Part IV of this book takes you through a myriad of information about using WordPress and BuddyPress themes within your community. If you have a burning desire to know more, hop over to that part of the book and read all about it.

Options

The fifth item on the Site Admin menu is Options. The Site Options page contains the operational settings (such as the site name, administrator e-mail address, and the welcome text sent to new users) for your entire WordPress MU–powered community, as shown in Figure 3-5.

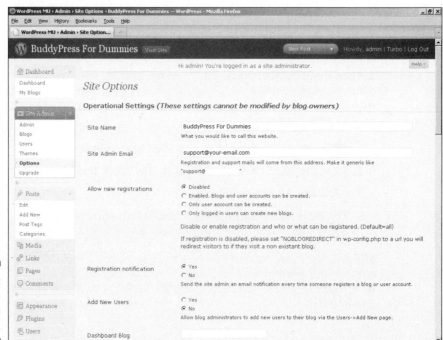

Figure 3-5: The Site Options page.

The following steps take you through each option:

1. **Type the name of your site in the Site Name text box.**

2. **Type your e-mail address in the Site Admin Email text box.**

   You use this e-mail address to send site registration notices, password reminders, and support e-mails to users within your community. Just a suggestion: Make the e-mail address an easy, generic address, such as `support@yourdomain.com`. Some users might e-mail you back at this address seeking support or assistance.

3. **Select an Allow New Registrations option:**

   • *Disabled:* Disallows new user registration completely. When selected, this option prevents people who visit your site from registering for a user account.

   • *Enabled. Blogs and User Accounts Can Be Created:* Gives users the ability to create a user account or a blog during the registration process.

   • *Only User Accounts Can Be Created:* Gives people the ability to create only a user account; users will not be able to create a blog within your network.

   • *Only Logged In Users Can Create New Blogs:* Allows only existing users — that is, those who are already logged in — to create a new blog within your network. This also disables new user registration completely. Select this option if you don't want just anyone registering for an account. Instead you, as the site administrator, can add new users at your own discretion.

4. **Select registration notification preferences.**

   Choose Yes or No to whether you want to be notified via e-mail each time a new user registers in your community.

5. **Select whether to allow blog administers to add new users to their blog(s).**

   Choose Yes or No to whether you want to allow your community blog owners to add new users to their own community blog via the Users page within their individual dashboards.

6. **Type the name or ID of the dashboard blog.**

   The dashboard blog is the main blog for your Web site. If this field is left blank, the main blog for your site will default to your main domain (`yourdomain.com`) when people visit your site. New users are added as subscribers to the dashboard blog if they don't have a blog within your community.

7. Set the default role for new users on the dashboard blog.

Your drop-down menu choices are

- *Subscriber:* Users can access their profile only and cannot access any of the back-end features or settings of your main blog.

- *Contributor:* Users can upload files and write, edit, and manage posts on your main blog. However, when a contributor writes a post, the post is saved as a draft to await administrator approval. Contributors cannot post to the blog without approval, which is a nice way to moderate content written by new authors.

- *Author:* In addition to having the same access and permissions as a contributor, an author can publish posts without administrator approval. Authors can also edit and delete their own posts.

- *Editor:* In addition to having the same access and permissions as an author, an editor can moderate comments, manage categories, manage links, edit pages, and edit other author's posts. Editors can also read and edit private posts.

- *Administrator:* This user has access to all menus and settings within the WordPress dashboard and has the authority to change any of those options and settings, as well.

I would highly recommend leaving the default role set to Subscriber because you don't want community users to have access to any of the back-end settings and options for your main blog (unless that's your intention, then by all means, change it!).

8. Type disallowed user names in the Banned Names text box.

By default, WordPress MU bans several user names from being registered within your community, including *www, web, root, admin, main, invite, administrator, members, register, activate, search, blog, activity, blogs, forums,* and *groups.* For good reason, you don't want a random user to register a username, such as *admin,* because you don't want that person misrepresenting himself as an administrator on your site. You can enter an unlimited amount of usernames that you do not want to allow on your site in the Banned Names text box.

9. Limit registration to certain e-mail addresses.

This option allows you to enter an unlimited amount of e-mail addresses to limit new user registration to only certain e-mail addresses. For example, if I wanted to create a community of people from my publishing company, Wiley Publishing — I can put *wiley.com* in this field to restrict registration to only people with access to that e-mail domain. People who try to register with an e-mail that is not on the list cannot register.

To keep registration open to everyone, regardless of their address, leave this field blank.

10. **In the Welcome Email text box, type the text of the e-mail you want new users to receive when they register with your site.**

    Alternatively, you can leave this area alone and use the default text provided for you by WordPress MU.

    A few variables you can use in this e-mail aren't explained entirely on the Site Options page, including

    * `SITE_NAME`: Inserts the name of your WordPress site.
    * `BLOG_URL`: Inserts the URL of the new member's blog.
    * `USERNAME`: Inserts the new member's username.
    * `PASSWORD`: Inserts the new member's password.
    * `BLOG_URLwp-login.php`: Inserts the hyperlinked login URL for the new member's blog.
    * `SITE_URL`: Inserts the hyperlinked URL for your WordPress MU site.

11. **In the First Post text box, type the text that you want to appear in the first post on every blog that's created in your community.**

    You can use this area to provide useful information about your site and services. This also serves as a nice guide for new users, as they can view that post in their dashboard, on the Edit Post page, and see how it was entered and formatted and use that as a guide for creating their own blog posts. You can also use the variables mentioned in Step 10 to have WordPress automatically add some information for you.

12. **Select media upload buttons.**

    The choices are Images, Videos, and Music. Select the media that you'll allow community users to upload to their own blog (assuming you're integrating community blogs on your site).

13. **Type the number for the maximum storage space allowed for blog uploads.**

    The amount is in megabytes (MB), and the default storage space is 10MB. This amount of hard drive space is what you give users to store the files they upload to their blog.

14. **Select upload file types.**

    Users cannot upload any file types that do not appear in this text box. By default, WordPress includes the following file types: `.jpg`, `.jpeg`,

.png, .gif, .mp3, .mov, .avi, .wmv, .midi, .mid, and .pdf. You can remove any default file types, and add new ones.

15. **Set the maximum uploaded file size.**

   This amount is in kilobytes (K), and the default file size is 1500K. This means that a user cannot upload a file that is larger than 1500K. Adjust this number as you see fit.

16. **Set the Admin Notice Feed.**

   If you want to display the latest post from your main blog within the dashboard of each of your users, type the RSS feed of the blog into this text box. By default, the text box is blank.

17. **Type the usernames that are allowed administrative access to your dashboard.**

   The usernames in this text box are allowed to log in to the main blog dashboard and access the Site Admin menu.

18. **In the Menus section, select the Plugins check box.**

   The Plugins page will be visible to users on their own blog dashboard. If you leave this option deselected, users will not have access to the plugins list. For more information about using plugins with WordPress and BuddyPress, see Chapter 13.

19. **Click the Update Options button.**

   When you finish the Site Options settings, don't forget to click the Update Options button to save your settings. This reloads the Site Options page with your saved settings.

Upgrade

The final item on the Site Admin menu is Upgrade. You use the Site Upgrade page to upgrade the WordPress MU software. When WordPress MU releases a new version of their software, a message is shown at the top of your WordPress dashboard alerting you that you need to upgrade. This easy process is described in the "Tools" section, later in this chapter. However, upgrading the main software isn't enough; you have to make sure each blog within your community is upgraded also. To accomplish this upgrade, simply click the Upgrade Site button on the Upgrade Site page. After you do that, WordPress MU runs a script that upgrades each blog within your community, assuming that you've chosen to integrate community blogs.

Depending on the size of your community — particularly if there are several blogs — this could take a very long time.

Setting general site options

Many of the remaining items in the navigation menu on the left side of the page are general settings for your site, but others allow you to accomplish tasks, such as publishing new posts, writing and publishing pages, creating link lists and categories, and installing themes and plugins for your site.

Posts

The Posts menu is directly beneath the Site Admin menu. Hover your cursor on Posts and then click the drop-down arrow that appears to the right. The Posts menu expands to display the following options:

- ✔ **Edit:** Click this link to visit the Edit Posts page so you can edit existing posts in your blog.

- ✔ **Add New:** Click this link to visit the Add New Post page where you can create a new post on your blog, as shown in Figure 3-6.

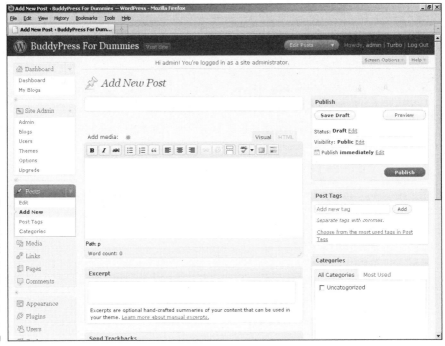

Figure 3-6:
The Add New Post page where you write and publish blog posts to your site.

✔ **Post Tags:** Click this link to visit the Tags page where you can create and manage tags on your blog.

✔ **Categories:** Click this link to visit the Categories page where you can create and manage categories on your blog.

Media

Beneath the Posts menu is the Media menu where you can upload and manage media files, such as photos, videos, and audio files. Hover your mouse on Media and then click the drop-down arrow that appears to the right. The Media menu expands to display the following options:

✔ **Library:** Click this link to visit the Media Library page where you manage your previously uploaded media files.

✔ **Add New:** Click this link to visit the Upload New Media page where you can use the built-in WordPress file upload feature to upload new media files to your Web site.

Links

The Links menu is where you can add and manage link lists (known as *blog-rolls*) on your Web site. Hover your mouse on Links and then click the drop-down arrow that appears to the right. The Links menu expands to display the following options:

✔ **Edit:** Click this link to visit the Edit Links page where you manage, edit, and delete links you've added to your Web site.

✔ **Add New:** Click this link to visit the Add New Link page where you add new links to include on your Web site.

✔ **Link Categories:** Click this link to visit the Link Categories page where you add and manage link categories. Link categories allow you to categorize links on your site by topic (much like post categories).

Pages

Beneath the Links menu is the Pages menu where you can add and manage pages on your Web site. Hover your mouse on Pages and then click the drop-down arrow that appears to the right. The Pages menu reveals the following options:

✔ **Edit:** Click this link to visit the Edit Pages page where you edit, delete, and manage pages on your site.

✔ **Add New:** Click this link to visit the Add New Page page where you create and publish new pages to your site.

Comments

The Comments menu doesn't have any options; therefore, it doesn't have a drop-down arrow. Simply click Comments to visit the Edit Comments page where you can edit, display, and manage comments that visitors have left on your blog.

Appearance

The Appearance menu is where you can add, activate, and delete themes on your site, as well as edit existing themes. You also work with WordPress widgets in this section. Hover your mouse on Appearance and then click the drop-down arrow that appears to the right. The Appearance menu expands to display the following options:

- **Themes:** Click this link to visit the Manage Themes page where you can manage installed themes and activate or de-activate themes to change the appearance of your blog.

- **Widgets:** Click this link to visit the Widgets page where you can configure the widgets you want to use on your site, including

  - A listing of recent posts

  - A listing of recent comments

  - A listing of categories you've created

  - The link lists you've added

- **Editor:** Click this link to visit the Edit Themes page where you find a listing of all the templates that make up your WordPress theme. You can click on each template on this page to edit them.

- **Add New Themes:** Click this link to visit the Install Themes page where you can browse the official WordPress Free Themes Directory from within your WordPress interface. You can search for new themes based on color, format, and style; and then install and activate a new theme from this page.

Plugins

The Plugins menu is where you can add, activate, de-activate, delete, and edit plugins for your WordPress site. Additionally, you find and install the BuddyPress suite of plugins here (see Chapter 4).

Hover your mouse on Plugins and then click the drop-down arrow that appears to the right. The Plugins menu expands to display the following options:

✔ **Installed:** Click this link to visit the Manage Plugins page where you find a listing of all the plugins currently installed on your WordPress site. Here you can activate, de-activate, or delete plugins as needed.

✔ **Add New:** Click this link to visit the Install Plugins page where you can browse the official WordPress Plugins Directory from within your WordPress interface. You can search for plugins based on terms, plugin author name, and popularity; and then install and activate the plugin from this area.

✔ **Editor:** Click this link to visit the Plugin Editor page where you will find a listing of all the plugin files currently installed on your WordPress site. If you are comfortable with editing PHP programming, you can edit plugin files to adjust them to your needs.

Users

The Users menu is where you can manage, edit, delete, and add users to your WordPress site. Hover your mouse on Users and then click the drop-down arrow that appears to the right. The Users menu expands to display the following options:

✔ **Authors & Users:** Click this link to visit the Users page where you find a listing of registered users on your site. You can edit their profiles, e-mail addresses, passwords, and roles. You can also delete users from your site in this section.

✔ **Add New:** Click this link to visit the Add New User page to do just that: add a new user by typing her username (also her login), first and last name, e-mail address, Web site address, and password; and then assigning her an Administrator, Editor, Contributor, Author, or Subscriber role.

✔ **Your Profile:** Click this link to visit the page where you can edit your own profile information, including

• The preferred color scheme (gray or blue) you want for the dashboard display

• Your first and last name

• Your e-mail address

• Your Web site address

• Your biographical information

• Your password

Tools

The Tools menu is where you can take advantage of some useful tools included in your WordPress installation by clicking through the following options:

✔ **Tools:** Click this menu item to visit the Tools page where you can install and use Google Gears to speed up the page load time of your Web site. You can also take advantage of an application called Press This that allows you to post clips of text, images, and videos from any Web page you visit on the Web.

✔ **Import:** Click this menu item to visit the Import page where you can import data from another blogging platform into your WordPress site. This is especially nice if you've been blogging on another site and you want to import that data (posts, comments, and so on) into your new WordPress site. WordPress gives you the ability to import from the following platforms:

- Blogger
- Blogware
- DotClear
- GreyMatter
- LiveJournal
- Movable Type and TypePad
- RSS
- Textpattern
- Another WordPress blog

✔ **Export:** Click this link to visit the Export page where you can create an export (XML) file to transfer the data from your current WordPress Web site to another WordPress-powered Web site.

✔ **Upgrade:** Click this link to visit the Upgrade page where you can find out whether a newer version of WordPress is available. If there is, you can click the Upgrade Automatically button to upgrade your WordPress software to the latest version without ever leaving your WordPress dashboard. This is very handy because WordPress releases a new upgrade approximately every 120 days.

Settings

The final item on the navigation menu is Settings where you can set up the general options and basic configurations that determine how your WordPress Web site functions. Hover your mouse on Settings and then click the drop-down arrow that appears to the right. The Settings menu expands to display the following options:

✔ **General:** Click this link to visit the General Settings page where you configure some basic settings for your WordPress Web site, such as:

- Blog title
- Blog URL

- Admin e-mail address

- Membership options

- Time zone and date format

✔ **Writing:** Click this link to visit the Writing Settings page where you configure how your WordPress site handles publishing options, such as:

- Formatting

- Default post and default link categories

- Posting via e-mail

- Update settings, such as Ping-O-Matic, which is set up by default

✔ **Reading:** Click this link to visit the Reading Settings page where you configure the options for how your WordPress site handles content display, such as:

- Whether the front page displays blog posts or a static page

- The number of blog posts to display on one page

- The number of blog posts to display in the RSS Feed

✔ **Discussion:** Click this link to visit the Discussion Settings page where you configure options for how your WordPress site handles comments and trackbacks, including spam and moderation settings.

✔ **Media:** Click this link to visit the Media Settings page where you tell WordPress how to handle images on your Web site.

✔ **Privacy:** Click this link to visit the Privacy Settings page where you find the privacy control settings for your Web site.

✔ **Permalinks:** Click this link to visit the Permalink Settings page where you set up the URL structure on your Web site. The permalink settings control how the individual URLs look for each of your posts and pages.

✔ **Miscellaneous:** Click this link to visit the Discussion Settings page where you configure the folder and directory path WordPress uses to store files that you upload to your Web site through the WordPress file upload interface.

Part II
Getting Up and Running with BuddyPress

The 5th Wave   By Rich Tennant

"You should check that box so they can't profile your listening and viewing habits. I didn't do it and I'm still getting spam about hearing loss, anger management and psychological counseling."

In this part . . .

After you lay the WordPress foundation, you're ready to download, install, and configure the BuddyPress suite of plugins that enable you to design a social community on your Web site. In this part, you install the BuddyPress plugins and configure the initial settings and required options.

Chapter 4

Setting Up Base Camp

In This Chapter

▶ Reviewing basic requirements

▶ Installing BuddyPress

▶ Automatic and manual installation methods

▶ Activating BuddyPress

▶ Using the default themes

▶ Discovering the BuddyPress menu

After reading this chapter, you'll find that installing BuddyPress on your WordPress MU–powered Web site is relatively easy to accomplish. In Chapter 2, I cover all the basic requirements that you need in order to run BuddyPress on your Web site. By this point in the book, you should have accomplished the following:

✔ Registered a domain name for your Web site

✔ Obtained a Web hosting provider to house your Web site data

✔ Uploaded the WordPress MU files to your Web hosting account

✔ Set up the WordPress MU MySQL database

✔ Installed the WordPress MU software on your Web site

✔ Configured the correct Apache/DNS settings on your Web server

✔ Have a very good idea of the navigation structure of the WordPress MU dashboard

If you haven't completed one, or more, of these steps, revisit Chapter 2 to review the sections where I discuss these items in detail. If you've met these requirements, then you're ready to set up your BuddyPress community.

This chapter takes you through the installation and activation process for BuddyPress, and includes information on the two installation methods: automatic and manual. This chapter also introduces you to the default BuddyPress themes that ship with the BuddyPress suite of plugins. You also discover the basics of the BuddyPress menu to understand your WordPress

MU dashboard and the available BuddyPress components and settings. Additionally, at the end of this chapter, you find some online BuddyPress resources to help you along your way.

You must already have WordPress MU functioning on your Web site before you can install and use BuddyPress to build a social community on your Web site. (Chapter 2 covers the installation and setup of WordPress MU.)

In addition to the information provided in this chapter on installing BuddyPress on your Web site, you might also want to visit the official BuddyPress Codex to reference a nice checklist of installation steps: `http://codex.buddypress. org/getting-started/setting-up-a-new-installation`.

Installing BuddyPress

You can use two methods to install BuddyPress on your WordPress MU–powered site:

✔ Automatic installation, using the WordPress MU auto-installer

✔ Manual installation, using FTP (File Transfer Protocol) to upload files to your Web server

Using either of these installation methods will get BuddyPress up and running on your Web site. The automatic installation is, by far, the easiest; however, the manual installation method is good to know in case the automatic installation method fails (machines are not infallible, you know).

Using the automatic installation method

The easiest method to install BuddyPress on your Web site is to use the automatic installer that's built into the WordPress MU platform. This method takes the guesswork out of installing BuddyPress because the installer does all the heavy lifting for you, including the following:

✔ Downloads the latest version of BuddyPress to your Web server

✔ Places the BuddyPress files in the correct directory (or location) on your Web server

✔ Verifies that BuddyPress files are viable and in the right spot before you can use them

If something bad happens during the automatic installation process, such as an interruption in Internet service, WordPress MU warns you that BuddyPress is not ready to be activated on your site. The automatic installer knows whether the pieces and parts of a plugin, like BuddyPress, are correctly in place. If they aren't, the installer simply will not let you activate and use the plugin until it verifies that the installation went smoothly.

By using the automatic installer to install and activate BuddyPress, you save yourself valuable time that can be spent building your Web site content and community. If it sounds too good to be true (something so geeky can't really be that easy, can it?), then give the automatic installer a shot and experience its goodness! The following steps take you through installing BuddyPress on your WordPress MU–powered site with the built-in automatic plugin installer:

1. **Log in to your WordPress MU dashboard.**

   Point your browser to `http://yourdomain.com/wp-login.php`, enter your WordPress username and password, and then click the Log In button.

2. **Expand the Plugins menu.**

   On the left side of your WordPress MU dashboard, click the drop-down arrow that appears on the Plugins menu. This expands the Plugins menu and shows several links beneath the menu title.

3. **Click the Add New link.**

   The Install Plugins page appears, as shown in Figure 4-1.

4. **Search for the BuddyPress plugin.**

   Make sure Term is selected in the drop-down menu and then type **BuddyPress** in the field to the right.

5. **Click the Search Plugins button.**

   This reloads the Install Plugins page with a listing of search results for the term *BuddyPress*. Figure 4-2 illustrates the plugin search results page.

6. **Click the Install link for the BuddyPress plugin.**

   A pop-up window appears with a description of the BuddyPress plugin. (In Figure 4-2, the BuddyPress plugin on the Install Plugins search results page is the fifth listing.)

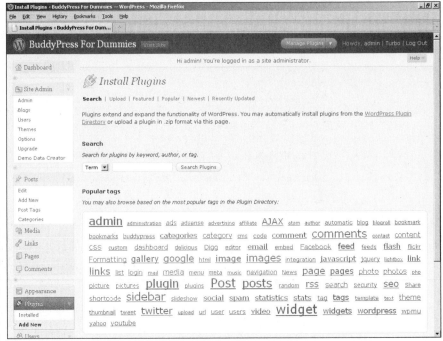

Figure 4-1:
The Install
Plugins
page on the
WordPress
MU dash-
board.

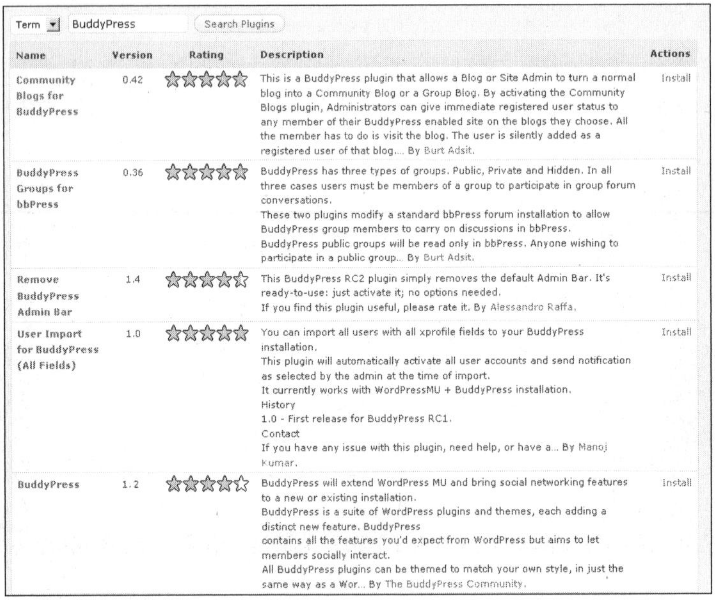

Figure 4-2:
The Install
Plugins
search
results
page.

7. Install BuddyPress.

Click Install Now in the top-right corner of the BuddyPress pop-up window, as shown in Figure 4-3. This loads the Installing Plugin: BuddyPress page and displays each step of the successful plugin installation process:

- Downloading install package from `http://wordpress.org/ extend/plugins/buddypress`

- Unpacking the package

- Installing the plugin

- Successfully installed the plugin BuddyPress

8. Activate BuddyPress.

Two links display after the plugin installation: Activate Plugin and Return to Plugin Installer. Click the Activate Plugin link to activate BuddyPress on your Web site. You return to the Manage Plugins page where you see a listing of plugins currently installed on your Web site; BuddyPress is now among the plugins listed.

Figure 4-3:
Pop-up
page for
Installing
BuddyPress.

The WordPress MU automatic plugin installer comes in handy for any plugin you want to install and use on your Web site. However, the only plugins that are available through the plugin installer are listed in the official WordPress Plugin Directory located at `http://wordpress.org/extend/plugins`.

After you install WordPress MU, the site admin (that's you) needs to enable the display of the Plugins menu for users within your community if you want to allow your users to access the menu to choose which plugins they want to activate on their community blog. When you visit the Manage Plugins page to activate the BuddyPress plugins, a red status message tells you, the site admin, that the Plugins page is not visible to normal users and must be activated (see Figure 4-4). You do not need to activate the Plugins menu to activate BuddyPress. The only reason to do this is if you want your normal users (non-admin users) to see and use the Plugins page to manage plugins on their own community blog. For more about the use of plugins, see Chapter 13.

The next part of this chapter deals with the manual installation of the BuddyPress plugin files — you might want to stick around for these instructions because they are good to know in a pinch. Additionally, this information gives you a solid idea of where the BuddyPress plugin files live on your Web server, which comes in handy when you dig deeper into customizing your BuddyPress community by creating or tweaking theme designs (see Part IV).

Error message

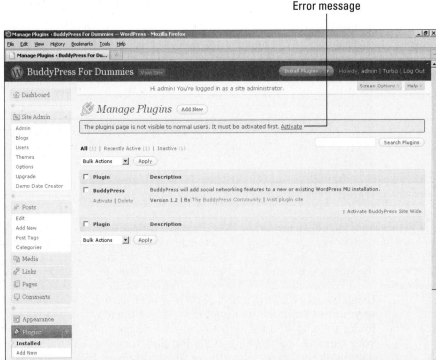

Figure 4-4: Status message on the Manage Plugins page.

Installing BuddyPress manually

The manual installation process of BuddyPress requires quite a few more steps than the automatic installation method I cover. However, this method gives you a good understanding of the directory structure of the BuddyPress files and the location of the files on your Web server, including the names of the folders and files that make up the suite of BuddyPress plugins.

Before you start, make sure you have an FTP program ready because you'll need it to transfer the BuddyPress files from your computer to your Web server. Chapter 2 covers the information you need to use an FTP program if you want to make sure you have the information and tools necessary to perform the manual installation.

Downloading the BuddyPress files

To download the BuddyPress plugins from the official BuddyPress Web site:

1. **Browse to the BuddyPress Web site at `http://buddypress.org`.**

2. **Choose Download on the top navigation menu on the BuddyPress Web site.**

   The Download BuddyPress page (`http://buddypress.org/download`) appears where you download the latest release of BuddyPress.

3. **Click the Download BuddyPress link.**

   A dialog box appears where you choose a location on your computer to store the BuddyPress Zip file.

4. **Decompress (or unzip) the BuddyPress plugin files.**

   Use a program like WinZip for the PC, or the built-in tool for compressed files on a Mac.

Be sure to remember where you store the BuddyPress files on your computer because you need to know that for the next step in the manual installation procedure.

Uploading the BuddyPress files

To upload the BuddyPress files to your host, within your FTP program open the location on your computer where you unzipped the BuddyPress plugin files that you downloaded earlier. The left side of Figure 4-5 shows all the files in the `\buddypress` folder. I'm using an FTP program called Filezilla; the program you use might look different but will still list the same files and folders you see here.

Using your FTP client, connect to your Web server, and upload all the files to your hosting account's root directory. Upload the entire `\buddypress` folder to your Web server into the `/wp-content/plugins/` folder within your existing WordPress installation directory. The right side of Figure 4-5 illustrates the correct location of the BuddyPress files on your Web server.

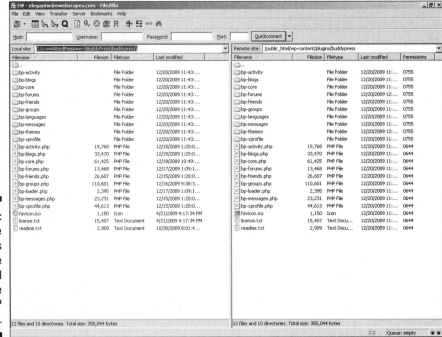

Figure 4-5:
The
BuddyPress
file structure
displayed
in the
Filezilla FTP
program.

Most FTP client software allows you to select all the files and drag and drop them to your Web server. Other programs have you highlight the files and click a Transfer button.

In Chapter 2, I give you several tips and things to keep in mind when uploading files to your Web server via FTP, including transfer mode and file permissions. Review that section if you experience any problems during the manual installation process.

Activate BuddyPress after manual file installation

After you have the necessary BuddyPress files uploaded to your Web server, you can activate BuddyPress on your Web site. To activate BuddyPress, follow these few easy steps:

1. **Log in to your WordPress MU dashboard.**

   Point your browser to `http://yourdomain.com/wp-login.php`, enter your WordPress username and password, and then click the Log In button.

2. **Browse to the Manage Plugins page.**

   Choose Installed on the Plugins menu on the left side of your WordPress MU dashboard. This loads the Manage Plugins page where you find a listing of all the installed plugins on your site.

3. **Activate BuddyPress.**

   Click the Activate link that displays beneath the BuddyPress plugin. The Manage Plugins page reloads, and BuddyPress appears at the top of the page under the Currently Active Site Wide Plugins heading, as shown in Figure 4-6.

BuddyPress admin bar

One thing you might immediately notice after successfully installing and activating BuddyPress is the admin bar at the top of your site, as shown in Figure 4-7.

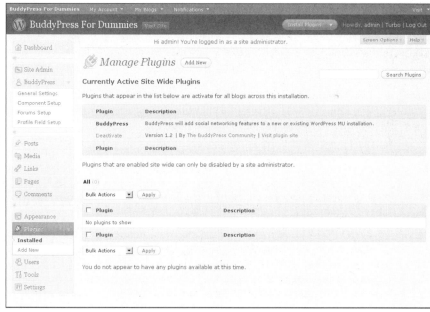

Figure 4-6:
When activated, BuddyPress appears under Currently Active Site Wide Plugins.

Admin bar

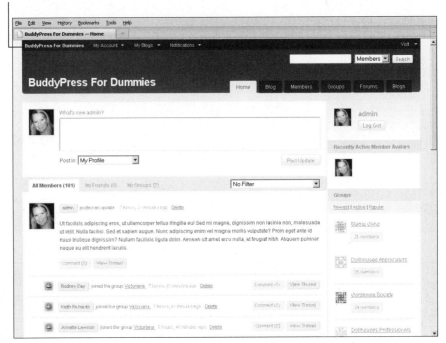

Figure 4-7:
The
BuddyPress
admin bar.

The admin bar is a navigation menu that you and your community of users can use to navigate the different pages and features of your social community after logging in.

Using Default BuddyPress Themes

BuddyPress comes with default themes that you can use for the visual look of your social community's Web site. One theme framework is the parent theme that all other (child) themes are built from. That might sound a little confusing, but in Part IV of this book, I unravel the mysteries surrounding parent and child themes, frameworks, and using them to create your BuddyPress social community Web site's custom design. For right now, however, getting the default themes installed and running on your site is the important issue.

Moving theme folders

After you install and activate BuddyPress on your site, the theme files are in the /wp-content/plugins/buddypress/bp-themes folder on your Web server.

Whether you chose the automatic or manual method of installing BuddyPress, the theme files need to be moved before you can use the themes on your Web site. You use your FTP program to move the theme folders to the correct location on your Web server. The three theme folders to move are

- ✔ Move `/wp-content/plugins/buddypress/bp-themes/bp-sn-parent` to `/wp-content/themes`

- ✔ Move `/wp-content/plugins/buddypress/bp-themes/bp-classic` to `/wp-content/themes`

- ✔ Move `/wp-content/plugins/buddypress/bp-themes/bp-default` to `/wp-content/themes`

Keep an eye out for a new release of the WordPress MU software in the early months of 2010. The planned upgrade for WordPress MU will eliminate the need for you to move the BuddyPress theme files to the `/wp-content/themes/` folder; this action will be done for you when you install and activate the BuddyPress suite of plugins.

Every FTP program differs in the way it allows you to move files and folders from one directory to another. Some allow you to utilize the drag-and-drop method; others require that you right-click the file or folder with your mouse, select the Move option, and then type the directory that you want to move the files or folders to.

Activating themes

The final step in making sure that you can use the default BuddyPress themes on your Web site is to activate them within your WordPress MU dashboard. Two concepts are at work:

- ✔ **Enabling themes on your WordPress MU dashboard**

  The BuddyPress installation process places the BuddyPress themes where they need to be on your Web server; however, you still need to take the extra step of activating those themes for use on your WordPress MU site. Part IV of this book covers BuddyPress themes in depth; however, to use themes on your WordPress MU and BuddyPress site, the theme files need to exist in the `/wp-content/themes` folder in your WordPress MU installation directory on your Web server. Having the themes installed in that directory isn't enough, however; you also need to enable the themes for use on your WordPress MU site.

- ✔ **Activating a theme to display on your main site**

  Once enabled, themes can be activated. You can have only one active theme on your Web site at a time. The active theme is what displays when you, and other people, view your Web site in a Web browser.

The following steps enable the BuddyPress themes in WordPress MU and activate the BuddyPress Default theme on your Web site:

1. **Log in to your WordPress MU dashboard.**

   Point your browser to `http://yourdomain.com/wp-login.php`, enter your WordPress admin username and password, and then click the Log In button.

2. **Browse to the Site Themes page.**

   Choose Themes on the Site Admin menu on the left side of your WordPress MU dashboard. The Site Themes page appears, showing a listing of available themes installed in your `/wp-content/themes` folder.

3. **Enable the BuddyPress themes for use on your WordPress MU site.**

   Select the Yes radio button to the left of either the BuddyPress Classic theme or the BuddyPress Default theme. The BuddyPress Social Network Parent theme does not get enabled, because it acts only as a framework for the other child themes.

4. **Click the Update Themes button.**

   The Site Themes page reloads and displays a message telling you that the Site Themes options are saved, as shown in Figure 4-8.

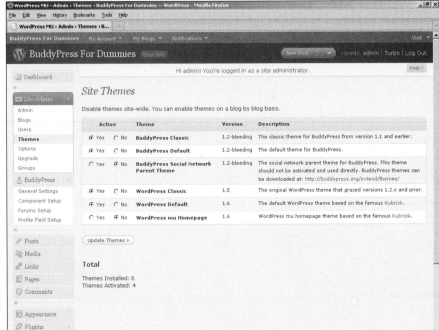

Figure 4-8: Site Themes options save after selecting themes and clicking the Update Themes button.

5. **Browse to the Manage Themes page.**

   Choose Themes on the Appearance menu on the left side of your WordPress MU dashboard. The Manage Themes page loads where you activate the theme you want to display on your site.

6. **Activate the BuddyPress Default theme.**

   Click the Activate link that appears beneath the BuddyPress Default or the BuddyPress Classic theme thumbnails — you can use either the Default or Classic theme, the choice is yours. I've chosen to activate the BuddyPress Default theme. When it's activated, the BuddyPress Default theme (see Figure 4-9) displays when you visit your site.

You can preview how a theme will look on your site before activating it on the Manage Themes page. Click the Preview link beneath the theme image, and a pop-up window shows you how your site looks with that particular theme active. To activate the theme from the pop-up window, just click the Activate link that appears in the top-right corner of the window. To close the window without activating the theme, click the X that appears in the top-left corner of the pop-up window.

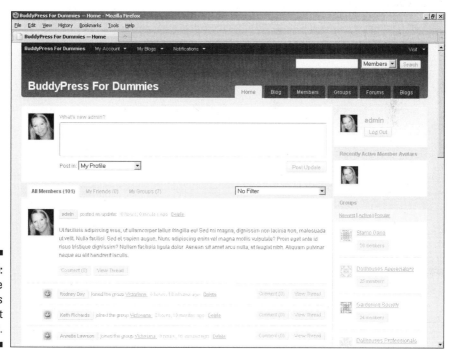

Figure 4-9:
The
BuddyPress
Default
theme.

The BuddyPress themes use built-in WordPress and BuddyPress widgets to display content on your Web site. I don't cover widgets in this chapter; however, Chapter 9 has a great deal of information on how to use widgets, including the built-in BuddyPress widgets that enable you to add dynamic and interactive features to your social community Web site.

Finding the BuddyPress Menu

In Chapter 2, I cover the basics of navigating through the WordPress MU dashboard. The left side of the dashboard is where you find all the menus of options and settings that you need to set up and configure your WordPress MU site. Once installed and activated, BuddyPress has its own menu in the WordPress MU dashboard directly beneath the Site Admin menu. Figure 4-10 shows you exactly where the BuddyPress menu is found.

The next chapter in this book, Chapter 5, goes through the options and configurations in detail; however, to give you a very basic idea of the navigation options and configuration settings in the BuddyPress menu, here's a brief rundown:

The BuddyPress menu

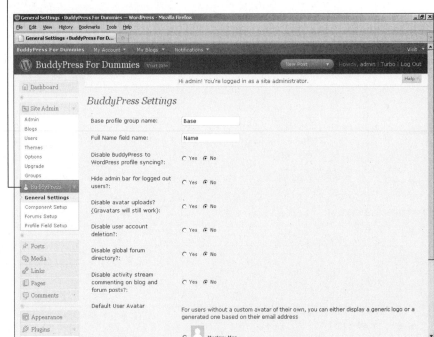

Figure 4-10: The BuddyPress menu on the WordPress dashboard.

✔ **General Settings:** Click this link to load the BuddyPress Settings page where you define basic settings of your BuddyPress social community, such as its wire, admin bar, and avatar handling.

✔ **Component Setup:** Click this link to load the BuddyPress Component Setup page. Components are the modules that you can use to enable the following features within your community:

- Activity Streams

- Blog Tracking

- bbPress Forums

- Friends

- Groups

- Private Messaging

- Extended Profiles

You can enable all the components or just the ones you want to use; you do not need to enable all the components for BuddyPress to work on your site. Enable the components that you might want to use; the disabled ones will not be accessible to users on your site. You can, however, come back later and enable the components if you choose.

✔ **Forums Setup:** Click this link to load the Forums Setup page where you can set up a new bbPress installation or use an existing one to integrate discussion forums into your social community. bbPress is a discussion forum software (created by the same folks behind WordPress and BuddyPress) that's separate from WordPress MU or BuddyPress. However, bbPress integrates with both platforms. For more information about this option, see Chapter 7.

✔ **Profile Field Setup:** Click this link to load the Profile Field Setup page where you can create information fields that your community users fill out about themselves and display on their member profiles within your community pages. See Chapter 5 for in-depth information about extended user profiles.

Various sites on the Web offer additional information, resources, and assistance to help you with all things related to BuddyPress and WordPress MU. Table 4-1 lists some of the more popular Web sites where WordPress and BuddyPress geeks hang out to talk, swap stories, and help one another.

**Table 4-1   Helpful WordPress MU and BuddyPress
Web Resources**

WordPress MU Resources

Web Site Name	Web Site Address (URL)
WordPress MU — Official Site	`http://mu.wordpress.org`
WordPress MU Support Forum	`http://mu.wordpress.org/forums`
WordPress MU Codex (documentation)	`http://codex.wordpress.org/ WordPress_MU`

BuddyPress Resources

Web Site Name	Web Site Address (URL)
BuddyPress.Org — Official Site	`http://buddypress.org`
BuddyPress Codex	`http://codex.buddypress.org`
BuddyPress Forums	`http://buddypress.org/forums`
BuddyPress Developer Community	`http://buddypress.org/ developers`

Chapter 5

Configuring BuddyPress

In This Chapter

▶ Configuring the general settings

▶ Setting up BuddyPress components

▶ Installing and enabling group forums

▶ Encouraging user friendships

▶ Using private messaging

▶ Setting up extended profiles for users

*T*he very foundation of a BuddyPress-powered social community is the BuddyPress suite of plugins. These components help create the "social" part of your network by allowing your community to participate in your Web site by building personal profiles, creating friendships with other users, and communicating with other users via private messaging, forums, wires, and groups.

In this chapter, you configure the initial general settings of BuddyPress via the BuddyPress menu on your WordPress MU dashboard. Additionally, you step through the setup of each BuddyPress component, and gain insight about why you may or may not wish to use the component in your community.

You do not have to use all of the components that come with BuddyPress for it to work on your Web site. You can choose which components you want to use by enabling them on the BuddyPress menu and leaving the rest disabled. Just like the salad bar at your local eatery — take what you want and leave the rest!

Configuring the General Settings

First things first, you need to visit the BuddyPress Settings page to configure the general settings of your BuddyPress community. BuddyPress comes packaged with several different components and features that you can enable within your community. (See Chapter 6 for information on BuddyPress components and what they do). You do not have to use all of the available components — as a site administrator, you have the option to use only what you need and leave the rest. The following steps take you through the basic settings. Later in this chapter I show you the different components you can use in your BuddyPress community site.

1. **Log in to your WordPress MU dashboard.**

   Point your browser to `http://yourdomain.com/wp-login.php`, enter your WordPress admin username and password, and then click the Log In button.

2. **Expand the BuddyPress menu.**

   On the left side of your WordPress MU dashboard, click the drop-down arrow on the BuddyPress menu. This expands the BuddyPress menu and displays several links beneath the menu title.

3. **Browse to the BuddyPress Settings page.**

   Click the General Settings link on the BuddyPress menu. This loads the BuddyPress Settings page, as shown in Figure 5-1, where you set up the initial general settings for your community.

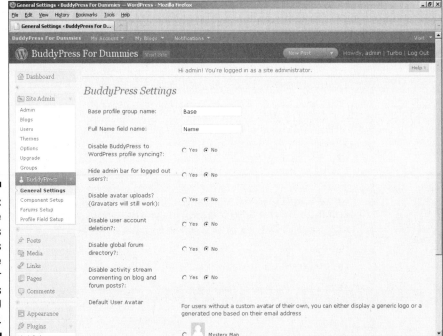

Figure 5-1: The BuddyPress Settings page on your WordPress MU dashboard.

On the BuddyPress Settings page, you're presented with seven settings. Each of these options already has a default setting, which you can leave or change according to your tastes:

✔ **Base Profile Group Name:** By default, the Base Profile Group Name value is Base, but you can change the value to anything you want by typing a new name in the text field. I cover profile groups in the later "Building Profile Groups and Fields" section; in short, however, the profile group name is the title that displays on member profiles above the information they provide at signup.

Figure 5-2 shows my member profile where I've changed the default profile group name to Information. (You can see that the title bar above the details in my profile now reads *Information*.) If I had left the default profile group name Base, the title on my profile would read *Base* instead.

✔ **Full Name Field Name:** Just like the default profile group name, the Full Name Field Name value displays on member profiles as the member name label. By default, the Full Name Field Name value is Name — but you can change the value by typing a new phrase in the text field. A couple of examples might be Handle or Nickname.

In Figure 5-2, you see that the label to the left of my name reads *People call me* — so when visitors see my member profile, they read *People call me: Lisa Sabin-Wilson*. This is another small way to customize your BuddyPress social community.

✔ **Disable BuddyPress to WordPress Profile Syncing?:** Here you can choose to have BuddyPress synchronize users' profiles with the profile data they filled out in their WordPress profiles.

✔ **Hide Admin Bar for Logged Out Users?:** Select Yes or No to hide the admin bar for logged out users. The admin bar is a navigation menu that appears at the top of a WordPress MU Web site that has an additional BuddyPress social community added to it. The admin bar allows users to navigate to different areas of the community, such as profiles, groups, forums, and blogs. If you want this admin bar visible to users of your community who aren't logged in (or who aren't members), select No. If you want to hide it from visitors who aren't logged in, select Yes.

For more information about the admin bar and using it for easy navigation throughout your Web site and community, see Chapter 6.

✔ **Disable Avatar Uploads?:** Here you can choose to disable users' ability to upload their own avatar image. If you select Yes, users won't be able to add their own photos or pictures to their member profiles. If you select No, users will be able to upload their own photos to display on their profiles.

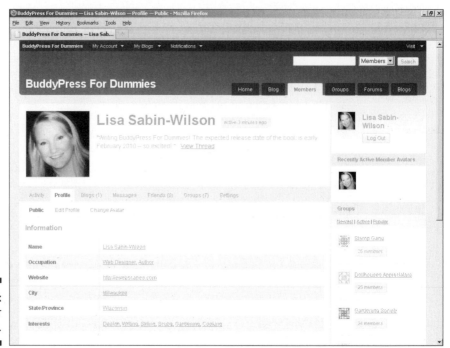

Figure 5-2:
My member
profile.

✓ **Disable User Account Deletion?:** This allows you to select whether you will allow your users to delete their own accounts within your community. The selection is No by default, which allows users to delete their own accounts whenever they want to — this is the recommended setting if you want to give your users full control over their accounts in your community.

✓ **Disable Global Forum Directory?:** By default, the selection here is set to No, which means the Global Forums Directory will display on your site. (See Chapter 6 for full information about BuddyPress Directories). If you prefer to disable this, select Yes.

✓ **Disable Activity Stream commenting on blog and forum posts?:** Here you can control whether community members can leave comments within Activity Streams on blog posts and forum posts. By default, this option is set to No — select Yes if you want to disable this feature.

✓ **Default User Avatar:** User profiles that don't have a custom avatar or photo uploaded display a default avatar. Your selection here determines the default avatar, and BuddyPress gives you four options to choose from, as shown in Figure 5-3.

Figure 5-3:
The four images you can choose from to set the default avatar.

When you complete selecting and setting the options on the BuddyPress Settings page, be sure to click the Save Settings button at the bottom of the page, otherwise your new settings will not be saved.

Discovering BuddyPress Components

The next step in configuring your new BuddyPress community is enabling the components that you want to use on your Web site. You can use all of them, or some of them, depending on your personal preference. This section gives you the details on each component to help you decide whether you'd like to use them to enhance your community. You can find further information on these components in Chapter 6, which takes you through how members of your community can use each feature.

To enable or disable components for your Web site, follow these steps:

1. **Log in to your WordPress MU dashboard.**

   Point your browser to `http://yourdomain.com/wp-login.php`, enter your WordPress admin username and password, and then click the Log In button.

2. **Expand the BuddyPress menu.**

   On the left side of your WordPress MU dashboard, click the drop-down arrow on the BuddyPress menu. This expands the BuddyPress menu and displays several links beneath the menu title.

3. **Browse to the BuddyPress Component Setup page.**

   Click the Component Setup link on the BuddyPress menu. This loads the BuddyPress Component Setup page, as shown in Figure 5-4, where you set up the initial settings for your community.

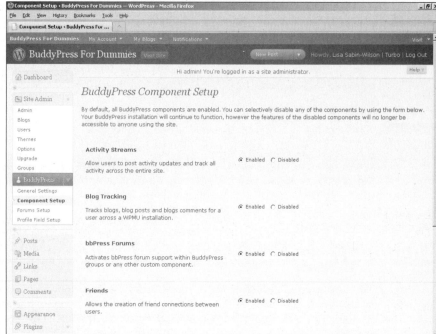

Figure 5-4:
The
BuddyPress
Component
Setup page
on your
WordPress
MU dash-
board.

Each component on the BuddyPress Component Setup page has two options that you can select: Enabled or Disabled. By default, each component is enabled — to change that for any of the components on this page, select the Disabled radio button and then click the Save Settings button on the bottom of the page to save your changes.

Activity Streams

You probably want to enable activity streams in your community because activity streams are the heart of almost every social community on the Web. Enabling activity streams in BuddyPress gives you the capability of publishing a page on your Web site that displays all of your community members' activities on your network. Every action is recorded on the activity stream, which gives your community members an easy way to discover what other members are doing and how they're using your community features.

Figure 5-5 shows a WordPress MU-powered Web site at the official test site for BuddyPress at `http://testbp.org`. The front page of the Web site, which uses the BuddyPress Default theme, shows recent member activity within their entire community.

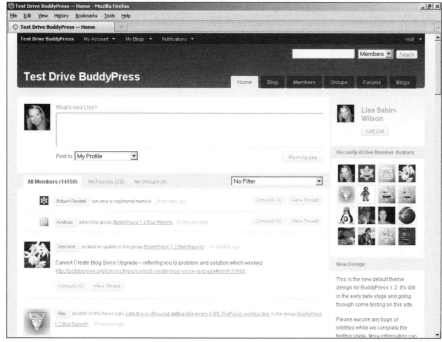

Figure 5-5:
Site wide
activity on
the front
page of
http://testbp.
org.

Additionally, activity streams collect individual activities on individual profiles so that members can see a running list of their own recent activities within your community, as well as a listing of their friends' activities.

What types of activities are recorded within the activity streams? Don't worry — the recorded activity is restricted to community activities only, so no one will know if you're picking your nose while browsing the Web. The following activities are some examples of what's recorded in activity streams:

✔ Wire posts

✔ Blog posts and comments

✔ New friendships

✔ Profile updates, including updates to a member's profile photo

Blog Tracking

One feature of a WordPress MU–powered blog that sets it apart from a Web site powered by the (single user) WordPress.org software is that the MU-powered blog allows users to create multiple blogs within the network. Adding BuddyPress to the mix doesn't remove this feature at all; it enhances and encourages the activity by providing the Blog Tracking component.

With the Blog Tracking component enabled, members' blogs, blog posts, and blog comments display in one spot on their member profile. This enables other members to easily find all the blogs that member belongs to, or owns, as well as all of their blog posts and comments. This handy feature encourages deeper navigation and conversation through member participation within your network on various member blogs. Figure 5-6 illustrates the Blog Tracking feature on the BuddyPress demo Web site (`http://testbp.org`). For additional information about integrating member blogs, see Chapter 7.

bbPress Forums

Discussion forums, or *message boards,* engage your community in communications, discussions, and debates about various topics. BuddyPress integrates discussion forums into your community to allow users to create, manage, and maintain their own message boards for groups they create within your network. Group and community members post and reply to topics right from the community's group pages — without leaving the member area.

bbPress (`http://bbpress.org`) is the discussion forum platform that integrates with a BuddyPress community. The reason for this is simple, bbPress is part of the WordPress family of software and it integrates seamlessly with the WordPress platform. Figure 5-7 shows a forum integrated on the BuddyPress demo Web site for the Group called BuddyPress Testers. Within this group, members can start discussion threads and encourage other group members to participate in the conversation. For more information about groups and forums, including technical details on how to install bbPress on your Web site, see Chapter 8.

Friends

A community wouldn't be social without friends, would it? The Friends component is really fun — it allows you and your users to add new friends that you've met within the community. Community friendships exist among people within the network who connect through requests. Each community member has a list of people who are "friends" that anyone can browse. Additionally, members can click a name on the list to view the full profile, and even add that person as a friend on their own list.

Every member profile displays an Add Friend button so you can add friends while you're browsing the Members Directory. Friend requests are e-mailed to the member, who then can log in to accept or decline your friendship request. After the request is accepted, your activity stream will appear on your friend's wire, and vice versa, so you can keep track of what your friends are up to. You can also send private messages to your friends.

Figure 5-6:
The Blog
Tracking
component,
as seen
on the
BuddyPress
demo Web
site.

Figure 5-7:
bbPress
discussion
forum inte-
grated into a
BuddyPress
community
group page.

Groups

The Groups component gives users the ability to create, well — *groups!* Think of groups as similar to cliques in high school— groups of kids who shared an interest in sports, music, theater, or chess; or even those geeks in the back of the room with their noses stuck to their computer monitors (you know the type . . . ahem). Groups in social communities like the one you're running on your Web site with BuddyPress allow members to band together with other people who share the same interests and ideas so they can interact, discuss, and communicate with one another in their own little corner of your Web site.

BuddyPress also has a built-in Groups Directory. This listing of groups within your community is browseable and searchable. Figure 5-8 shows you the Groups Directory on the official BuddyPress test site at `http://testbp.org/groups`. Using the drop-down menu above the Groups display (on the right), you can sort the Groups display by the following sorting methods:

✔ Last Active

✔ Most Members

✔ Newly Created

✔ Alphabetical

Additionally, BuddyPress ships with a Groups widget that gives you the ability to display a random listing of groups and that also includes navigation features to display groups by other criteria, such as newest, most active, and most popular.

For information on groups, including details on creating group forums, see Chapter 8.

Private Messaging

To re-use the high school analogy that I use in the Groups example, the Private Messaging component is just like passing notes to your best friend during Mr. Smith's 4th period Geometry class — some things just cannot wait until recess! The difference within a BuddyPress community is that these are virtual notes and there's no moderator standing by to reprimand you or asking whether you have something to share with the rest of the class!

Private messages sent among friends in a BuddyPress community are just that — private. When you send private messages to friends, the next time they log in to the community they see a notification that they have a new message. They can click the alert, read your message, and hit the Reply button to send a reply back to you, all within the confines of the network. And no one sees these messages except you and your friend.

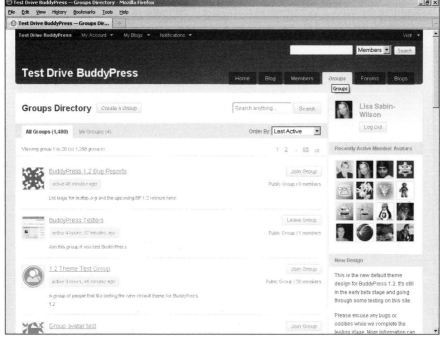

Figure 5-8:
The Groups
Directory
listing on
the official
BuddyPress
test site.

Members can set up their notification preferences in their profile settings
after they sign up and obtain an account. I cover these preferences in
Chapter 6, but for now, just know that members have the ability to be notified via e-mail whenever they receive a new message.

Extended Profiles

On a regular WordPress MU–powered Web site — that is, one without the
additional features of a BuddyPress community installed — users are asked
to provide just two pieces of information when they sign up:

✔ A username

✔ An e-mail address

With the Extended Profiles component enabled in BuddyPress, you can ask
your members to fill out all sorts of questions — beyond a username and an
e-mail address — when they sign up for membership on your Web site. You
can create your own questions or use the default ones. By default, there are
two items asked of your members at signup:

✔ Name

✔ Photo upload of themselves

On extended profiles, you can create an unlimited amount of information fields for your users to fill out that will display on their profiles. Some good examples of the information that you can ask your users to provide are

- ✓ Location, such as city, state, province, and country
- ✓ Birth date (you can exclude the year if you want to)
- ✓ Interests
- ✓ Occupation
- ✓ Web site addresses
- ✓ Other social network memberships, such as Twitter or Facebook

The more information fields that you provide on your users profiles, the more users can share about themselves with other members of your community, which allows everyone to get to know each other beyond just a photo and a username. The only required bits of information are the user's name, username, and e-mail address; sharing anything else is optional. Figure 5-9 shows extended profile fields on my member profile, including Company, Job Title, Website, and Interests.

You're asking your new members to share their e-mail address for signup and site administration notifications only. Member e-mail addresses are private and not shared within the public forum or community.

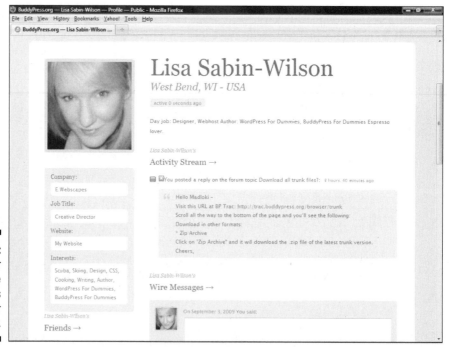

Figure 5-9:
My member profile in the BuddyPress developer community.

The upcoming "Building Profile Groups and Fields" section covers everything you need to set up profile groups and fields for your community members to share their information.

Setting up bbPress Forums

The Forums Setup link on the BuddyPress menu takes you to where you set up the bbPress discussion forum software so your BuddyPress community can create group forums, which I discuss in Chapter 8. For more information on bbPress, see the following "What is bbPress" sidebar.

To navigate to the Forums Setup page on your WordPress MU dashboard, follow these three simple steps:

1. **Log in to your WordPress MU dashboard.**

   Point your browser to http://*yourdomain.com*/wp-login.php, enter your WordPress admin username and password, and then click the Log In button.

2. **Expand the BuddyPress menu.**

   On the left side of your WordPress MU dashboard, click the drop-down arrow on the BuddyPress menu. This expands the BuddyPress menu and displays several links beneath the menu title.

3. **Browse to the Forums Setup page.**

   Click the Forums Setup link on the BuddyPress menu. This loads the Forums Setup page, as shown in Figure 5-10, where you set up the initial settings for your community.

The Forums Setup link appears on the BuddyPress menu only when you enable bbPress Forums on the BuddyPress Component Setup page. If bbPress Forums is disabled, the Forums Setup link does not appear in the menu at all.

You have two options on the Forums Setup page:

- ✔ **Set Up a New bbPress Installation:** Use this option if bbPress is not installed on your Web server.

- ✔ **Use an Existing bbPress Installation:** Use this option if bbPress is installed on your Web server.

The next section of this chapter takes you through the steps of installing and setting up bbPress for use within your community.

What is bbPress?

bbPress is an open source discussion forum, or Internet message board, platform created by the folks at Automattic who created the WordPress, WordPress MU, and BuddyPress platforms and plugins. On the bbPress Web site at `http://bbpress.org`, you can read about bbPress, join in its discussion forum about the software, read the bbPress blog to learn about updates and upcoming releases of the software, and download the latest version of bbPress and related plugins and themes.

People use bbPress to run forums on their Web sites to encourage participation in discussions

and debates on topics of interest to community members. You don't need WordPress or BuddyPress to use bbPress; however, bbPress integrates seamlessly with the WordPress and BuddyPress platforms, and allows site owners to share user information between the installations of WordPress or WordPress MU (with or without BuddyPress).

Perhaps the largest and most popular implementation of the bbPress software is the WordPress community support forum at `http://wordpress.org/support`.

Figure 5-10: The Forums Setup page on the WordPress MU dashboard.

Setting up a new bbPress installation

To set up a brand new bbPress installation, follow these steps:

1. **Click the Set Up a New bbPress Installation button.**

   The Forums Setup: New bbPress Installation page appears with a message telling you that you need to complete the installation process, which is usually a fast and easy, one-click process.

2. **Complete the installation of the bbPress software.**

   Click the Complete Installation button. The Forums Setup page appears with a message telling you that you need to create a configuration file before you can use the Forum feature.

3. **All Done!**

   No, really — it is that quick and easy! BuddyPress writes a new file to your BuddyPress plugin directory into your WordPress installation directory called `bb-config.php`. This file contains the necessary information the software bbPress needs to connect to your existing WordPress MU database; for your reference, here is an example of what the `bb-config.php` file looks like:

   ```
   $bb->custom_user_table = "wp_users";
   $bb->custom_user_meta_table = "wp_usermeta";
   $bb->uri = "http://yourdomain.com/wp-content/plugins/buddypress/bp-forums/
           bbpress/";
   $bb->name = " Forums";
   $bb->wordpress_mu_primary_blog_id = 1;
   define('BB_AUTH_SALT', "947e3f84ddfb12eda897156a25f8dd2898380993d27d1a3dbc5
           5408ebe986a3a");
   define('BB_LOGGED_IN_SALT', "d2e88a14f2fc60b99dcc080e4de2646b4173273d694df5
           e14f110b132d5b5e04");
   define('BB_SECURE_AUTH_SALT', "b1d425584cb97341dfa1fdbed80f7fe516ea6f1bcd60
           6dce82d08f050f815d56");
   define('WP_AUTH_COOKIE_VERSION', 2);
   ?>
   ```

4. **Return to the Forums Setup page.**

   Click the Forums Setup link in the BuddyPress menu again. A successful installation of bbPress will result in a new message on the Forums Setup page that reads *bbPress forum integration in BuddyPress has been set up correctly. If you are having problems, you can re-install.*

Integration . . . what's that?

I use the word *integration* several places in this chapter, and you might be wondering what that means, exactly. Integration means that the bbPress forum software shares the same data that WordPress MU and BuddyPress uses to define user accounts, such as usernames, passwords, e-mail addresses, and avatars (or photos). Data sharing is integral in creating a smoothly run social community that allows users to log in to their member account only once to access the various features within your network.

If, for example, you were running the bbPress forum software as a stand-alone message board without WordPress or BuddyPress, users would need to log in to the bbPress forum to participate. On a Web site running WordPress MU and BuddyPress in tandem with bbPress, requiring bbPress users to log in to use the forum after they already logged in to your community would be annoying. This is where integration comes into play.

When a user logs in to your community, a cookie stores in his browser directory that tells all the integrated pieces of software on your Web site (WordPress MU, BuddyPress, and bbPress) that the user is logged in. This means that the user's credentials as a logged-in member are shared and recognized throughout the entire network.

Using an existing bbPress installation

In the previous "What is bbPress" sidebar, I point out that bbPress can function as a stand-alone discussion forum platform on hundreds of sites across the Web without the presence of WordPress or BuddyPress. In fact, you might already have bbPress installed and running on your Web site, in which case, you don't need to do a brand new installation. In cases like this, BuddyPress gives you the option to use an existing bbPress installation to integrate forums into your community. To accomplish this, follow these steps:

1. **Click the Use an Existing bbPress Installation button.**

   This button appears on the Forums Setup page and when clicked, loads the Forums Setup: Existing bbPress Installation page.

2. **Type in the location of the `bb-config.php` file.**

   The Forums Setup: Existing bbPress Installation page appears with a message telling you to provide the location of the `bb-config.php` file from your existing bbPress installation directory. Type that file location in the `bb-config.php` File Location field. Your file location might look similar to `/home/public_html/yourdomain/bbpress/`.

3. Finish the installation procedure.

Click the Complete Installation button at the bottom of the page to finish the installation of bbPress on your Web site. The Forums Setup page appears with a message telling you the bbPress integration in BuddyPress was successful.

With the bbPress forums installed on your Web site, along with WordPress MU and BuddyPress, your community setup is complete. Figure 5-11 shows an example group forum, as seen on the BuddyPress demo Web site at `http://testbp.org`. Your community members can use the Forum feature to add discussion forums to groups they create within your network. (See Chapter 6.)

At this point, no more software needs to be installed on your Web server to run your community unless you want to extend the functions and features of your community by using special add-ons called *plugins*. For information about using plugins on your WordPress MU and BuddyPress Web site, see Chapter 13. Additionally, Chapter 15 contains a list of ten popular BuddyPress plugins that you can use to enhance your Web site.

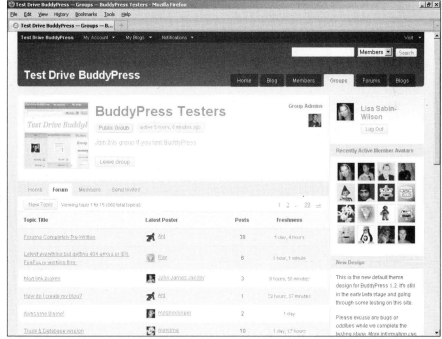

Figure 5-11:
The Groups Forum feature on the BuddyPress demo Web site.

Building Profile Groups and Fields

Within any social community on the Web, members share information about themselves through profiles so that community members can get to know each other a little better.

The final item in the BuddyPress menu is Profile Field Setup. Clicking this link loads the Profile Field Setup page where you set up new profile groups and fields to display on the user sign-up page and member profiles. These groups and fields allow your community members to share additional information about themselves with the rest of your community.

Profile groups are groupings of profile questions. By default, BuddyPress creates the first group, Base, for you. The earlier section, "Configuring the General Settings," gives you instructions on how to change the name of the default profile group. In that section, I change the name from Base to Information; but you can call the group whatever you want, I won't stop you. Also by default, the Name field — users provide their name upon signup — is created for you and can be changed per your preference, too.

Although you can create as many profile groups as you want, the first profile group contains the fields that users fill out when registering for your Web site. All other profile groups are available for users to fill out, at their leisure, after they successfully sign up and log in. At that point, they can edit their profile and fill out the other profile fields that you provide within the different groups.

Adding new profile fields

Figure 5-12 shows the Profile Field Setup page on my WordPress MU dashboard. Notice that the profile group name, Information, displays at the top of the group, and the following fields (that I created) are within that group:

- **People Call Me (Core):** This field is actually the default Name field on a new installation of BuddyPress. You can change the name of this field on the BuddyPress General Settings page, but you cannot delete this field because it contains information that BuddyPress uses to create the base of a member's profile.

- **Occupation:** Asks users to provide information on what they do for a living.

- **Web Site:** Gives members a chance to publicize their own Web site on their profile.

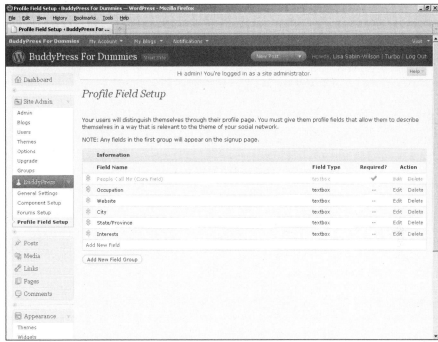

Figure 5-12:
The
BuddyPress
Profile Field
Setup page.

✔ **City:** Asks members to tell everyone the city they live in.

✔ **State/Province:** Asks members to provide the state or province they reside in.

✔ **Interests:** Asks members to provide a list of items that interest them, such as hobbies they like to do in their free time.

You start by adding a field to the default profile group; from there, you can create additional new fields as needed. The following steps add an Occupation field to the default profile group:

1. **Click the Add New Field link.**

   The Add New Field link is located at the bottom of each Profile Group box, as seen in Figure 5-12. The Add Field page appears.

2. **Type** Occupation **in the Field Title text box.**

   This field name will display on the Edit Profile page.

3. **Type a description of your new field in the Field Description text box.**

   The description is a short line of text that tells the user what type of information you're asking for. For example, the Field Description for the Occupation field could read *What do you do for a living?*

4. **Choose the required status on the Is This Field Required? drop-down menu.**

   To require this information from your members when they register for your Web site, choose Required on the drop-down menu; to make the information optional, select Not Required.

5. **Choose the field type on the Field Type drop-down menu.**

   BuddyPress gives you seven Field Type options. Select the option that best fits the type of answer you want your members to provide:

   - *Text Box:* For answers that require only single lines of text, such as Occupation.

   - *Multi-Line Text Box:* For answers that require multiple lines, or maybe a paragraph of text, such as Your Bio.

   - *Date Selector:* For answers that require dates (day, month, year), such as Birthday.

   - *Radio Buttons:* For answers that require one selection from a few possible answers, such as a yes/no question.

   - *Drop-Down Select Box:* For answers that require a drop-down menu where users can select one of several possible answers, such as a listing of all 50 states where the member need only pick the one they reside in.

   - *Multi Select Box:* For answers that require a drop-down menu where members can select more than one answer from a drop-down list of several possible answers, such as a listing of languages the member currently speaks.

   - *Checkboxes:* For answers where more than one response can be selected from a checklist of items, such as Pets: Dog, Cat, Fish, Bird, in which case, members can check one, or all, answers for this question.

6. **Save your changes.**

   Click the Save button at the bottom of the page to save the changes you've made to your new profile field.

Figure 5-13 illustrates how the profile fields that I created look on my member profile in my community.

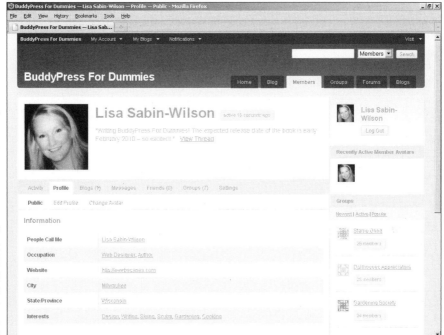

Figure 5-13:
Answered
profile fields
displayed on
a member
profile.

Creating new profile groups

In the previous section, I mention that the default profile group contains the profile fields presented to a member when they go through the sign up process. Figure 5-14 shows the Sign Up page where each of the profile fields that I created are displayed and just waiting for a new member to come along and answer.

The fields from new profile groups that you create do not appear on the registration page. They appear on the member's profile on the Edit Profile page (see Figure 5-15) where members can fill out the remaining fields at their leisure. Links to each profile group you create appear as tabs on the Edit Profile page. For example, I created two new profile groups for testing purposes called Profile Group 2 and Profile Group 3, which display as links in the tab menu navigation.

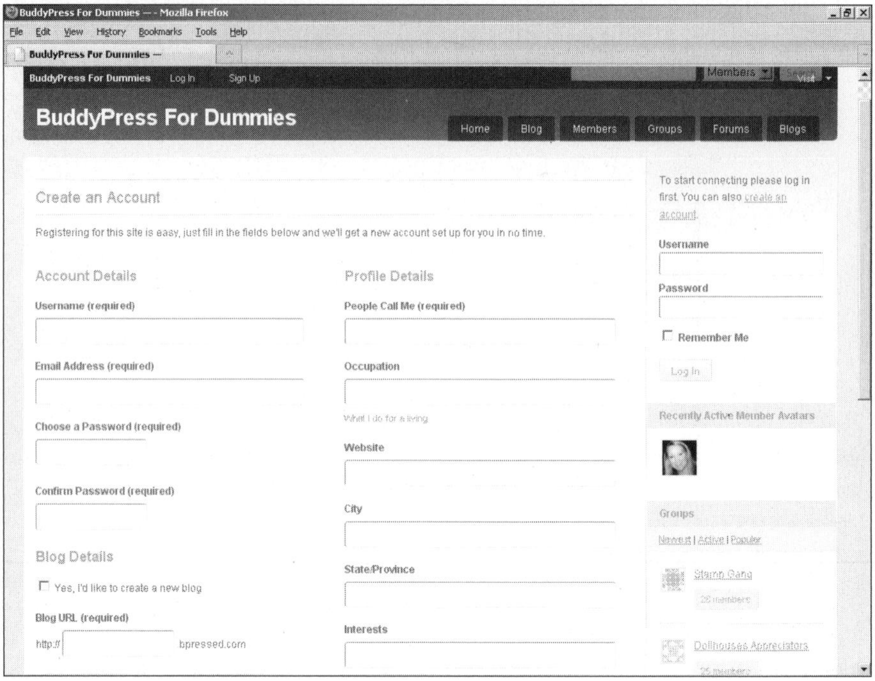

Figure 5-14:
Profile fields
on the
community's
Sign Up
page.

To create new profile group, make sure you're on the Profile Field Setup page and follow these steps:

1. **Click the Add New Group Link.**

   You find this link at the bottom of the page. Once clicked, the Add Group page appears.

2. **Name the new profile group.**

   Type the name you want assigned to this new group in the Profile Group Name text box.

3. **Add the new group.**

   Click the Add Group button; you return to the Profile Field Setup page and see your new profile group displayed. You can add new profile fields to this new group by following the step-by-step instructions in the previous section.

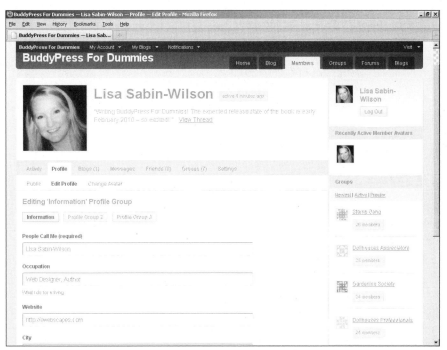

Figure 5-15:
Profile fields
on the Edit
Profile page.

Using extended profiles, you can tailor the personal details shared by members to the theme (or genre) of your social community. For example, a sports community could create profile groups and fields that encourage members to share details about their favorite sports teams and players. A music community could ask members to share their preferences about music groups, genres, and artists that they enjoy. Members can update their profile information as often as they want, too. Additionally, the answers your members provide are searchable within member directories. Therefore, if you want to see members who live in Wisconsin, you can search for the term *Wisconsin* and get a listing of all members who have that state listed in their member profile. Figure 5-16 shows the search results on the BuddyPress test site at http://testbp.org — I used the search term *Wisconsin* all members in that community from Wisconsin. Of the 14,550 total members, 4 are from Wisconsin — I was surprised to find so many!

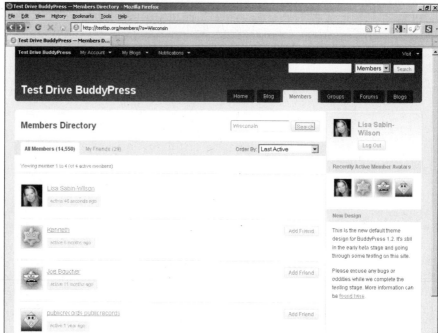

Figure 5-16:
Searching
for
members
in a
BuddyPress
community.

Part III
Understanding BuddyPress Features

The 5th Wave   By Rich Tennant

ADVANCED COMMUNICATIONS IN THE LUPINE COMMUNITY

MyDen

"Woo!"

In this part . . .

Okay! You've installed WordPress, and BuddyPress is up and running — time to explore all the features BuddyPress has to offer you and your community members. In this part, you explore extended member profiles, avatars, activity streams, friends, groups and forums. You also discover the multiple blog option in WordPress to enable your community members to build their own blogs in your community.

Chapter 6

Exploring Your New Community

In This Chapter

▶ Registering as a new member

▶ Using the admin bar

▶ Editing your profile

▶ Managing messages

▶ Making and adding new friends

▶ Creating and joining new groups

▶ Discovering your activity stream

▶ Browsing community directories

*W*hen you're familiar with the BuddyPress components and know how to set them up in your community, it's time to have a look at how those components will appear on the front end of your site. In other words, what will users see on your site after they sign up to become a member?

This chapter steps you through registering as a new member on your site; setting up and editing your member profile; uploading and cropping your avatar (or photo); using the admin bar to navigate the areas of your community; making and adding new friends within the community; understanding activity streams, groups, and forums;, and using the Members, Groups, and Blogs directories.

When you're done with this chapter, you'll understand how all the BuddyPress components work together to form a fun and interactive social community on your Web site, and you'll have the knowledge you need to support your member community.

In this chapter, and all subsequent chapters, I am using the BuddyPress Default theme. Because BuddyPress has two different themes available — the BuddyPress Default and BuddyPress Classic — some of the things I describe in this chapter may look different on your system if you are using the Classic theme on your site.

Signing Up as a New Member

The first step any prospective member of your community must take is registering to become a member of your site; without that step — she cannot enjoy the benefits of membership. It's a good idea for you to go through the process of signing up as a new member so you can experience what your members will experience. To accomplish this, be sure you log out of your WordPress dashboard by clicking the Log Out link in the top-right corner.

New member registration

The following steps assume that you're using the default BuddyPress themes. If you're not using those themes, then some of these steps may vary, and you'll have to make adjustments based on the theme you are using. (See Part IV of this book for more information about BuddyPress themes.) To sign up as a new member, proceed with the following steps:

1. **Browse to your site at `http://yourdomain.com`.**

   Replace *yourdomain.com* with your own domain name, where you installed WordPress MU and BuddyPress.

2. **Click the Sign Up link in the Site Admin menu.**

   The Sign Up page (`http://yourdomain.com/register`) appears with several fields of information that need to be filled out, including the profile fields that you created for the default profile group in Chapter 5. Figure 6-1 shows the Sign Up page.

3. **Type your desired user name in the Username field.**

   This required field needs to be at least four characters in length. Because this account is for your testing purposes only, enter **tester** in the Username field. This username becomes part of the URL for the member profile. For example, with the username of *tester*, the member profile URL is `http://yourdomain.com/members/tester`.

4. **Type your e-mail address in the Email Address field.**

   This required field needs to be an e-mail account that you can access. The e-mail address entered here is the one in which members receive all community-related notifications, including their account username and password login information. Additionally, member accounts are limited to one e-mail address, so if you're already using an e-mail address for a member account, you cannot develop another account using the same e-mail address. For your testing purposes, enter a different e-mail address than the one you're using for your WordPress MU admin user account.

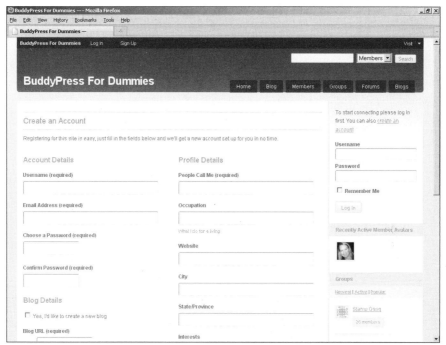

Figure 6-1:
The default
BuddyPress
Sign Up
page.

5. Type your desired password in the Choose a Password field.

Your password can be anything you want it to be, but make sure the password is difficult for other people to guess. After you type the password into the Choose a Password field, you have to re-type the same password into the Confirm Password field — both are required.

6. Select the Yes, I'd Like to Create a New Blog check box.

This causes the system to create a blog for your test account when you sign up. Users can choose not to create a blog and bypass this selection altogether; they are not required to set up a blog within your network. If they don't select this box, users will have a member profile only, but can choose to create a blog within your network later if they want to.

7. Type your desired Blog address in the Blog URL text box.

The Blog URL is the Web address of your blog within your community. For your testing purposes, type **testblog** in the Blog URL field. This creates the Blog URL of http://testblog.*yourdomain*.com if you're using the WordPress MU subdomain setup, or http://*yourdomain*.com/testblog if you're using the WordPress MU subdirectory setup. (See Chapter 2 regarding subdomains versus subdirectories for member blogs in WordPress MU.)

8. **Type your desired title in the Blog Title text box.**

   Here is where you can give your blog a name. The Blog Title displays at the top of your blog so everyone knows what your blog is about. For your testing purposes, type **My Test Blog** in the Blog Title field.

9. **Select Blog privacy options.**

   This selection states, "I would like my blog to appear in search engines and in public listings around this site." Select Yes to make your blog public and viewable in your community profile and blog directories, and to allow search engines (such as Google or Yahoo!) to see your blog and record it in their search directories. Select No if you want to hide your blog from community profiles, directories, and search engines.

10. **Type your name in the Name text box.**

    This is a required field. Type your name the way you want it to appear on your member profile.

11. **Fill out the remaining profile fields.**

    The profile fields that you add to the default profile group (see Chapter 5) will appear on the registration page. Fill in the requested information and keep in mind that the answers you provide display on your member profile.

12. **Click the Complete Sign Up button.**

    A new page appears with a message that reads, "Sign Up Complete!" Your new account is created and you receive an e-mail at the address you provided in Step 4.

13. **While you wait for the e-mail from Step 12 to arrive — upload your avatar.**

    An *avatar* is a photo or graphic image that visually represents you in the community. It appears on your member profile, in all comments you leave on member blogs and wires, and next to your activity streams throughout the community site. A default image displays for you, but you probably want to change it to something a little more personal and specific to you. To change your default avatar, follow these steps:

    a. *Click the Browse button.*

       A dialog box appears where you select a photo that you want to use from a directory on your computer. Select the file and click Open (or just double-click the file); the dialog box closes.

    b. *Click the Upload Image button.*

       The file uploads from your computer to your Web server where it is stored in a folder in your WordPress installation directory.

    c. *Resize your image.*

BuddyPress provides a built-in cropping tool that allows you to crop your chosen file to a size of your preference. To use the cropping tool, you drag the edges of the box, shown in Figure 6-2, to the size you prefer. Everything inside the borders of the box displays as your avatar within the community. When you're done, click the Crop Image button; the page reloads and shows your new avatar. If you're unhappy with the image, you can follow these steps again to upload and crop a new image.

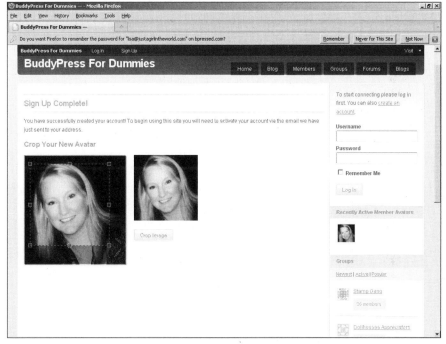

Figure 6-2: The cropping tool allows you to crop and resize your avatar.

Activating a new member account

During the signup process, an e-mail is sent to an address you provide that contains a link that you must click to activate the new user account. Skipping this step prevents the user account from creating fully. When you click the link, a browser window opens, and the Account Activate page on your community Web site appears with a message that reads, *"Your account was activated successfully! You can now log in with the username and password you provided when you signed up."* At that point, you can log in to your site using the username and password that you created by following these steps:

1. **Type your username in the Username field.**

   The login area is located in the top right of your Web site. Type the username that you designated when you signed up for this account; if you followed the steps in the preceding section, the username you created is *tester.*

2. **Type your password in the text box to the right of the Username field.**

   Type the password that you designated during the signup process.

3. **Click the Log In button.**

   The front page of your site reloads. At this point, the login area disappears and your avatar and username display. When you click your username, your member profile appears at `http://yourdomain.com/members/tester`.

Figure 6-3 shows my "tester" profile complete with avatar and the information I filled out during the sign-up process.

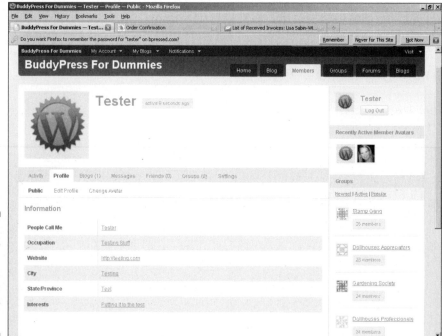

Figure 6-3:
A member
profile on a
BuddyPress-
powered
community
site.

Now you have a regular member account. You can use this account to test all the features in your community the way a regular member would. The next sections of this chapter cover those features in detail from a member's perspective.

Navigating the Admin Bar

You might have already noticed the admin bar located at the top of every page on your Web site (see Figure 6-4). Community members use the admin bar to navigate through the areas and sections of your Web site, and throughout your community.

Admin bar

Figure 6-4:
The admin bar appears at the top of every BuddyPress community page.

Table 6-1 provides a description of the menu items found on the admin bar. I discuss the My Account options more fully in the next few sections.

Table 6-1		Admin Bar Menu Items	
Main Menu	Submenu Item(s)	Destination Page	Description
Site name	None	Front page	Returns you to the front page of your Web site.
My Account	Activity	Activity page	Lists your recent activity within the community.
	Profile	Profile page	Displays your community profile.
	Blogs	Blogs page	Lists blogs that you own within the community.
	Wire	Wire page	Shows recent posts to your wire.
	Messages	Messages page	Displays messages sent to you by community members.
	Friends	Friends page	Lists friends you've added within the community.
	Groups	My Groups page	Lists community groups you've joined.
	Settings	General Settings page	Displays settings you can change, or you can delete your account completely.
	Log Out	Logout page	Logs you out of the community and returns you to the front page of the Web site.
My Blogs	*Blog name*	Dashboard for your blog	If you have a community blog, clicking your blog's name takes you to its dashboard.
	Create a Blog	Create a Blog page	Displays a form you can use to sign up for and create a new community blog.
Notifications	None	None	When certain activities happen, a small red alert appears here.
Visit	Random Member	Community member profile	Takes you to a randomly selected profile.
	Random Group	Community group page	Takes you to a randomly selected group page.
	Random Blog	Community member blog	Takes you to a randomly selected member blog.

In Chapter 5, I describe an option available to the site administrator that hides the admin bar from logged-out users. If you want site visitors, including ones who aren't logged in as a member, to see the admin bar, then be sure to select No on the Hide Admin Bar for Logged Out Users? option on the BuddyPress Settings page. If you want only members who are logged in to see the admin bar, then select Yes for that setting. The choice is yours — I report, you decide!

Exploring Your Profile

When you activate a community account, your profile is your gateway into the community's features. When you're logged in, your profile gives you menu options in the navigation bar above your profile information. Notice the options are the same as those in the My Account menu on the admin bar. You can choose whichever menu is more comfortable for you to use when navigating the features.

Your profile page looks slightly different when you aren't logged in to the community. Figure 6-3 shows a profile of a member who's logged in. Figure 6-5 shows a profile of a member who's logged out. When logged out, you are not able to see the menu options in the navigation bar above your profile, and a login form appears at the top of the sidebar on the right of the page.

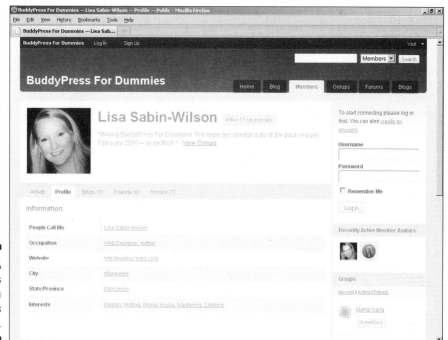

Figure 6-5: A BuddyPress profile of a user who's logged out.

A light gray menu with several navigation options appears above your profile information (refer to Figure 6-3). When you're navigating your profile, another subnavigation menu appears beneath those navigation options, which gives you the ability to edit or view different options for your account. For example, when you choose Profile in the navigation menu, the subnavigation menu displays any options you have for the Profile feature.

Activity

The first menu item is the Activity feature. Click Activity and the Activity page loads in your browser window and lists only your recent activity within the community. The types of activities listed here include

- **Blog posts:** When you publish a new blog post on your community blog, the title of the blog post displays in you're Activity stream with a link to your new blog post. If my new blog post were titled, "BuddyPress is really neat!" the My Activity stream would display *Lisa Sabin-Wilson wrote a new blog post: BuddyPress is really neat!* Additionally, the time since that activity happened would display, such as *1 hour ago* or *2 months ago*.

- **New friendships:** When you add a new friend to your network, it displays in you're My Activity stream. Figure 6-6 shows a listing on my Activity page that reads, "You and Tester are now friends." The name *Tester* links to Tester's profile, too.

- **Group activity:** All activity related to groups posts to your My Activity stream, such as new groups you create or join, new comments you leave on a group wire, and any topics you comment on (or create) in a group forum.

- **Profile updates:** Updates you make to your profile list in your My Activity stream. For example, your Activity page will mention if you change your avatar or update your profile fields.

- **Status updates:** All status updates you make post to your My Activity stream. (See the upcoming "Updating your status" section for more info about updating your status.)

Navigating the Activity page

The Activity page lists the 25 most recent updates per page — click the Load More link at the bottom to automatically load the next 25 most recent updates on the page.

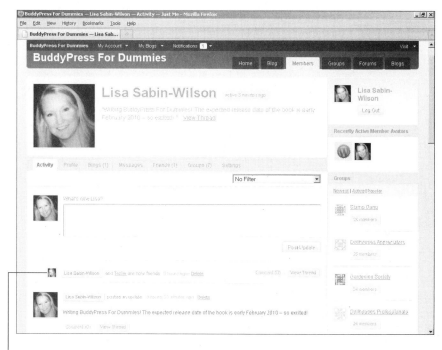

Figure 6-6:
The My
Activity
stream
displays
new friend-
ships I've
made.

New friendship listing

Above the My Activity stream, on the right side, you see a drop-down menu. (By default, the menu says, No Filter.) This menu gives you, and anyone else browsing your community pages, the ability to sort and filter the display of Activity listings on this page. The options provided within that drop-down menu include:

- ✔ **No Filter:** This option creates an Activity listing of all possible activities within the community. This is the default option.

- ✔ **Updates Only:** Choosing this option changes the display on the page to a list of status updates. (See the upcoming section, "Updating your status," for more information about status updates.)

- ✔ **New Blog Posts Only:** Choosing this option changes the display on the page to a list of new blog posts.

- ✔ **New Blog Comments Only:** This option filters the activity listing to display only new blog comments.

- ✔ **New Group Forum Topics Only:** This option filters the activity listing to display only new topics created within Group forums.

✔ **New Group Forum Replies Only:** Choosing this option changes the display on the page to list only new replies made within Group forums — which is nice way of keeping track of new discussions going on within the different forums within your community.

✔ **New Friendships Only:** This menu option filters the activity listing to display newly created friendships between members within the community.

On each activity listing, a Comment link appears after the update. When clicked, this link opens a text box that allows any member to leave a comment. Figure 6-7 shows the comment text box beneath an activity listing of a new friendship.

Figure 6-7:
Members can easily leave a comment on any activity listing with the Comments link.

Updating your status

Above the Activity listings is a text box where you can provide a quick status update. Status updates are usually short one- to two-line statements you write to update your friends and other community members about what you're doing. If you've ever used the Twitter platform, you know exactly what I'm talking about. Twitter is considered a "micro-blogging'" service where members of the Twitter community can update their status, 140 characters at a time, to provide their friends and followers with details of exactly what they're doing at that moment.

You can use status updates in various ways:

✔ **Give a quick update on what you're doing right this moment.** For example, if I were to update my status right now in a BuddyPress community, I would probably write something like *I'm about halfway done with writing Chapter 6 of my BuddyPress latest book: BuddyPress For Dummies!,* as seen in Figure 6-8.

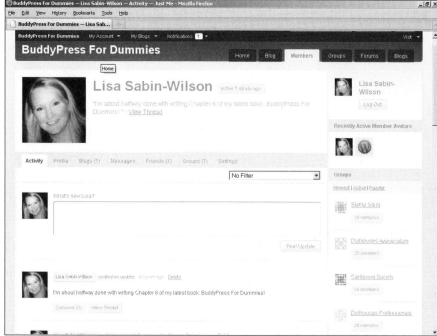

Figure 6-8:
My latest
status
update
on the
BuddyPress
demo Web
site.

✔ **Ask a question that community members will see.** You can ask a question like *Does anyone have any good examples of a live BuddyPress community site?* — and with any luck, you'll get a good answer. Community members an respond to you by clicking the Comment link on your status update. (By the way, you can find some great examples of live BuddyPress community sites in Chapter 17.)

✔ **Share a helpful tip or resource with your friends in the community.** For example, *Hey! I just found this great book called BuddyPress For Dummies — everyone should read it!*

There are no rules for status updates, you can use them any way you want. The following steps show you how to update your status on your profile:

1. **Visit your profile.**

   You need to be logged in to update your status. You can view your profile at `http://yourdomain.com/members/tester` (where *your domain.com* is the domain of your Web site).

2. **Click the Activity link in the navigation menu.**

   The Activity page loads, showing a text box at the top.

   3. Type your update in the What's New? text box.

   4. Click the Post Update button.

   This saves and then displays the text of your status update with a time-
   stamp of how long ago you made the update (for example, 1 minute ago,
   1 hour ago, 10 days ago, and so on).

You can update your status as often as you want; there are no time restric-
tions on when you can do it. Your status update also appears to the right of
your Member Avatar on your Profile page. That status update will change the
next time you type in a new status update on the Activity page.

Profile

The second menu item is the Profile feature. Click Profile, and the Profile
page loads in your browser window. Earlier in this chapter, you see what a
profile looks like in a BuddyPress community (refer to Figure 6-3). A member
profile displays the following items:

   ✔ The amount of time since you were last active in the community (for
     example, as shown in Figure 6-6, Active 1 Minute Ago)

   ✔ Your avatar (or photo)

   ✔ Your latest status update

   ✔ The Add Friend button, which allows other community members to
     request your friendship

   ✔ The Send Message button, which allows your established friends to send
     you a private message

   ✔ The information from the profile fields that you fill out when you sign up.

On the subnavigation menu on the Profile page, you see three additional
options that you can use to sort the Profile menu:

   ✔ **Public:** This Profile menu default view shows you exactly how your pro-
     file looks to others when they view your profile page.

   ✔ **Edit Profile:** Where you can edit the details in your profile, including the
     profile fields that you set up previously.

   ✔ **Change Avatar:** Where you can edit your avatar by uploading a new one,
     or re-cropping the one you currently have.

Editing your profile information

On the subnavigation menu on the Profile page, the second option, Edit Profile, is where you can update and add new profile information as often as you like. To create new profile groups and fields for your members to fill out so they can add information to their profile, see Chapter 5.

Figure 6-9 displays the Editing page for my profile.

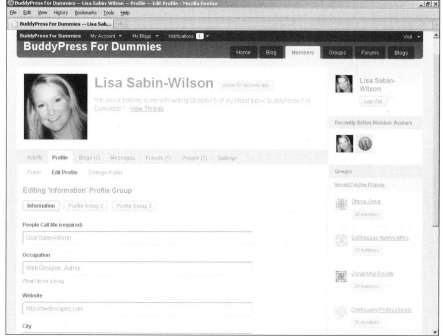

The profile group contains the questions I filled out when I signed up as a member. (As I discuss in Chapter 5, this default profile group is set up for you when you install BuddyPress on your site.) The remaining questions contain profile information that I can fill out after I log in and choose Profile⇨Edit Profile.

To edit your profile, fill out the profile fields with the information requested. Be sure to click the Save Changes button at the bottom of each profile group when you finish. If you visit your public profile (by choosing Public on the subnavigation menu), you see your information is updated. Notice that some of the words in your profile are hyperlinked. Check out the following "Profile data — filtered" sidebar to find out why hyperlinks are a great feature for your community members.

Changing your avatar

On the subnavigation menu on the Profile page, the last option, Change Avatar, is where you upload and crop a new avatar to display on your profile. The method of accomplishing this is the same one you use during the user registration process; see the earlier "New member registration" section to change your avatar.

Blogs

The third menu item is the Blogs feature. Click Blogs, and the Blogs page loads in your browser window where you see a listing by title of the blogs that you own, or are a member of, within the community. The blog titles are hyperlinked, meaning you and other community members can click a blog's title to load it in your browser window.

Above the Blogs listing is a drop-down menu that allows you to filter the display of your blogs by the following sort methods:

- Last Active
- Newest
- Alphabetical

Filtering the display of Blogs on the page is especially helpful if you own or are a member of several different blogs within the community.

Profile data — filtered

On your profile, you see that some of the words and phrases are a different color and are underlined (if you're using the BuddyPress Default theme). When you click such text, called a *hyperlink,* a page that lists other members who have the same words in their profile appears. This feature is helpful because it gives you the opportunity to discover members within the community who have the same interests, live in the same area, or do the same type of work that you do. For example, when I click Author on my profile, a directory of community members who have the word *Author* in their profile appears. From there, I can communicate with other authors and share experiences, resources, and information about a field and activity that we have in common.

Messages

The next menu item is the Messages feature. After you add community members as friends, you can send private messages to them, and they can send messages to you. Click Messages, and the Messages page loads in your browser window where you can read, send, and manage messages for your user account. Three options appear in the subnavigation menu: Inbox, Sent Messages, and Compose.

Managing your Inbox

When you choose Messages⇨Inbox, you can read messages sent to you by your community friends. A short excerpt of the messages displays with your friends' avatars (photo), their names, the dates the messages were sent, and the title of their messages. Click a message title to read the full content of the message.

You can sort your Inbox by using the Select drop-down menu on the Inbox page. BuddyPress gives you three options to sort messages by:

✔ **Read:** Displays messages that you've read.

✔ **Unread:** Displays messages that you haven't read.

✔ **All:** The default displays all messages sent to you, read or unread.

Managing messages in your Inbox is a pretty easy task. Figure 6-10 illustrates that I have two messages in my Inbox. The number to the right of the Inbox option in the subnavigation menu changes depending on the amount of messages you have in your Inbox. If there are no messages in your Inbox, nothing displays next to the Inbox option.

On the Inbox page, you can delete a message by clicking the Close button (the small red box with the white X in the middle), shown to the right of the message excerpts in Figure 6-10.

You can further manage the messages in your Inbox by using the links above the Inbox section and the check boxes shown to the right of the message excerpts in Figure 6-10. Select the check box next to the message you want to manage, and then choose one of the following links from the menu:

✔ **Mark as Read:** BuddyPress displays that message as one that you've already read. Additionally, the notification icon on the admin bar that tells you the number of unread messages you have in your Inbox turns off.

✔ **Mark as Unread:** BuddyPress displays that message as one that you haven't read. The notification icon in the admin bar remains active as a reminder that the message is in your Inbox.

✔ **Delete Selected:** BuddyPress deletes the selected message from your Inbox. Be careful with this one, though, because there's no confirmation message asking you whether you're sure that you want to delete the message. When you click the Delete Selected link, the Inbox page reloads and states the message has been deleted — and sure enough, the message is gone forever.

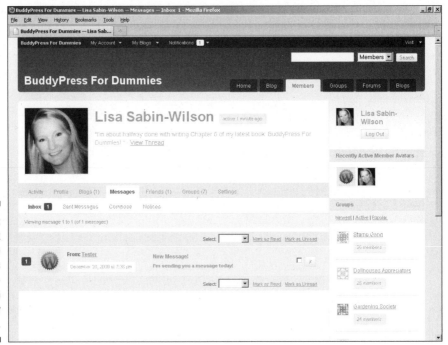

Figure 6-10: The Inbox page displays private messages from community friends.

Reading and replying to Inbox messages

To read a message listed in your Inbox, click the message's title. A new page loads and displays the full content. This page also keeps a record of your conversations with the message sender regarding this message, so when you send a reply, it lists on this page, too. Figure 6-11 shows a message thread between a friend within the community and me. The original message is at the top, followed by any subsequent replies and a text box at the bottom for you to easily add more to the private conversation.

Viewing messages you've sent

When you choose Messages⇨Sent Messages, you see only the messages sent by you to other community friends. You can view and manage those messages the same way you do on the Inbox page; review the previous section and apply that information to the Sent Messages page.

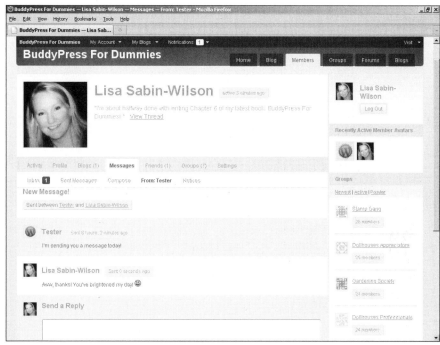

Figure 6-11:
The entire conversation thread for a private message.

Composing a new message

The next option in the Messages menu is Compose. When you choose Messages⇨Compose, the Compose page appears where you can compose a new message to send to a community friend. To compose a new message, follow these steps:

1. **In the Send To field, type the username of the friend you want to send the message to.**

2. **(Optional) Send as a notice to all users,**

   Underneath the Send To field is the This Is a Notice to All Users checkbox — check this box if you want your message to be sent to all users within the community.

3. **In the Subject field, type a message subject.**

   The subject also serves as the message title that displays in your friend's Inbox.

4. **In the Message text box, type the body of your message.**

   There are no character or word count limits here, so your message can be as short or as long as you need it to be.

5. **Click the Send Message button at the bottom of the Compose page to send the message to your friend.**

Notifications

The final option in the Messages menu is Notices. When you click the Notices link, the Notices page loads and lists all new notifications you have received. Notices can include several items, such as

- ✔ New friendship requests

- ✔ Newly received, unread messages

- ✔ Replies to messages you have sent

- ✔ New Group invitations

Additionally, when you have new notices waiting for you, you will see a notification alert. This alert — a bright white circle with a number in the center — appears in the admin bar at the top of every BuddyPress community page next to the Notifications item. The number within the circle indicates how many new notifications you have. You can see this in play in Figure 6-10.

Friends

Friendships are made and lost in social communities around the Web, and a BuddyPress-powered community is no different.

The next menu item is the Friends feature. Choosing Friends⇨ Friends loads the My Friends page, which lists all the friends you've added within the community. Figure 6-12 shows my Friends list on a BuddyPress community Web site.

Viewing and sorting your My Friends list

The My Friends page, by default, displays your newest friends in the community first. The Friends list reveals your friends' avatars, names, and times since their last recorded community action, and a button giving you the option to cancel your friendship with each person.

You can further sort your friends by using the drop-down menu above the listing. This drop-down menu allows you to sort your Friends list by:

- ✔ Last Active
- ✔ Newest Registered
- ✔ Alphabetical

Figure 6-12:
My friends
list on the
BuddyPress
demo Web
site.

Groups

If membership in the exclusive community on your site isn't enough, you and other community members can create new groups and join existing groups within your community. In Chapter 5, I describe groups and using them in your BuddyPress community. The Groups feature is the place to go to view groups you belong to, create new groups, and invite your friends to community groups you're associated with.

Choosing Groups⇨My Groups loads the My Groups page, which lists community groups you either own or belong to. Figure 6-13 illustrates the My Groups page where the group's avatar, title, number of members, and description display for easy understanding and navigation.

Figure 6-13:
The My
Groups
page dis-
plays the
community
groups you
belong to or
own.

Viewing and sorting your My Groups list

Above the My Groups section is a drop-down menu of options that allow you
to further sort your list by the following sort methods:

- **Last Active:** The My Groups page, by default, displays your most
  recently active groups first.

- **Most Members:** Sorts your My Groups list to display the groups with the
  highest amount of members.

- **Newly Created:** Sorts your My Groups list to display the groups creation
  date, from newest to oldest.

- **Alphabetical:** This option sorts the My Groups list in alphabetical order,
  A through Z.

Creating a new group

If you want to create your own group within a Buddypress community, click
the Groups link in the top-right navigation menu — then click the Create a
Group button. This loads the Create a Group page, where you can create a

community group on any topic, theme, or interest you want. Simply create the group and then invite other friends from the community to join. To create a new group, choose Groups⇨Create a Group, as shown in Figure 6-14, and then follow these steps:

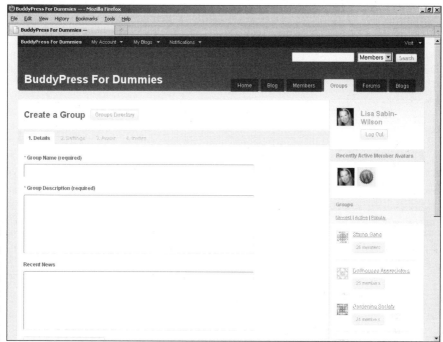

Figure 6-14: Creating a new group in your BuddyPress community.

1. **Type the name of your group.**

   The Group Name field is where you type in the name of the group you are creating.

2. **Type the group description.**

   The Group Description field is where you type a short description of your new group.

3. **Enter any recent group news.**

   If your new group has any recent news you want to share, type it in the Recent News field.

4. **Click the Create and Continue button.**

This loads the Create a Group — Settings page where you can choose whether to enable discussion forums for your group. If you do, place a check mark in the box labeled *Enable Discussion Forum*.

Additionally, you have three privacy options to choose from:

- *This Is a Public Group:* Any member of the community can join, and the group is listed in the community's group directory and in search results. Additionally, the group content (wire posts, members, forum topics, and discussions) are viewable by any member of the community.

- *This Is a Private Group:* Requires that community members request to join the group. Requests are sent to the group administrator (or creator) for approval. The group is listed in group directories and search results; however, the group's content is viewable to only approved members of the group.

- *This Is a Hidden Group:* Allows membership by invite only; the site administrator (or creator) has to invite the members before they can join. This group is not included in group directories or search results, and the group's content is viewable to only approved members of the group.

5. Click the Next Step button.

This loads the Create a Group — Avatar page where you can upload and crop an avatar that represents the group within the community.

6. Upload and crop the group avatar.

The steps for uploading and cropping a group avatar are the same as the steps to upload an avatar for your profile. Follow the steps in the earlier "New member registration" section to upload and crop your group's avatar.

7. Click the Next Step button.

The Create a Group — Group Invites page appears where you can select from your friends list who you want to invite to join your new group.

8. Click the Finish button.

Your new group's page loads in your browser window. The group I created during this process is shown in Figure 6-15.

Managing a newly created group

After you create a new group, as the group administrator, you need to know a few things about managing the group. The Groups menu provides easy navigation to the Admin, Forums, and Members options, as shown in Figure 6-16, but it also links to helpful options that are available to only the site administrator. Your options on the Groups subnavigation menu are

Figure 6-15:
A newly
created
group on a
BuddyPress
community
site.

✔ **Home:** This link is visible to all members of the group and returns you to the Groups front page.

✔ **Admin:** This link is visible to only the group administrator and contains the following options for group management, as shown in Figure 6-16:

• *Edit Details:* Edit the group name, description, news, and notification preferences.

• *Group Settings:* Edit the settings for enabling the comment wire or discussion form and set the privacy options for the group.

• *Group Avatar:* Change the group avatar by uploading and cropping a new image.

• *Manage Members:* View a listing of all members of the group and manage their settings.

You can also "Kick/Ban" a member, which removes the member from the group and disallows them from re-joining the group in the future. You would do this for a group member who is being particularly difficult, or who has been harassing other members of the group, and so on. The decision to ban a member from the group is at the discretion of the group administrator.

Additionally, you can promote a member to Moderator or Administrator status, which increases the member's access to administrative group settings. Usually, group administrators promote another member to help moderate a particularly busy group where the administrator might need help with member and topic management. Additionally, you are able to demote a member from moderator or administrator to a normal member, with no advanced privileges.

- *Delete Group:* Delete the group completely from the community. Be careful using this option because it deletes everything — group wire comments, group forum discussions, and member lists — and removes the group from site directories, search results, and activity streams. Be aware that deleting a group is permanent — once you do this, all group data is completely lost and there is no way to get it back — so be careful with this option!

✔ **Forum:** This link is visible to all group members and loads the group forum page where you and other members of your group can view and create forum topics and discussions within the group.

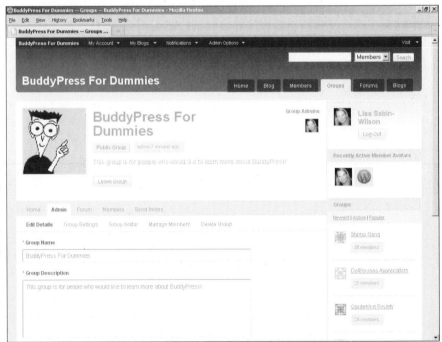

Figure 6-16:
The group administrator can edit the group's details and settings on the Admin menu.

- ✔ **Members:** This link is visible to all group members and loads the group Member Directory for the group, which displays members' avatars and names. Each name is a hyperlink that takes you to that member's profile.

- ✔ **Send Invites:** This link is visible to only the group administrator and loads a listing of your friends that you can select and send group invites to. The members you invite get a notification via e-mail and a notification in the admin bar at the top of the site.

- ✔ **Leave Group:** This link is visible to all community members and gives them the option of leaving the group completely. They can rejoin the group later if they choose to. Group administrators aren't allowed to leave their own group, so Group administrators will not see the Leave Group option in the navigation menu.

Above the Group listings is a drop-down menu that allows you and other group members to sort the display of group activity by the following methods:

- ✔ **Updates Only:** Choosing this option displays a listing of updates made by group members.

- ✔ **Group Forum Activity Only:** Choosing this option displays a listing of group forum topics and discussion.

- ✔ **Blog Activity Only:** Choosing this option displays a listing of blog activity (posts and comments) from group members.

Settings

The next menu item is the Settings feature. Choose Settings⇨General to

- ✔ Change your account e-mail address.

- ✔ Change your password by typing a new password in the Change Password text box, re-typing it in the second text box, and then clicking the Save Changes button.

The second option on the Settings subnavigation menu is Notifications where you can set your community e-mail notification preferences, as shown in Figure 6-17. Select Yes if you want notifications by e-mail; select No if you'd rather not receive e-mail notifications. Notifications are sent for the following events:

- ✔ **Messages:** You receive an e-mail when another member sends you a private message or a new site notice is posted.

- ✔ **Friends:** You receive an e-mail when another member sends you a friendship request or accepts your friendship request.

✓ **Groups:** You receive an e-mail when another member invites you to join their group, when group information updates, when a member posts a wire message to a group you belong to, when you're promoted to group administrator or moderator, and when a member requests to join a group that you marked private in the group settings.

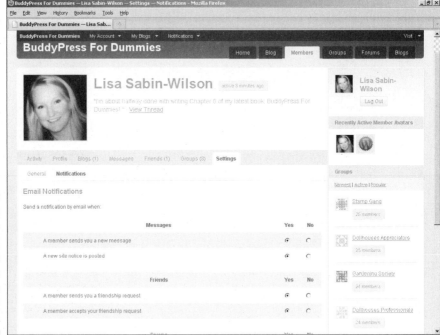

Figure 6-17:
Set your
e-mail
notification
preferences
on the
Notifica-
tions page.

By default, all e-mail notification preferences are marked as Yes; you'll automatically receive e-mail notifications whenever any of those events occurs unless you go to the Settings page and change your e-mail notification preferences.

Discovering Site Wide Activity, Directories, and Searches

What good is a community of active, social members if they cannot find activities or other members within the community? About as good as photographer without a camera, I'd say. That's why BuddyPress communities come with the following features:

✔ **Site Activity stream:** A listing of activities that have happened through-out the entire community that includes the following:

- Wire posts on member profiles and group pages

- New friendships between community members

- New blog posts and comments

- New forum topics and discussions

- New groups

- New members to a group

- Status updates by community members

- Profile updates by community members (new avatars, new profile data, and so on)

When a community member performs an action within the community, it appears in the Site Wide Activity stream. Figure 6-18 displays the Site Wide Activity stream on the BuddyPress demo Web site at `http://testbp.org`.

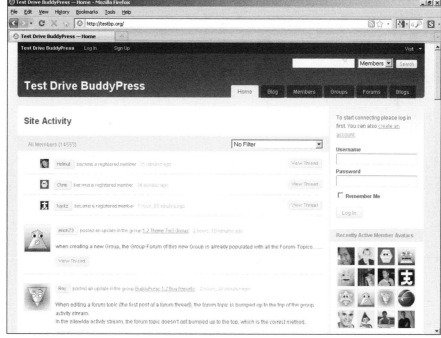

Figure 6-18:
The Site Wide Activity stream at `http://testbp.org`.

✔ **Members Directory:** A full listing of community members sorted from the most recently active member to the least recently active member where you can view names, profiles, and avatars. Additionally, you can use the drop-down menu shown above the Members listing to sort the directory by the following sort methods:

- Last Active

- Newest Registered

- Alphabetical

By default, the Members Directory lists the ten most recently active members, as shown in Figure 6-19. Other members appear, ten per page, on subsequent pages. Also, to the right of each member's name is an Add Friend button, which you can click to send friend requests to members from the directory page. (If you're already a friend of the member listed, the Cancel Friendship button appears instead.)

✔ **Groups Directory:** Similar to the Members Directory, a full listing of groups within the community sorted by the most recently active groups, which appear on the first page before the listing paginates. This pagination feature keeps the directory pages from becoming too unwieldy. To the right of each group listing is a Join Group button, which you can click to join that group. (If you're already a member of a group, the Leave Group button appears instead.) Also similar to the Members Directory, you can use the drop-down menu to sort the Group listing by the following sort methods:

- Last Active

- Most Members

- Newly Created

- Alphabetical

✔ **Forums Directory:** A directory listing of all forums created within the community, sorted by the most recently active forums. With the drop-down menu displayed above the forums listing, you can filter forum topics by the following sort methods:

- Last Active

- Most Posts

- Unreplied

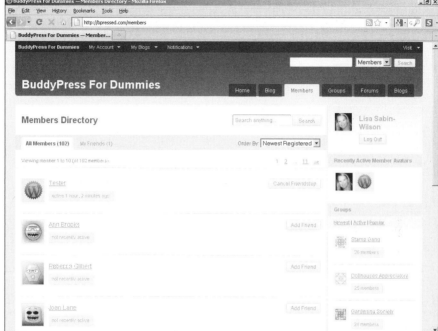

✔ **Blogs Directory:** A directory of all blogs within the community sorted by the most recently active blogs, which appear on the first page before the listing paginates. As with the Members Directory and Groups Directory, you can sort community blogs using the drop-down menu at the top by the following sort methods:

- Last Active
- Newest
- Alphabetical

To the right of each blog listing is a Visit Blog button, which takes you to that community blog. Additionally, beneath the Visit Blog button is a link to the most recently posted article on that blog, as seen in Figure 6-20.

Another easy way to navigate the community is to use the built-in Search feature that appears on the top right of every page within the community. Figure 6-21 shows the Search feature on a BuddyPress community site.

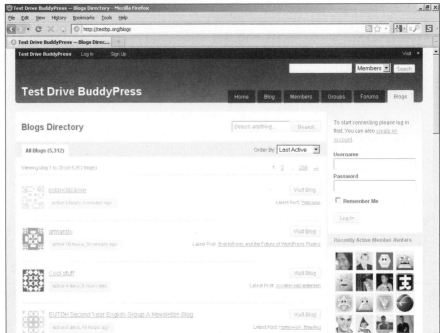

Figure 6-20:
The Blogs
Directory
listing.

The Search field

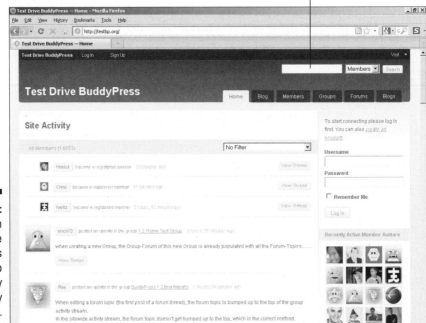

Figure 6-21:
The Search
feature
appears
at the top
of every
community
page.

To use the Search feature, follow these steps:

1. **Type a keyword in the Search field.**

   The keyword you use should correspond with the criteria for your search. For example, if you want to search the community for members, groups, or blogs related to the subject of coffee, type **coffee** in the Search field.

2. **Choose the type of search you want to perform.**

   The drop-down menu to the right of the Search field allows you to narrow your search results to the following directories:

   - *Members:* Returns search results within the Members Directory.

   - *Groups:* Returns search results within the Groups Directory.

   - *Forums:* Returns search results within the Forums Directory.

   - *Blogs:* Returns search results within the Blogs Directory.

3. **Click the Search button.**

   BuddyPress performs a search based on the keyword criteria that you specified in the Search field. When the search is complete, a new page loads in your browser window with the results that meet your criteria.

Using the Site Activity stream; the Members, Groups, Forums, or Blog directories; or the Search feature within your BuddyPress community enables you and your community members to discover new members, new activity, and new information within your community.

You can also discover people and activities within your community by using widgets. Chapter 9 fully covers how to use widgets in your community.

Chapter 7

Enabling Blogs

● ●

In This Chapter

▶ Enabling user blogs

▶ Configuring WordPress MU for member blogs

▶ Setting up blog options

▶ Displaying directories

▶ Tracking blogs in member profiles

▶ Listing blog comment activity in activity streams

● ●

*B*logs are a benefit to a social community and allow members to manage and maintain articles, publish ideas and photos, and share information — all of which becomes part of the content flow within the community's activity streams. Enabling user blogs is just another tool you can provide to your community to encourage the sharing of information and interactivity between members. The advantage to you, the site owner, is that the more your users publish to their community blogs, the more content they provide within your community, which increases the value of your site has as a whole.

The WordPress MU software is what allows you to enable your community users to create blogs within your network. However, in BuddyPress, you have the option to track user blogs and blog activity within the member profiles and directories. Every community is different; whether you want your community members to create and manage blogs is a decision only you can make. This chapter gives you the information to help you make that decision, along with details on how to make it happen.

Managing User Blogs in Your Community

In Chapter 2, you download, install, and set up the WordPress MU software, which is required to run BuddyPress. You also choose whether you want blogs created in a subdirectory of your Web site, or a subdomain, as follows:

✔ **Subdirectory**: Using this configuration, users' blogs are created in a dirrctory on your Web server and the Web addresses of the blogs look similar to `http://yourdomain.com/username`.

✔ **Subdomain**: Using this configuration, a new subdomain is created and the Web addresses of the users' blogs look similar to `http://user name.yourdomain.com`. Subdomains require configuring the DNS on your Web server, and Chapter 2 gives you the information and steps you need to make that happen.

Enabling user blog creation

Chapter 2 gives you a tour of the WordPress dashboard, where you manage all the settings for your WordPress MU-powered Web site. On the WordPress dashboard, you can enable or disable the creation of blogs within your network. The following steps take you through the procedure:

1. **Log in to your WordPress dashboard.**

   The URL for your WordPress dashboard is `http://yourdomain.com/wp-login.php` (where *yourdomain.com* is your actual site domain name.)

2. **Choose Options on the Site Admin menu.**

   The Site Options page appears, as shown in Figure 7-1, and you're presented with several configuration options for your WordPress MU installation.

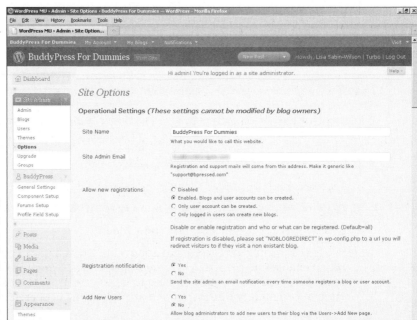

Figure 7-1:
The Site Options page on your WordPress dashboard.

3. **Select an option under Allow New Registrations:**

   - *Disabled:* Disallows new user registration completely. People visiting your site will not be able to register for a user account.

   - *Enabled. Blogs and user accounts can be created:* Gives users the ability during the registration process to create a user account and a blog.

   - *Only user accounts can be created:* Gives people the ability to create only a user account; they will not be able to create a blog within your network.

   - *Only logged in users can create new blogs:* Allows only users who are already logged in to create a new blog within your network. This also disables new user registration completely.

4. **Save your settings.**

   Click the Update Options button at the bottom of the Site Options page to save the options you configure. (The Site Options page reloads in your browser with your new settings saved.)

In Figure 7-1, I chose the Enabled. Blogs and User Accounts Can Be Created option because I want people who visit my site to be able to create an account, and a blog, when they register.

With blog creation enabled, users have the option on the user registration page to select whether they would like to create a blog. The user registration page for my community (shown in Figure 7-2) displays the Yes, I'd Like to Create a New Blog check box. When users check this box during the sign-up process, a blog is created for them.

If the user doesn't check this box, then only a user account that accesses all the BuddyPress member profile areas is created. However, users can create a blog later from within their BuddyPress member profile settings. These steps show you how to create a blog from your member profile:

1. **Login to the community using your username and password.**

2. **Hover your mouse over the My Blogs item on the Site Admin bar.**

3. **Click Create a Blog! from the drop-down menu.**

4. **Type the address for your new blog in the Blog Domain text box.**

5. **Type the title of your new blog in the Blog Title text box.**

6. **Choose Privacy options for your new blog.**

   Select Yes if you want the blog to appear in community directory listings and to enable it to be discovered by search engines, such as Google. Select No if you want your new blog to be private. Private blogs aren't listed in community directories and are not visible to search engines.

Check this box to create a blog during the sign-up process

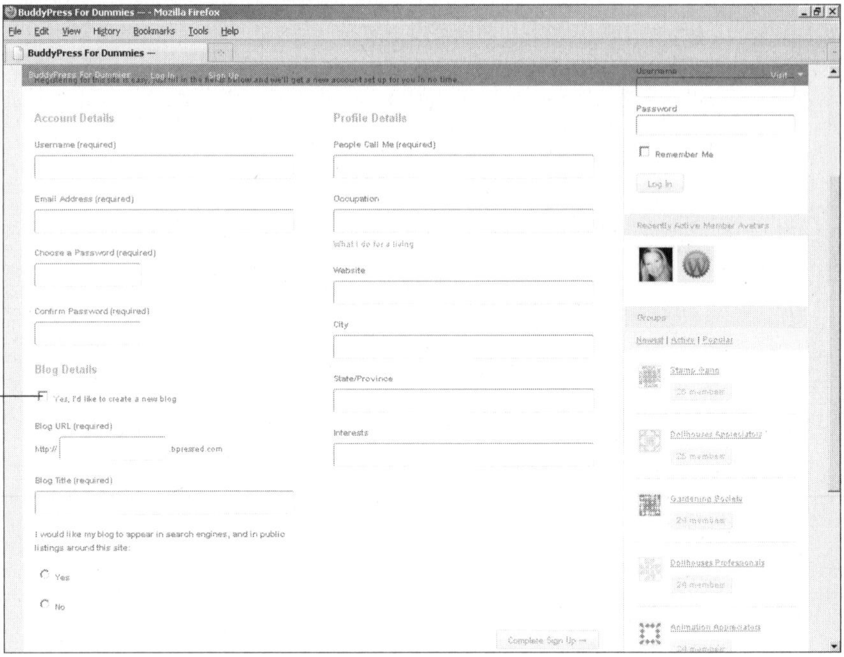

Figure 7-2:
The user registration page on a site with user blogs enabled.

7. Click the Create Blog button.

The Create a Blog page reloads with a message congratulating you on the creation of your new blog. The page displays a link to your new blog, as well as a dashboard link that you click to log in, manage your new blog, and publish new blog posts.

Remember that your community members can only create blogs within the community if you have that option enabled within the WordPress MU Site Admin options, found in your WordPress MU Dashboard (see Chapters 2 and 3 for information on setting site options in WordPress MU).

Managing user blogs

As the site owner, you have full access to all user blogs created within your community. Choosing Blogs on the Site Admin menu loads the Blogs page, which lists all the blogs in your community, with options for managing each blog.

Searching for specific blogs

At the top of the Blogs page is a Search feature you can use to search for blogs by name, blog ID, or IP address. This is very helpful if you have a large

community and one of your users e-mails you with a problem or question —
you can visit the Blogs page and pull up the information on his blog pretty fast.

Managing individual blogs

The Blogs page lists the blogs in your community by ID. (User blogs are
assigned a specific ID at the time of their creation.) The listing of user blogs
also displays the following information about each blog:

- **ID:** Blog ID number
- **Domain:** The name associated with this blog
- **Last Updated:** The date the blog was last updated (or posted to)
- **Registered:** The date the blog was registered within your community
- **Users:** The e-mail address associated with the user(s) of the blog

When you hover on any of the blogs listed on the Blogs page, an options
menu appears that allows you to manage the blogs within your community.
Figure 7-3 shows the options that appear when I hover my mouse on the 'testblog' user blog in my community.

Figure 7-3:
Options to
manage
individual
user blogs
on the Blogs
page.

The available options and the ways they can help you manage your blogging
community are as follows:

- **Edit:** Opens the Edit Blog page, which allows you to view and edit settings for this users blog. You use this more for diagnostic and troubleshooting purposes than for altering user settings.
- **Backend:** Opens the user's blog Dashboard, allowing you (the community administrator) to view the Dashboard as if you were the ower of this
  blog. It's excellent for troubleshooting purposes, as it allows you to view
  how the user has set up the different options in their blog Dashboard.
- **Deactivate:** Deactivates the user's blog, but does not delete it. When you
  choose Deactivate, you confirm that you're certain you want to deactivate this blog. After you confirm you want to deactivate the blog, the

Deactivate link changes to Activate, allowing you (the community administrator) to reactivate the blog at any time. Visiting the user's blog after it's deactivated displays a message that reads, "This user has elected to delete their account and the content is no longer available."

✔ **Archive:** Suspends the user's blog and deactivates it. When you choose Archive, you confirm that you're certain you want to archive the blog. After you confirm you want to archive the blog, the Archive link changes to Unarchive, allowing you (the community administrator) to unarchive the blog at any time. Visiting the user's blog after it's archived displays a message that reads, "This blog has been archived or suspended."

✔ **Spam:** Marks the blog as spam and archives/suspends it from your community. When you choose Spam, you confirm that you're certain you want to mark the blog as spam. After you confirm you want to mark the blog as spam, the Spam link changes to Not Spam, allowing you (the community administrator) to mark the blog as Not Spam at any time.

✔ **Delete:** Deletes the user's blog from your community. When you choose Delete, you confirm (twice!) that you're certain you want to delete the blog. If you confirm that you want to delete the blog, you cannot undo this action. This doesn't delete the user's account, however; the user can create new blogs with his or her existing user account.

✔ **Visit:** Opens the user's blog in a new browser window.

When you delete a blog within the community (or if one of your users delete their own blog), it's permanent; so be absolutely, 100 percent positive that you really, really want to delete the blog before you confirm the action. This is why the WordPress MU software provides not one, but two, confirmation messages, forcing you to think twice before you act.

Deleting multiple blogs at one time

Figure 7-4 shows a check box to the left of each blog listing. You can delete or mark as spam multiple blogs from your community at one time by selecting the check box next to each blog you want to delete and then clicking the Delete button at the top of the page. This is very helpful if you have a number of spam blogs appear in your community.

Adding a blog to the community

You can manually add blogs to the system from your WordPress dashboard, as shown in Figure 7-4. This feature is especially helpful if you want to create your own blogs within the community, or if you want to set up a blog for a friend and save him the trouble of creating a blog on his own. (We all have friends like that, don't we?)

In the Add Blog section of the Blogs page, take the following steps to create a blog:

1. **Type a username in the Blog Address text box.**

2. **Type the title of the blog in the Blog Title text box.**

3. **Type the user's e-mail address in the Admin Email text box.**

4. **Click the Add Blog button.**

   The Blogs page reloads, and the blog you just set up appears in the list of blogs.

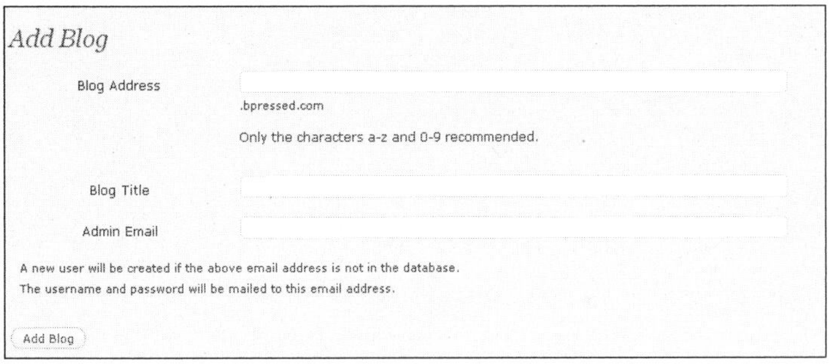

Figure 7-4:
WordPress
MU allows
you to
create
blogs
within the
Dashboard.

Add Blog

Blog Address

.bpressed.com

Only the characters a-z and 0-9 recommended.

Blog Title

Admin Email

A new user will be created if the above email address is not in the database.
The username and password will be mailed to this email address.

Add Blog

BuddyPress includes a default theme (see Figure 7-5) that your users can use for their blogs within the community.

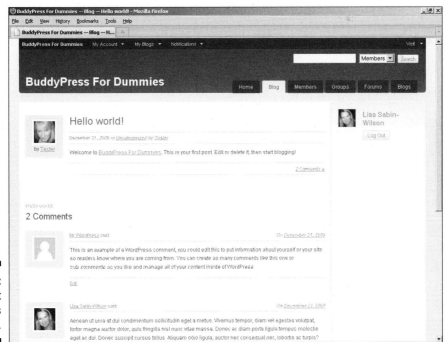

Figure 7-5:
The default
BuddyPress
blog theme.

What displays on the default BuddyPress theme depends on the use of the built-in WordPress and BuddyPress widgets. Chapter 9 covers widgets, including information about installing new themes and tweaking the default BuddyPress themes with basic HTML and CSS to make them unique to your social community.

Tracking Community Blog Activity

Part of what makes a social community so informative and fun is that you can find out what community members are up to through activity streams and tracking. With BuddyPress installed on a WordPress MU site, you can track blog activity within your community. This section shows you the ways a BuddyPress social community Web site keeps track of blog activity within your user community.

The blog activity tracked in activity streams includes

- ✔ **Creation of new blogs:** Any time a user creates a new blog in your community, it broadcasts to the entire community.

- ✔ **Newly published blog posts:** When a user posts to their community blog, the entire community knows.

- ✔ **Newly published blog comments:** When a user comments on a public community blog, it's noted throughout the community.

Before any blog activity can be tracked within your community, however, you have to enable blog tracking in the BuddyPress options:

1. **Log in to your WordPress dashboard.**

2. **Choose Component Setup on the BuddyPress menu.**

   The BuddyPress Component Setup page appears.

3. **Enable Blog Tracking.**

   Select the Enabled option to turn on blog activity tracking across your entire network.

4. **Save your settings.**

   Click the Save Settings button at the bottom of the BuddyPress Component Setup page to save the blog tracking settings.

With blog tracking enabled, your users can easily discover all the new blog activity occurring within your community. Figure 7-6 shows an activity stream listing new blog posts made within a BuddyPress social community.

Figure 7-6: A BuddyPress activity stream shows community blog activity.

The Site Activity stream shown in Figure 7-6 displays on a page within your site by using either the BuddyPress Default theme (the code for this is built into the theme itself) or with the BuddyPress Classic theme, using the built-in BuddyPress widget called Site Wide Activity. With this widget, you can control how many activity items display on the page at one time. Chapter 9 covers BuddyPress widgets and displaying information and content on your community Web site.

A user's blog activity also displays on the member's Activity page in his or her own activity stream. As shown in Figure 7-7, some of my most recent blog activity displays on my profile's Activity stream.

Each blog has privacy options, which I cover in the earlier "Enabling user blog creation" section. If the privacy options are set to disallow the blog from appearing in search engines and public listings, then that blog will not be included in blog activity listings throughout the community.

A BuddyPress-powered social community also has the added advantage of providing a directory of blogs within the community. In the BuddyPress Default theme, click Blogs on the navigation menu displayed to the right of the site title for a directory of the community's blogs, as well as a drop down manu navigation feature that allows you to browse community blogs by the latest active, newest and alphabetically. Figure 7-8 shows the Blog Directory listing in a BuddyPress community using the BuddyPress Default theme.

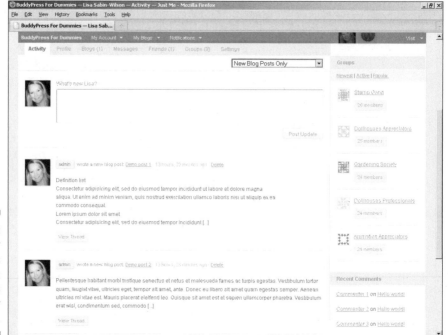

Figure 7-7:
Member
profiles
show an
individual's
community
blog activity.

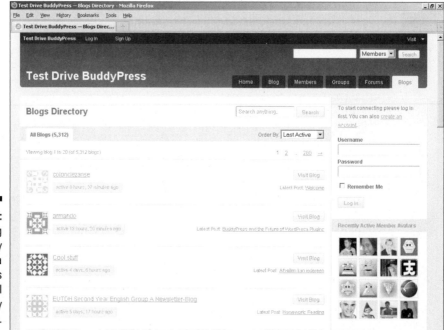

Figure 7-8:
The Blog
Directory
listing in a
BuddyPress
social
community
site.

Publishing Blog Posts

In this book's Introduction, I state that I expect readers to have a certain level of experience with blogging on WordPress. However, part of the responsibilities of owning a social community is supporting users and letting them know how they can use the different features.

All the chapters of this book give you insight into using WordPress and BuddyPress as a site owner/administrator and as a member of your site so that you can give your members direction and instruction. This section briefly looks into how you and your users will use the WordPress MU blog feature to write, categorize, and publish blog posts on the community blogs.

Here are the steps to compose and write a basic blog post from your WordPress dashboard:

1. **Choose Add New on the Posts menu.**

   The Add New Post page appears, as shown in Figure 7-9, where you write and publish a new blog post to your community blog.

2. **Type the title of your post in the title text box.**

3. **Type the content of your post in the body text box.**

   Just as you would type an e-mail, you type the content of your post in the text box on this page. You can use the formatting menu above the text box to format your content with bold or italicized text, hyperlinks, and text alignment. Additionally, you can insert photos and images into your blog post by using the Add Media icons.

4. **Publish your post.**

   Click the Publish button to publish the post to your blog.

You and your users can manage posts published to your blog by choosing Edit on the Posts menu. The Edit Posts page appears, and lists all the posts.

For specific details on managing a WordPress-powered blog, refer to my book, *WordPress For Dummies*.

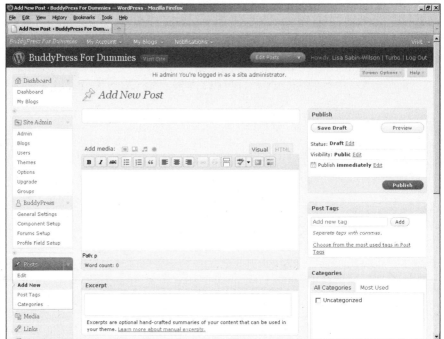

Figure 7-9:
The Add
New Post
page on the
WordPress
dashboard.

Chapter 8

Using the Groups Feature

In This Chapter

▶ Introducing the BuddyPress Groups feature

▶ Enabling groups and forums

▶ Creating new groups

▶ Joining an existing group

▶ Participating in a group

▶ Exploring group administration, member management, and activity

*I*magine you are the host of a large house party and you've invited 100 of your closest friends to attend. When the party gets started, there's a lot of noise while everyone tries talking to one another — talking over the music, and talking over other people. In a short time, you notice that the people at your party start to break out into smaller groups having conversations in different rooms. A group in the kitchen is discussing their favorite food and wine, while another group in the TV room is engaged in a heated conversation over their favorite contestant on the latest reality TV show.

The concept is the same for the BuddyPress Groups feature. As the site owner, you invite the public to gather in your space on the Web to take part in the sharing of content and the overall conversation. Inevitably, your community members will break out into smaller groups to discuss shared topics of interest. Sometimes, in large gatherings, smaller groups of conversation make it easier to participate and engage other members.

This chapter introduces you to the BuddyPress Groups feature. I show you how to enable groups and forums in your social community; how to create, join, and participate in new groups within the community; and how to administer and manage your own groups.

Enabling Groups and Forum Options

In a BuddyPress community site, you can think of groups as micro-communities that exist within the larger community. Groups are where members of your community can come together to discuss and share ideas. Group members can use the forums feature to start discussions on different topics and to invite other group members to participate in those discussions. Enabling forums allows your members to create discussion forums within the groups they create in your community.

Just because the Groups feature exists doesn't mean you need to use it. Plenty of great Web sites thrive without allowing members to create groups and forums within the network. However, if you who want to give your community members this ability, you can create an unlimited number of group and forum discussions on an unlimited amount of topics to keep the conversations within your community lively and active. All you have to do is follow these steps:

1. **Log in to your WordPress MU dashboard.**

2. **Choose BuddyPress⊃Component Setup.**

   This loads the BuddyPress Component Setup page where you can enable or disable the available BuddyPress components.

3. **Select Enabled under bbPress Forums.**

   This gives your community members the ability to create discussion forums within the groups they create in your network.

4. **Select Enabled under Groups.**

   This gives your community members the ability to create, join, and participate in groups within your community.

5. **Click the Save Settings button at the bottom of the page to save the Component Setup settings you've selected.**

bbPress is a discussion forum platform created by the folks behind the popular WordPress platform, so it makes perfect sense for the developers of BuddyPress to choose bbPress to provide the framework for the group's forums.

In Chapter 5, I cover setting up and installing the bbPress Forums feature to allow you to enable forums on your community site. If the forums have not yet been set up on your site, review Chapter 5.

bbPress is a discussion forum platform that many people use as a stand-alone solution for hosting a discussion forum on their Web site. However, bbPress is part of the BuddyPress suite of plugins and installs along with BuddyPress when you do the initial installation (see Chapter 4). bbPress exists within the

BuddyPress directory of files in the `/wp-content/plugins/buddypress/bp-forums/bbpress/` folder on your Web server and integrates completely with your WordPress MU and BuddyPress installation.

Participating in community groups

Like everything else within a BuddyPress community site, group activity is tracked and displayed within the community's activity stream. The type of information tracked includes

- ✓ **Creation of new groups:** When a member creates a new group, it appears on community activity wires and in the Group Directory listing. The creation of the group is broadcast on that member's profile, as well.

- ✓ **Posts made to a group's wire:** When a member comments on the group's wire, it appears in the Site Wide Activity listing and on that member's profile.

- ✓ **Creation of new forum topics:** When a group member starts a new forum topic, it appears in the Site Wide Activity listing and on that member's profile.

- ✓ **Posts made to a forum discussion:** When a group member participates in a forum by posting a comment, the comment appears in the Site Wide Activity listing and on that member's profile.

The type of tracked information depends in part on the options you choose when you create the group. When a new group is created, the group administrator (or owner) can set the group's privacy options to Public, Private, or Hidden. (See Chapter 6.) If a group is set to Hidden, then the group activity items will not publish in the community activity wires and directories.

Groups Directory

Figure 8-1 shows the community's Groups Directory in the BuddyPress Default theme. The Groups Directory can be viewed by clicking Groups on the upper-right navigation menu of the Web site.

By default, the Groups Directory lists all groups by most active to least active and displays a maximum of tengroups per page. Additionally, the Groups Directory gives you a drop-down menu that allows you to sort the Groups listing by the following methods:

- ✓ **Last Active:** Choosing this option displays the Groups listing by the most recent to the least active groups within the community.

- ✓ **Most Members**: Choosing this option displays the Groups listing by the groups with the most members to the groups with the least members.

✔ **Newly Created:** Choosing this option displays the Groups listing by the newest groups to the oldest groups created within the community.

✔ **Alphabetical:** Choosing this option displays the Groups listing in an alphabetical manner.

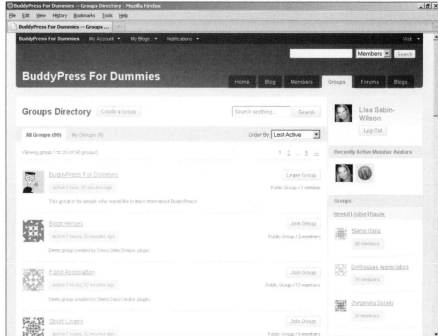

Figure 8-1:
The Groups Directory in a Buddy Press social community site.

Groups listed in the directory display the following information:

✔ **Avatar:** When members create new groups, they can choose an avatar, or photo, to represent the group.

✔ **Name:** This name is given to the group by the group administrator.

✔ **Time last active:** This shows the time of the group's last activity, such as a new member, new wire comment, or forum post. This will display something similar to "Active 1 hour, 30 minutes ago."

✔ **Description:** Two or three lines of text that describe what the group is about.

✔ **Number of members:** Total number of group members.

✔ **Join/Leave option:** This button gives you the ability to join a group or leave a group you're already a member of.

Groups widget

You can use the widgets that come packaged within BuddyPress to display specific content on your community site; check out Chapter 9 to find out how. One of the widgets is the Groups widget, which displays a listing of community Groups on the site to help other members easily discover existing groups they can browse and join. The Groups widget allows users to sort the list of groups by the following criteria:

✔ **Newest:** The latest groups created within the community.

✔ **Active:** The most active groups in the community, determined by the amount of discussion occurring within the group.

✔ **Popular:** The most popular groups in the community, determined by the number of group members.

The links to sort the groups are located in the upper-right corner of the widget, as shown in Figure 8-2.

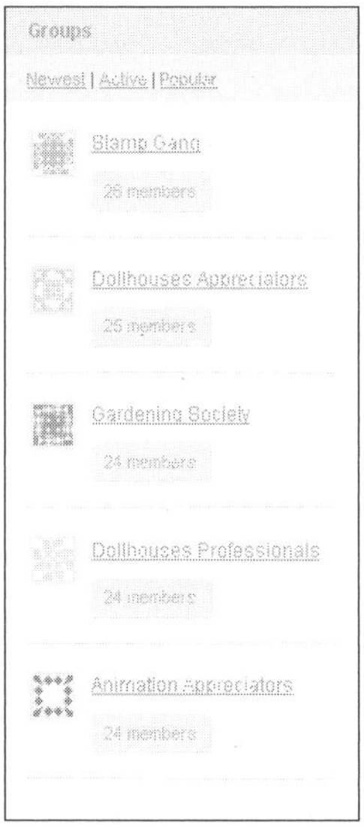

Figure 8-2:
The Groups widget displays a list of groups, sortable by Newest, Active, and Popular.

Site Activity

The Site Activity listing is part of the front page of a BuddyPress site (if you're using the BuddyPress Default theme), or powered by the Site Wide Activity widget (if you are using the BuddyPress Classic theme). (You can find out more about widgets in Chapter 9.) This widget gives you a list of all community activity in your network, including group activity items. However, if you're using the BuddyPress Default theme, you don't really need to use the widget — Figure 8-3 shows the Site Activity listing from the official BuddyPress demo site, filtered by new Group forum replies within the community. (Information about filtering the Site Activity listing can be found in Chapter 6.)

Figure 8-3:
The Site Wide Activity listing filtered by Groups.

Viewing group activity in the Site Activity listing allows community members to discover new and active groups within the community. From the Site Activity listing, members can click the name of the group to view the group's front page, find out more about the group and, if they desire, join the group.

Finding out about a community group

Every group within a BuddyPress community has its own page. Figure 8-4 shows a group in the BuddyPress demo site community.

The front page of a group displays the following information:

Figure 8-4:
A group's front page in a BuddyPress social community.

✔ **Avatar:** The group *administrator* — the person who created the group — can choose a photo, called an *avatar,* to represent the group. The group page displays the large version of the group avatar. (See Chapter 6 for information on how to create a group avatar.)

✔ **Join/Leave option:** This button gives users the options to join or leave a group.

✔ **Administrator:** The photo and name of the person who created the group. The administrator's name links to his/her profile. Additionally, if the administrator has assigned any other administrators or moderators of the group, they will appear in this section, as well. (See Chapter 6 for information on assigning other administrators and moderators to a group you own.)

✔ **Title:** The title of the group, determined by the group's administrator.

✔ **Publicity:** Indicates whether the group is public or private. Chapter 6 covers information on group privacy options.

✔ **Description:** A short, two-to-three line description of what the group is about.

✔ **News:** Administrators and moderators can post news items that appear in the News section.

✔ **Recent activity stream:** All group activity is listed in the group's activity stream. This includes new members, new wire comments, and new forum topics. By default, recent activity items appear ten per page.

✔ **Recent forum topics:** A list of all forum topics. By default, forum topics appear five per page, in chronological order.

✔ **Members:** The avatars and names of the group members. By default, members appear five per page, but a See All link is available in the upper right of this section.

✔ **Forums**: If the administrator of the group has enabled a discussion forum for this group, a Forums link is shown in the navigation menu options above the group activity listing.

Joining community groups

After you discover a group that you want to join, visit the group's front page. Every group's front page has a Join/Leave button directly below the group's avatar. The following buttons display, depending on the group's publicity status:

✔ **Join Group:** Click this button to join a group. When you do so, you become a member of the group and the text on the button changes to "Leave Group."

✔ **Request Membership:** This button appears on private groups. When you click this button, the administrator of the group receives notification that you want to join and the text on the button changes to "Membership Requested." You have to wait for the administrator to approve your membership before you can participate.

✔ **Leave Group:** This button appears on groups that you are a member of. When you click this button, you cancel your membership to that group and the text on the button changes to "Join Group." You can click the Join Group button if you want to re-join the group later.

Joining the Discussion

The Forums feature is popular in BuddyPress communities because it allows members to host their very own discussion forums. Discussion forums give members the ability to create new topics for discussion and invite other members to comment on and provide feedback on that particular topic. Members can create an unlimited amount of topics to encourage discussion and conversation between all the members within the group. In BuddyPress, discussion forums are referred to as Group Forums. On any group's front page that has the Forum feature enabled, choose Groups⇨Forum on the navigation menus to the left. The group's Forum page appears, as shown in Figure 8-5, where you find a listing of the most recent topics started by members.

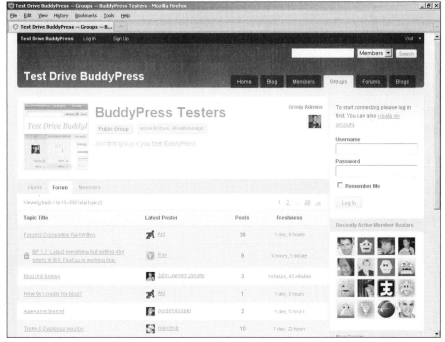

Figure 8-5: A group's Forum page lists the 15 most recent topics.

By default, the group's Forum page lists the 15 most recent topics; additional topics appear 15 per page.

Posting new topics in a forum is easy. Here's how:

1. **Click the Forums link in the Group navigation menu.**

   Scroll down to the bottom of the page and you find the Post a New Topic form, as shown in Figure 8-6.

2. **Type the title of your topic in the Title text box.**

   You can give your new topic any title you want.

3. **Type the topic message (or *body*) in the Content text box.**

4. **Tag your topic by typing keywords in the Tags text box.**

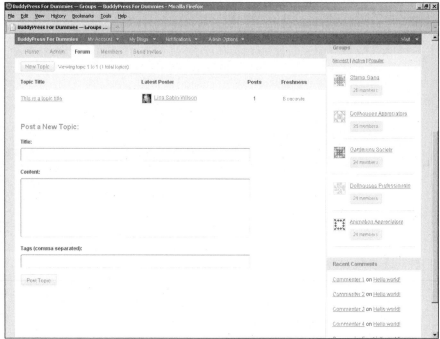

Figure 8-6:
This form
allows you
to post a
new topic in
a forum.

Members can browse forum topics by *tags* — one to two keyword
descriptions of what the topic is about. Tags organize topics. For
example, if your topic is about pet goldfish, the tags for your topic could
be *goldfish*, *fish*, and *pet fish*. Always separate each tag by a comma so
BuddyPress knows where one tag ends and another one begins.

5. Click the Post Topic button.

Your new topic displays in a new window with a text box underneath it
where other members can come along and add to the discussion of your
new topic.

Topics and discussions

When talking about group forums, you hear
phrases like *forum topics* and *discussion
threads,* but what is the difference between
the two? A *forum topic* is a proposed subject
of discussion. Similar to being in a group at a
party, you can start a conversation by bringing
up a topic for people to talk about. A *discussion
thread* is the conversation that results from the
topic. Every forum topic in BuddyPress has a
text box that members can use to submit their
thoughts on the topic; therefore, adding to the
conversations going on in the forum.

Exploring the Groups Menu

The navigation menu on the left side contains links for browsing your community's features, including the Groups feature. Within a group, the Groups menu has six options, as shown in Figure 8-4:

- ✔ **Home:** Displays the group's home page.

- ✔ **Forum:** Displays the Forum page where you can read and participate in forum topics and discussions.

- ✔ **Members:** Displays all the current group members; this page displays the member's avatar and name, linked to their individual profile. It also indicates how long the person has been a member of this particular group.

- ✔ **Send Invites:** Displays in the Groups menu only if you are a member of the group. This link loads the Send Invites page that lists community members you've added as friends. You can select which of your friends you want to invite to join the group by checking the box to the left of their name and then clicking the Send Invites button, as shown in Figure 8-7.

- ✔ **Leave Group:** Displays in the menu only if you are a member of the group. This link removes you from the group.

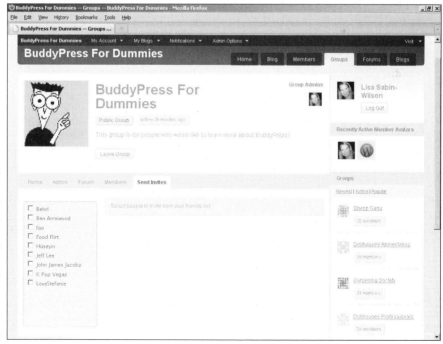

Figure 8-7:
Invite your
friends
within the
community
to join
groups of
which you
are a
member.

Part IV
Customizing
BuddyPress

The 5th Wave   By Rich Tennant

@RICHTENNANT

"Here's an idea. Why don't you start a social
network for doofuses who think they know
how to set a broken leg, but don't."

In this part . . .

This part is all about individualizing and customizing your BuddyPress themes and templates to create a completely unique look that's all your own. I tell you where to find existing free BuddyPress themes, how to tweak existing themes using basic HTML and CSS, and how to use BuddyPress template tags and functions to help you put together a nicely designed theme to suit your needs and style.

Chapter 9

Default Theme and Widgets

In This Chapter

▶ Installing BuddyPress themes

▶ Choosing between the Default and Classic theme

▶ Creating a Site Activity listing with the Classic theme

▶ Using a widget to display members

▶ Displaying community groups

▶ Create a warm welcome message with a widget

▶ Knowing the difference between blog widgets and community widgets

*B*uddyPress comes with two nicely designed themes that you can use on your site after you install and set up the BuddyPress plugin. The BuddyPress Default and Classic themes are included so you can get your site up and running right away.

You can customize the BuddyPress themes to create a visual design unique to your own community, which I cover in Chapter 11. You can also find, download, and install different themes created by designers in the BuddyPress community, which I describe in Chapter 10. Additionally, in Chapter 16, I list ten great free themes I've come across in my travels that you can use in your BuddyPress community.

This chapter gives you an overview of the BuddyPress themes, including how to install and activate it, and how and when to use the included BuddyPress widgets to display different content and information on your community Web site.

Installing the Themes

In Chapter 4, I show you how to install the BuddyPress suite of plugins into your existing WordPress MU installation. To perform this installation, you need to move the Default theme folders into the `/wp-content/themes/` folder on your Web server. (If you need to review how to move these files, check out Chapter 4.)

Keep an eye out for a new release of the WordPress MU software in the early months of 2010. The planned upgrade for WordPress MU will eliminate the need for you to move the BuddyPress theme files to the `/wp-content/ themes/` folder; this action will be done for you when you install and activate the BuddyPress suite of plugins.

The first theme included in the BuddyPress plugin is the BuddyPress Classic, as shown in Figure 9-1. This theme has a three-column layout and an orange-and-gray color scheme. The BuddyPress Classic theme requires the BuddyPress Parent theme in order to work.

The second theme is the BuddyPress Default theme, the newest theme to be created by the BuddyPress developers. You can see how the BuddyPress default theme looks in Figure 9-2; it has a two-column layout with a blue-and-white color scheme.

The third theme bundled in the BuddyPress suite of plugins is the BuddyPress Social Network Parent Theme. This theme should never be activated and used directly on your site. Rather, this theme is a parent theme, or a theme framework, that other themes are built from, including the BuddyPress Classic theme. I cover the parent/child theme relationship in more depth in Chapter 12.

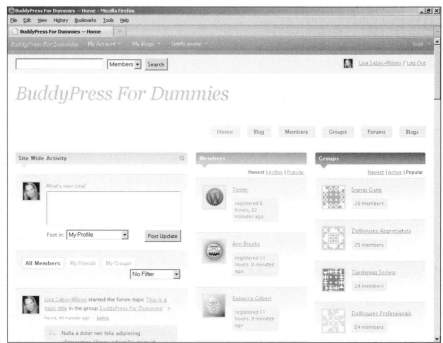

Figure 9-1: The BuddyPress Classic theme.

Figure 9-2:
The
BuddyPress
Default
Theme

I mentioned early on in this book that BuddyPress has undergone some pretty massive new development since it burst onto the blogging scene in 2008. The BuddyPress Classic theme, built on the BuddyPress Parent theme, was the first theme that users were able to use. For this reason, the BuddyPress developers left the Classic and Parent themes in place so that sites already running BuddyPress wouldn't fail when the new Default theme was added. I recommend you use the Default theme to build your community site — the Classic theme, while functional, is a bit more challenging to work with.

In this book I work exclusively with the BuddyPress Default theme, but the concepts and ideas introduced can be applied toward the Classic theme, if you care to go that direction. In this chapter, I mention some features that are used only with the Classic theme, but for the most part I stick with the Default theme.

Using BuddyPress Widgets

Widgets are helpful and handy tools found in all WordPress installations. BuddyPress adds some additional widgets to help you display the content you want to show on your community Web site. Widgets allow you to easily arrange the display of content, such as activity wires, member listings, and blog posts, on your Web site using drag-and-drop technology.

Have a look again at Figure 9-2. It shows the BuddyPress Default theme with the Site Activity listings on the left side; however, on the right side, you see my avatar, name, and a log out button at the top (if you were the one logged into the site, of course, you would be seeing your own avatar and name). The rest of the right sidebar is empty — that is because we haven't yet added widgets to the sidebar. I show you how to do that next.

To add widgets in the BuddyPress Default theme, log in to your WordPress MU dashboard and choose Appearance➪Widgets. This loads the Widgets page, shown in Figure 9-3, where the WordPress and BuddyPress widgets display beneath the Available Widgets heading, and the available sidebar appear on the right. In the BuddyPress Default theme, you can add widgets to

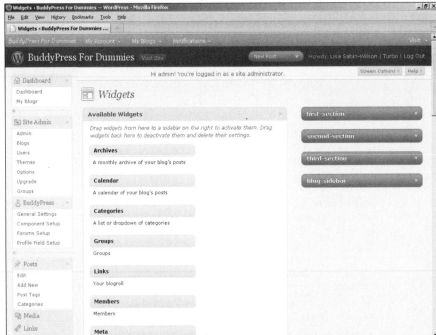

Figure 9-3:
The Widgets page is where you add widgets to your BuddyPress Default theme.

In a default WordPress MU installation with BuddyPress added, you have access to several widgets. However, the Widgets page on your WordPress dashboard doesn't indicate whether the widgets are WordPress widgets or BuddyPress widgets, so I've compiled a listing of widgets for you in Table 9-1, listed in order of appearance.

Table 9-1   Listing of WordPress MU and BuddyPress Widgets

Widget Name	Belongs to	Description
Archives	WordPress	Displays a monthly listing of blog post archives
Calendar	WordPress	Displays a monthly calendar with clickable links for blog post archives
Categories	WordPress	Displays a listing of categories on your blog that visitors can click to view blog posts filed in that category
Groups	BuddyPress	Displays a listing of groups within your community
Links	WordPress	Displays a listing of links you've added to the WordPress Link Manager
Members	BuddyPress	Displays a listing of members within your community
Meta	WordPress	Displays a list of administrative links, like login, logout and RSS links.
Pages	WordPress	Displays a listing of pages you've created
Recent Comments	WordPress	Displays a listing of the most recent comments left by visitors to your blog
Recently Active Member Avatars	BuddyPress	Displays a listing of avatars (photos) of the members who have been recently active in your community
Recent Posts	WordPress	Displays a listing of the most recent blog posts you've published to your blog
RSS	WordPress	Allows you to display an RSS Feed on your Web site
Search	WordPress	Displays a search box that allows your visitors to search your site using keywords
Tag Cloud	WordPress	Displays a listing of the tags you've created and posted to on your blog
Text	WordPress	Allows you to add a block of text to the sidebar of your Web site
Welcome	BuddyPress	Allows you to display a simple welcome message to visitors of your site
Who's Online Avatars	BuddyPress	Displays the avatars of members who are logged into your site

From Table 9-1, you can easily see that WordPress widgets deal mainly with your blog-related content, and BuddyPress widgets deal primarily with your community-related content.

One other BuddyPress widget is available — the Site Wide Activity widget — which is used only with the BuddyPress Classic theme. If you are using the Default theme, the Site Wide Activity widgets won't appeart on the WordPress Widgets page because it is used only with the Classic theme. I cover this widget in the next section.

Displaying site wide activity on the Classic theme

Within most community sites on the Web, there is a hub of activity where you can peek in and discover what's going on and who's doing what. On a BuddyPress-powered site, this hub of activity displays through a widget called Site Wide Activity.

After it's activated on the site, the Site Wide Activity widget displays a real-time listing of site activity, including:

✔ New friendships

✔ Recent posts on community blogs

✔ Latest forum topics and discussions

✔ Recent comments made to member and group wires

✔ Formation of new groups, forums, and blogs

✔ Latest member status updates

To add the Site Wide Activity widget to your site, using the Classic BuddyPress theme, follow these steps:

1. **Log in to your WordPress MU dashboard.**

2. **Choose Appearance➪Widgets.**

   The Widgets page displays the available widgets on the left and the available sidebars on the right.

3. **Expand the First-Section sidebar.**

   Clicking the drop-down arrow on the First-Section sidebar expands the sidebar and readies it to receive a new widget. This sidebar controls the content that displays in the left column of the BuddyPress Classic theme. (I like to place the Site Wide Activity Widget here because this section has the largest display on the BuddyPress Classic theme.)

4. **Locate the Site Wide Activity widget.**

   The Widgets page lists available widgets in alphabetical order; scroll down until you see the Site Wide Activity widget.

5. **Drag and drop the Site Wide Activity widget to the First-Section sidebar.**

   When you drag a new widget onto the First-Section sidebar, a dotted outline appears, indicating that you can now release the button on your mouse to drop the Site Wide Activity widget into place, as shown in Figure 9-4.

Figure 9-4:
Drag
and drop
widgets
into place
on your
WordPress
dashboard.

6. **Edit the Site Wide Activity widget's options.**

   After you drop the widget onto the sidebar, the widget expands to reveal available options, as shown in Figure 9-5. The Site Wide Activity widget has two options that you can configure:

   - *Number of Items per Page:* This option tells BuddyPress how many activity items you want to show on each page. The default setting is 25, but you can change the number by typing a new one in the text box provided.

   - *Max Items to Show:* This option tells BuddyPress how many items you want to display overall. By default, BuddyPress cuts off the listing at 200, but you can change the number by typing a new one in the text box provided.

By default, BuddyPress lists 25 activity items per page. The higher the number in the Max Items to Show option, the more page numbers that display.

7. **Save your widget settings.**

   Click the Save button within the Site Wide Activity widget to save the settings you just configured.

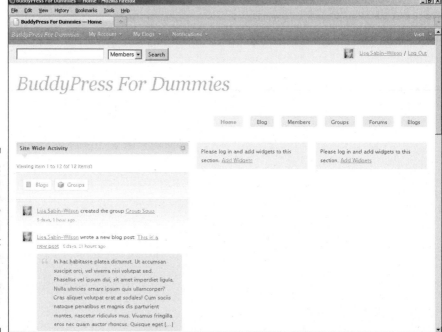

Figure 9-5:
Setting
options
for the
Site Wide
Activity
widget.

8. **Load your site to view the Site Wide Activity listing.**

When you load the main page of your site (`http://yourdomain.com`), you now see a listing of activity that has occurred within your community — the more activity, the larger the list. Figure 9-6 shows the Site Wide Activity listing on the home page of my BuddyPress community site.

Figure 9-6:
The Site
Wide
Activity
listing on
the front
page of site
using the
BuddyPress
Classic
theme.

The Site Wide Activity widget is available *only* if you have the BuddyPress Classic theme activated on your WordPress MU site; this widget will not appear as an available widget when you have the BuddyPress Default theme activated. The Site Wide Activity listing displays an array of activity within your community. Chapter 6 details what information accumulates in this listing and includes how you and your members can use it to navigate your community site.

Using the Members widget

One of the widgets I really like within BuddyPress is the Members widget, which allows you to display a listing of members within your community and sort the listing by the newest, recently active, and most popular members. The programming is in place — all you have to do is add the widget to the sidebar on your site by following these easy steps:

1. **Log in to your WordPress MU dashboard.**

2. **Choose Appearance⇨Widgets.**

   The Widgets page appears and displays the available widgets on the left and the available sidebars on the right.

3. **Expand the sidebar on the right.**

   Clicking the drop-down arrow on the sidebar expands the sidebar and readies it to receive a new widget (refer to Figure 9-3).

4. **Locate the Members widget.**

   The Widgets page lists available widgets in alphabetical order; scroll down until you see the Members widget.

5. **Drag and drop the Members widget to the sidebar.**

   Click the Members widget and while holding down your mouse button, drag it onto the sidebar.

6. **Edit the Members widget's options.**

   After you drop the widget onto the sidebar, the widget expands to reveal available options, as shown in Figure 9-7. The Members widget has one option that you can configure: Max Members to Show. This option tells BuddyPress how many members to display in the listing. By default, BuddyPress displays five, but you can change the number by typing a new one in the text box provided.

7. **Save your widget settings.**

   Click the Save button within the Members widget to save the settings you just configured.

8. **Load your site to view the Members listing.**

   When you load the main page of your site (`http://yourdomain.com`), you now see a listing of your community members in the right sidebar, as shown in Figure 9-8. You can sort the listing by using the links you see in the top-right corner of the Members listing:

   • *Newest:* The default display shows the newest members to register an account within your community.

   • *Active:* Displays the most recently active members within your community.

   • *Popular:* Displays the most popular members within your community, determined by the number of friends they've accumulated.

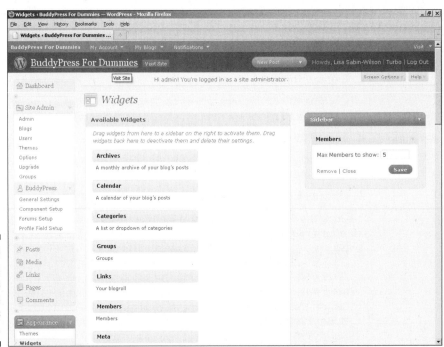

Figure 9-7:
Setting
options
for the
Members
widget.

The Members widget makes locating new members easy for you and your community because the Members widget shows the member's photo and name — both of which link directly to the member's profile.

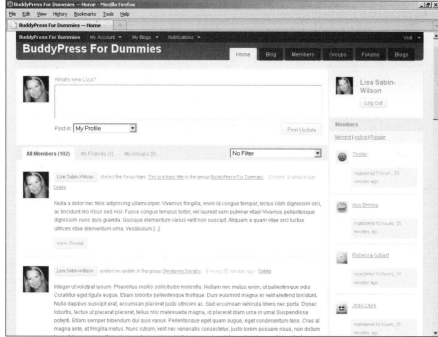

Figure 9-8:
The
Members
widget
in the
BuddyPress
Default
theme.

Displaying community groups

The Groups widget enables you to display a listing of groups within your community, which allows your members to discover new groups while they browse your Web site. The Groups widget displays the following information in the selected column of the BuddyPress Default theme:

✔ **The group's avatar:** A photo that the group administrator has chosen to represent the group that can be clicked by any site visitor to view the group's main page.

✔ **The group's title:** The title given to the group by the administrator that can be clicked by anyone to view the main page of the group.

  ✔ **The number of members:** The number of people who have joined the group.

You can display the Groups listing in any column on the BuddyPress Default theme using the Groups widget; here's how:

1. **Log in to your WordPress MU dashboard.**

2. **Choose Appearance⇨Widgets.**

   The Widgets page appears and displays the available widgets on the left and the available sidebar on the right.

3. **Expand the sidebar.**

   Clicking the drop-down arrow on the sidebar expands the sidebar and readies it to receive a new widget (refer to Figure 9-4). This sidebar controls the content that displays in the right column of the BuddyPress Default theme.

4. **Locate the Groups widget.**

   The Widgets page lists available widgets in alphabetical order; scroll down until you see the Groups widget.

5. **Drag and drop the Groups widget to the sidebar.**

   Click the Groups widget and while holding down your mouse button, drag it onto the sidebar.

6. **Edit the Groups widget's options.**

   After you drop the widget onto the sidebar, the widget expands to reveal available options, as shown in Figure 9-9. The Groups widget has one option that you can configure: Max Groups to Show. This option tells BuddyPress how many groups to display in this listing. By default, BuddyPress displays five, but you can change the number by typing a new one in the text box provided.

7. **Save your widget settings.**

   Click the Save button within the Groups widget to save the settings you just configured.

8. **Load your site to view the Groups listing.**

   When you load the main page of your site (http://yourdomain. com), you now see a listing of groups in the right column. You can sort the listing by using the links you see in the top-right corner of the Groups listing:

- *Newest:* The default display shows the newest groups created within your community.

- *Active:* Displays the most recently active groups within your community.

- *Popular:* Displays the most popular groups within your community, determined by the number of members they've accumulated.

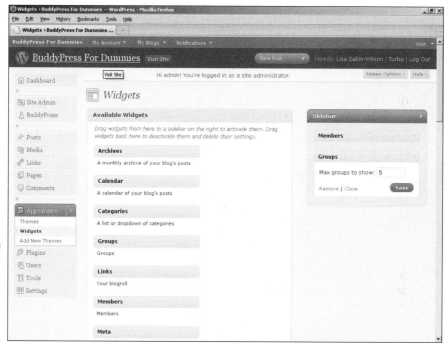

Figure 9-9: Setting options for the Groups widget.

Creating a warm welcome message

A warm welcome message tells visitors what your community is about and why they should join and begin interacting on your site right away!

You can accomplish this very easily by using the Buddypress Welcome widget. Just follow these steps:

1. **Log in to your WordPress MU dashboard.**

2. **Choose Appearance⇨Widgets.**

   The Widgets page appears and displays the available widgets on the left and the available sidebars on the right.

3. **Expand the sidebar on the right.**

   Clicking the drop-down arrow on the sidebar expands the sidebar and readies it to receive a new widget (refer to Figure 9-4).

4. **Locate the Welcome widget.**

   The Widgets page lists available widgets in alphabetical order; scroll down until you see the Welcome widget.

5. **Drag and drop the Welcome widget to the sidebar.**

   Click the Welcome widget and while holding down your mouse button, drag it onto the sidebar.

6. **Edit the Welcome widget's options.**

   After you drop the widget onto the sidebar, the widget expands to reveal available options, as shown in Figure 9-10.

   The Welcome widget has two fields for you to fill with information:

   • *Title:* Give your welcome message a title like *Welcome to Our Community!* — type your desired title into the Title text box.

   • *Content:* Come up with a short, effective paragraph of text that welcomes your visitors to your site and tells them what your site is about. Using a little HTML code, you can even provide a link inviting them to read more information on your site's Bio (or "About Us") page (as luck would have it, I cover basic HTML code in Chapter 10).

7. **Save your widget settings.**

   Click the Save button within the Welcome widget to save the settings you just configured.

8. **Load your site to view the Welcome message.**

   Figure 9-11 shows the welcome message displayed at the top of the right sidebar on my BuddyPress community site.

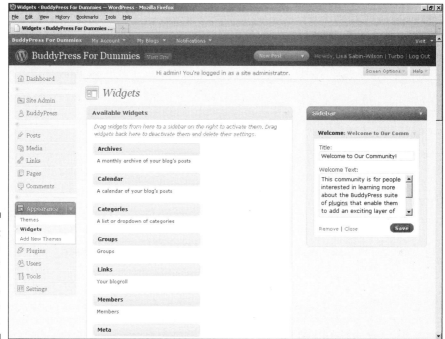

Figure 9-10:
Type a
welcome
message
with the
Welcome
widget.

Figure 9-11:
A Welcome
message
shown in
the right
sidebar
using the
Welcome
widget.

By now, you should understand the concept of widgets and adding them to your BuddyPress Default theme. The remaining BuddyPress widgets, and their options, include:

- ✔ **Recently Active Member Avatars:** Add this widget to display just the avatars (or photos) of the most recently active members within your community. By default, the number of avatars that displays is 15, but you can change the number by typing a new one in the text box provided in the widget's options.

- ✔ **Who's Online Avatars:** Add this widget to display avatars belonging to community members who are logged into your site; that is, their status is online. By default, the number of avatars that displays is 15, but you can change the number by typing a new one in the text box provided in the widget's options.

Blog versus Community Widgets

In Table 9-1, I list the widgets that are available within a default WordPress MU installation with BuddyPress added and indicate which widgets are default WordPress widgets, and which come with the BuddyPress suite of plugins. The difference between the two is the WordPress widgets are blog content–related, and the BuddyPress widgets are community-related. The WordPress widgets display information related to the content within your main site or blog, such as recent blog posts, categories, and lists you've created on your WordPress dashboard.

You can use the WordPress widgets to display content on your BuddyPress community — and you can mix and match WordPress and BuddyPress widgets to create content and navigation features that are unique to your site. Figure 9-12 displays my main blog page and the widgets I added by dragging and dropping them to the Sidebar section of the Widgets page:

- ✔ **Recent Posts:** A listing of the five most recent posts published to my blog.

- ✔ **Categories:** A listing of categories I've created on my blog.

- ✔ **Archives:** A listing of my monthly blog archives.

If you enable user blogs within your community, then these widgets are available for your users to drag and drop onto their own sidebars, too. On their blog, the information that displays relates to the content on their individual community blog.

Currently, widgets cannot be added to member profiles, but give those bright developers at BuddyPress.Org a little time. Down the road, I'm sure the wonder of widgets will be available to help you control the content that displays on your profile, too.

Other widgets can be added to a BuddyPress community by using plugins created just for BuddyPress community sites. For information on where to find, download, and install plugins for BuddyPress, see Chapter 13.

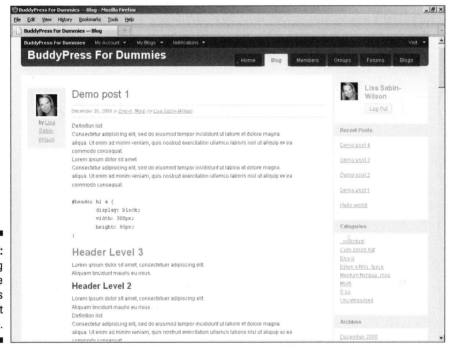

Figure 9-12:
My blog page in the BuddyPress default theme.

Chapter 10

Finding and Installing Themes

. . . .

In This Chapter

▶ Finding Free BuddyPress Themes

▶ Previewing a new theme

▶ Downloading and installing themes

▶ Activating and using a new theme on your community site

. . . .

*I*n previous chapters, I cover how to install and set up various BuddyPress features and components. You've discovered how to set up features like groups, forums, blogs, and extended member profiles. Chapter 4 shows you how to use the BuddyPress Default theme — a theme all ready for you to use right after you install and set up BuddyPress on your Web site. The default theme is great, but what if you're looking for something a little different?

This chapter steps you through finding free themes created for BuddyPress by members of the BuddyPress development community. You also find out how to download and install the theme on your site, and, finally, how to activate the theme for use.

Finding Free BuddyPress Themes

Unlike the parent WordPress community, the BuddyPress community does not yet have a solid theme development community, so finding quality free themes for BuddyPress at this time can be somewhat challenging. Still, it's not impossible, if you know where to look. The BuddyPress Default theme is meant to get you started, but you're certainly not limited to using only the default theme. You can download other themes and try them out on your site, which I talk about in this chapter. In Chapters 11 and 12, I discuss how you can customize your own BuddyPress theme, if you're the kind of person who likes to dip a bit into the techy side of things.

Free themes, such as the ones I spotlight in Chapter 16, are appealing to a wide audience of BuddyPress users because they offer an easy way to change the visual look and layout of your social community. They are also fantastic tools to use to teach yourself how to create and customize your own themes.

By using themes that are available for download from the BuddyPress Web site, you can get your social community site up and running at no additional cost because the themes you find there are free. You can find the directory of themes at `http://buddypress.org/extend/themes` (see Figure 10-1) to browse the offerings, view small screenshots of the themes, and download the theme files to your computer.

The themes that you find at the official BuddyPress site are compatible with the latest version of the BuddyPress software and free of any ugly code or obvious problems. In short, the themes are safe for your use because the BuddyPress development team has vetted them. Safe themes tend to be bug-free and contain the basic BuddyPress functions that are considered fundamental requirements to ensure that your theme, and ultimately your site, is able to take full advantage of all BuddyPress components and features.

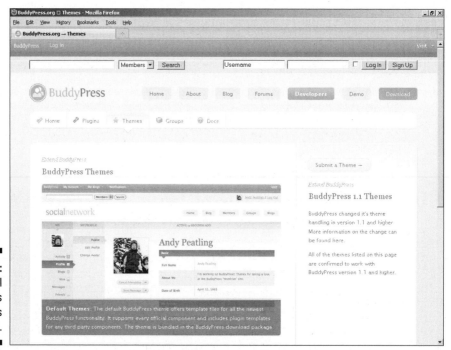

Figure 10-1:
The official
BuddyPress
themes
directory.

Table 10-1 gives you a few other places on the Web where you can find free BuddyPress themes. Be forewarned that BuddyPress developers check only themes listed on the official BuddyPress Web site, so I provide this list as a reference to you, with no guarantees.

Table 10-1	BuddyPress Theme Resources on the Web	
Name	*Web Address (URL)*	*Offering*
Free BuddyPress Themes	`http://freebpthemes.com`	Free BuddyPress themes and resource articles.
WPMU Dev	`http://premium.wpmudev.org/buddypress`	BuddyPress themes — but they are not free; there is a minimal cost for membership.
3oneseven	`http://3oneseven.com/topic/themes`	Free BuddyPress themes.

Downloading and Installing Themes

Each theme on the BuddyPress Themes page provides you with a link to download the theme. The following steps take you through the process of downloading, unpacking, and installing a free BuddyPress theme on your Web site:

1. **Click the Download link.**

   The download link appears on the image of the theme screenshot.

2. **Save the theme files to your computer.**

   After you click the download link, a dialog box opens, giving you the option to save a Zip file to your computer. Choose a location on your computer and save the file.

3. **Unpack the plugin Zip file.**

   All theme files are *zipped*, meaning they download to your computer in an archived format, either Zip or Tar.gz. Using your preferred decompression program (like WinZip, for example), unpack the files on your computer.

4. **Open your preferred FTP (File Transfer Protocol) program.**

5. **Connect to your Web server via FTP.**

   Check out Chapter 2 for detailed information on using FTP to connect to your Web server.

6. **Transfer (upload) the theme folder to your Web server.**

   Upload the unarchived theme folder from your computer into the /wp-content/themes/ folder within the WordPress MU installation directory on your Web server.

   The right side of Figure 10-2 shows that I uploaded the theme folder bp-music to the /wp-content/themes directory of my Web server.

After you download and unpack the theme on your computer, you should examine the theme's contents to make sure everything's okay. Most of the free themes that you download for use with BuddyPress will be a "child theme." (I go into more detail on the BuddyPress theme framework in Chapter 11, including the parent/child relationship, which you don't need to worry about in this chapter.) The directory structure of a child theme, at a minimum, contains the following:

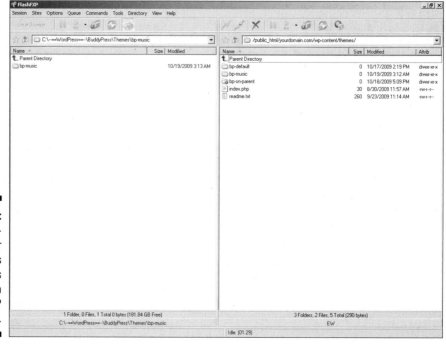

Figure 10-2:
A direc-
tory for
BuddyPress
themes files
shown in
an FTP
window.

✔ **A style sheet:** This is the `style.css` file that you see in the theme folder.

✔ **A screenshot:** This is the `screenshot.png` (or `screenshot.jpg`) image file that appears on the Manage Themes page on your WordPress dashboard.

✔ **A folder named `_inc`:** This folder contains, at a minimum, the following folders:

• `css:` This folder contains the various CSS (Cascading Style Sheet) files that drive the layout and formatting of the theme. (More information about CSS can be found in Chapter 12.)

• `images:` This folder contains all the image files that are used in the theme design.

The theme you download might contain additional files or folders not listed here, but check and make sure that it contains at least the files and folders that I've listed. If it does not, chances are the theme will not work with BuddyPress, and you may have to move on and find a different theme to use.

Activating a New Theme

You've browsed through a bunch of BuddyPress themes and have chosen the one you'd like to use. You have taken the big leap of downloading it, unpacking it, and uploading it to your Web server. You're on your way, but you still have two steps left to go before you can display your new theme on your Web site: enabling the theme and then activating it on your site.

Enabling a theme in WordPress MU

Because you are required to have the WordPress MU software running on your site to use the BuddyPress plugins, you always have to keep WordPress MU considerations in mind with every decision you make on running your community. These include any plugins you decide to use and any themes you install on your site.

In WordPress MU, to use a theme, it has to be enabled in the Site Admin menu first, which you can accomplish in these few steps:

1. **Log in to your WordPress MU dashboard.**

2. **Choose Site Admin⇨Themes.**

You find the Site Admin menu in the navigation on the left side of your WordPress MU dashboard.

3. **Find your new theme on the Site Themes page.**

   This page loads after you click the Themes link in Step 2.

4. **Make the theme active.**

   Select Yes to the left of the theme name to make the theme active on your site.

5. **Update your options.**

   Click the Update Options button to save your settings; the Site Themes page reloads and displays "Site themes saved."

Activating a new theme

After enabling the theme on your WordPress MU dashboard, the last step is activating the theme on your site. This step makes your new theme display on your site. To activate your new theme, follow these steps:

1. **Log in to your WordPress dashboard.**

2. **Choose Appearance➪Themes.**

   The Manage Themes page appears and displays small thumbnails of theme screenshots, as shown in Figure 10-3.

3. **Activate the theme.**

   In Figure 10-3, you see three links beneath the theme screenshot and name:

   • *Activate:* Click this to activate the theme on your Web site.

   • *Preview:* Click this to preview the theme.

   • *Delete:* Click this to delete the theme files from your Web server.

   Click the Activate link to activate the theme on your site.

4. **Visit the main page of your Web site to verify that the theme you selected is indeed displaying on your site.**

Many WordPress users enjoy the dashboard feature that allows them to browse the official WordPress Theme Directory to find, install, and activate themes. BuddyPress fans can use the same feature by clicking Add New Themes under the Appearance menu. Simply type the word **BuddyPress** in the search box to find themes compatible with BuddyPress; then click the Install link to install the theme on your site.

Figure 10-3:
The Manage
Themes
page on the
WordPress
dashboard.

Themes are always a hot topic of conversation in any discussion about the BuddyPress suite of plugins because most users are interested in more than just having the great BuddyPress features available on their Web site. Users also want to display a design that is aesthetically pleasing to the eye and, often, unique to their particular community. Using free themes is a nice way to get a different look and feel on your site than the standard BuddyPress Default theme.

If you're interested in individualizing your theme, check out the information on using CSS to style your BuddyPress community in Chapter 12. However, before you begin digging into the CSS for your theme, it's important to understand the BuddyPress theme architecture — including the parent/child framework that BuddyPress uses as its base — which I discuss in Chapter 11.

Finally, Chapter 16 of this book gives you a peek at ten nice BuddyPress themes that are available for you to download and try on your site for the price of absolutely nothing!

Chapter 11

Understanding Themes and Templates

In This Chapter

▶ Understanding parent/child theme relationships

▶ Exploring the BuddyPress Default theme

▶ Modifying parent theme files

▶ Using BuddyPress with an existing WordPress theme

*I*n Chapter 4, I take you through the process of installing BuddyPress on your WordPress-powered Web site, including installing the default BuddyPress themes. Refer to Chapter 4 if you feel like you need to review the default BuddyPress themes and their locations on your Web server.

In this chapter, you discover the concept of the parent/child theme framework that the BuddyPress themes are built upon. You can use this framework to build your own themes for BuddyPress. I provide you best practices in modifying the parent template files and integrating BuddyPress into an existing WordPress theme and include some helpful code snippets that will assist you in making your site a bit more dynamic and interactive.

 In Chapter 10, I discuss the history of the BuddyPress Classic and BuddyPress Parent theme and explained that in this book I will be working primarily with the BuddyPress Default theme. However, the concepts and ideas introduced can be applied toward the Classic theme, if you care to go that direction.

Understanding Parent/Child Theme Relationships

The concept behind parent/child themes is simple: The parent theme contains the core programming that creates the functions and features on your site, and the child theme contains the images and styles that provide the base for your site's layout and design. When someone visits your Web site, the theme customizations (in the form of Cascading Style Sheets, or CSS) and images stored in the child theme are loaded first, followed by the functions found in the parent theme.

Themes are divided into parent themes and child themes to keep the programming of the theme functions safe from user edits while still allowing full customization of the theme files by using custom CSS and images. This parent/child theme relationship has the advantage of safeguarding the BuddyPress themes for future upgrades because you do not edit the core functions in the parent theme files — *ever*. The nature of child/parent theme relationships means that the child theme pulls the functions from the parent theme, keeping the parent theme completely unaltered. Future upgrades to BuddyPress will overwrite the parent theme, keeping the style and formatting changes you've made in the child theme safe from breaking during an upgrade. You can still alter the function files from the parent theme, if you find you need to, and in that case, there are still safeguards in place for you, which I discuss a bit later in this chapter.

The BuddyPress Default theme is considered a parent theme, as it contains all the core template files required to display the different BuddyPress features and components on your Web site. If you want to change the Default theme, I recommend that you create a child theme that pulls from the Default theme framework. I explain more about this a bit later in this chapter.

Exploring the BuddyPress parent theme

The `bp-default` theme folder, shown in Figure 11-1, should be in the `/wp-content/themes/` folder on your Web server. Inside the `bp-sn-parent` theme folder, you find the following folders with templates that contain the base code for the BuddyPress features and functions:

- ✔ **_inc:** This folder contains all the base styles (CSS), JavaScript files, and images for the BuddyPress admin bar and for the default formatting of the theme.

- ✔ **Activity:** The templates in this folder provide the functions for the activity streams on member profiles.

- ✔ **Blogs:** The templates in this folder provide the functions for blog tracking on member profiles.

- ✔ **Forums:** The templates in this folder provide the functions for the Group forums within your community. This folder also includes the bbPress software that powers the discussion forum feature.

- ✔ **Groups:** The templates in this folder provide the functions for the groups listings on member profiles, as well as group pages, wires, and forums.

✔ **Members**: The templates in this folder provide the functions for the Members Directory listing in your community site.

✔ **Registration:** The templates in this folder provide the functions for the registration page that visitors use to register for your site.

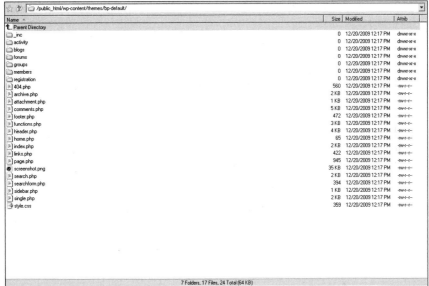

Figure 11-1:
The
BuddyPress
Default
theme
directory.

Within the `bp-default` theme folder, you also find several template files that power all the functions and features for your WordPress site — pages, posts, archives, comments, and search results.

Because these files create a solid framework of combined WordPress and BuddyPress functions, you should never have to edit them. Actually, I strongly recommend that you refrain from editing the files found in the `bp-default` theme folder because upgrades to BuddyPress will overwrite any changed files with the newer upgraded BuddyPress files, and any customizations you've done to your community Web site will be lost.

Exploring the child theme

In the previous section, I emphasize that customizations or changes to your BuddyPress theme should not be made in the parent theme folder. Rather, changes should be made in a child theme folder. This theme folder should contain very few files, as shown in Figure 11-2:

✔ **_inc:** This folder contains the CSS that define the style and layout of the site, as well as the images that create the visual look of the design.

✔ **screenshot.png:** This is the thumbnail representation of the BuddyPress child theme that you see in the gallery of available themes on the Manage Themes page in your WordPress dashboard.

✔ **style.css:** This is the main CSS for the child theme used to define all of the different CSS files that are used, from both the parent and child theme.

Figure 11-2:
The
BuddyPress
child theme
directory.

Creating a child theme folder

Now that you have the basic files that need to exist within a child theme folder - why not create one? Here's what you need to do:

1. **Create a new folder on your computer for your child theme.**

   Give the new folder the name you intend to call your new child theme. For our purposes here, I've created a folder called /child-theme — original, I know!

2. **Copy files from the Buddypress Default theme.**

   Download a copy of the following folders and files from the BuddyPress Default theme folder to the new /child-theme folder created on your local computer:

- /_inc folder and all files contained within

- style.css

- screenshot.png

3. **Connect the new child theme to the parent Default theme in the style.css file. Do this by following these steps:**

   a. *Open the* style.css *file in a text editor like NotePad. The first eight lines of the* style.css *file look like this:*

```
/*
Theme Name: BuddyPress Default
Theme URI: http://buddypress.org/extend/themes/
Description: The default theme for BuddyPress.
Version: 1.2
Author: BuddyPress.org
Author URI: http://buddypress.org
*/
```

Anything placed between the /* and */ characters in the style.css file is considered to be a comment — that is, a note left in plain English by the style sheet author to help readers understand the code. Comments do not affect the function of the code; in fact, browsers completely ignore them.

   b. *Edit the second line by giving your theme a new name.*

   For my example child theme, I've named it New Child Theme, so the second line of the style.css looks like this:

```
Theme Name: New Child Theme
```

   c. *Add a line to the* style.css *that tells BuddyPress that your new child theme is using the BuddyPress Default theme as the parent framework.*

   This line goes directly above the final comment closing mark. It is vital that this line gets included in your child theme style.css file because this is the line that connects your new child theme to the BuddyPress Default parent theme framework. The line is:

```
Template: bp-default
```

   When you are done, the final edits to the style.css look like this:

```
/*
Theme Name: New Child Theme
Theme URI: http://buddypress.org/extend/themes/
Description: The default theme for BuddyPress.
Version: 1.2
Author: BuddyPress.org
Author URI: http://buddypress.org
Template: bp-default
*/
```

4. **Save the new `style.css` file into your new `/child-theme` folder on your local computer.**

5. **Upload the child theme folder to your Web server.**

   Using your FTP client, upload the entire new `/child-theme` folder to your Web server into the `/wp-content/themes/` directory.

6. **Enable the New Child theme in the WordPress MU Site Admin menu.**

   Click the Themes link in the Site Admin menu in the WordPress MU Dashboard and enable the New Child Theme there.

7. **Activate the New Child Theme on your site.**

   Click the Themes link under the Appearances menu in the WordPress MU Dashboard and activate the New Child Theme.

8. **Customize the New Child Theme.**

   You can now customize the style, formatting, and images of your New Child Theme freely, without damaging the integrity of the base/core template theme files in the BuddyPress Default parent theme.

Chapter 12 takes you through the mechanics of tweaking your BuddyPress theme through CSS, including how to change the header image, background color, and font styles. This section simply shows you how the parent and child theme "talk" to one another. To understand that, you need to open and view the `style.css` file found in the root of the `bp-default` folder.

Because WordPress MU doesn't have a built-in theme editor, as the single user version of WordPress does, you have to open theme files with your FTP (File Transfer Protocol) program. Most FTP programs let you view files by right-clicking the file with your mouse and choosing View, which opens the file locally on your computer using a simple text editor, such as Notepad.

At the beginning of the file, you see information about the theme, such as the theme name, author, description, and version; the theme and author URLs; and theme *tags*, which are keywords that describe the theme. The last line of the opening information section of the `Template` file indicates: Template: `bp-default`. This portion of the child theme's `style.css` file is vital because it tells WordPress and BuddyPress what the parent theme is and where it needs to go to pull in all the features and functions for this theme. Without that line, WordPress and BuddyPress would not know which theme is the parent theme containing all the functions.

The other lines of code you see throughout the `style.css` file are commands that import different files and style sheets from the _inc folder within the theme, as well as from other directories within the child theme. For example, after the theme information section, the next line of the `style.css` file is

```
/* The default theme styles. */
@import url( _inc/css/default.css );
```

The @import command tells the program that you are importing another CSS file from a different directory location on your Web server. The second half of that command tells the program exactly where the file you're importing exists.

The style.css file imports information from several CSS files in the child theme folders; if you want to remove any of these calls, you can do so by simply deleting the entire line and then saving and re-uploading the file. The files (including full paths) from which information is imported are

- ✔ **@import url(_inc/css/default.css);** This style sheet formats the BuddyPress default layout and style.

- ✔ **@import url(_inc/css/adminbar.css);** This style sheet contains default styling and formatting for admin menu bar.

Using a custom CSS file in the child theme

Now you are ready to fully customize your BuddyPress child theme and keep it safe from being overwritten in future BuddyPress upgrades! All of the CSS files for you new Child Theme exist within the /_inc/css/ folder in your child theme. For the most part, you must edit the default.css file to customize the look and feel of your BuddyPress community site, but you can also edit the adminbar.css file to edit the look and feel of the Site Admin menu bar at the top of your site.

I cover tweaking your CSS to customize your theme more fully in Chapter 12. For now, all you need to know is that any CSS styling you add to the default.css file overrides all styles within the main style sheets in the parent theme. This is the main file you will use to customize the existing BuddyPress child theme with CSS styling of your own.

Using your own images in the child theme

As with the custom CSS file you create in the previous section, images for your theme design are found in the _inc/images folder in your child theme. Open the folder in your FTP application to find a number of images that make up the BuddyPress Default theme, as shown in Figure 11-3.

When you want to change any of the images that exist in the child theme, you create a new image (using your preferred graphic editor software, such as Photoshop or Paint Shop Pro); give it the same name as the file you are replacing; and then upload it to the _inc/images folder, which overwrites the original file. Likewise, if you delete any of the image files in the _inc/images directory in the child theme, the image will not load when your Web site loads in your browser. Any new images that you add need to be uploaded to this folder, and accounted for in the custom CSS file, which I discuss in Chapter 12.

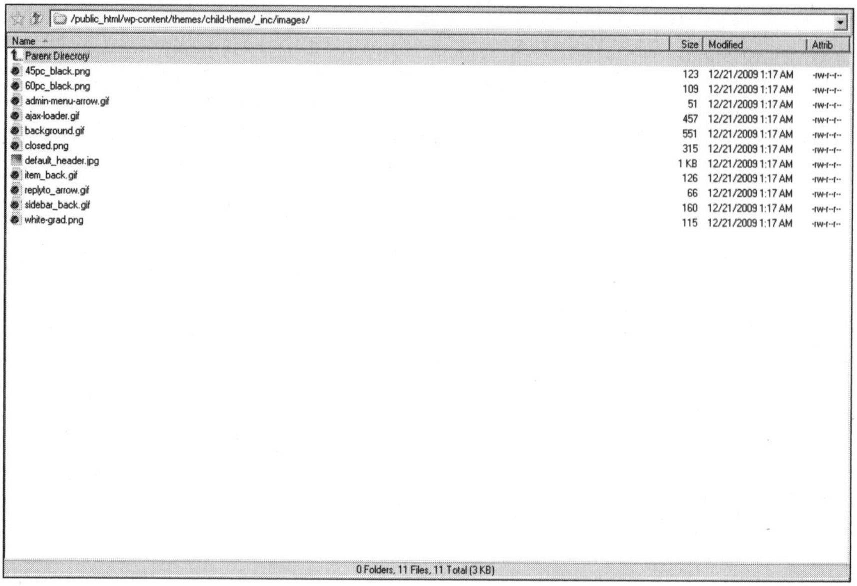

```
/public_html/wp-content/themes/child-theme/_inc/images/
```

Name	Size	Modified	Attrib
Parent Directory			
45pc_black.png	123	12/21/2009 1:17 AM	-rw-r--r--
60pc_black.png	109	12/21/2009 1:17 AM	-rw-r--r--
admin-menu-arrow.gif	51	12/21/2009 1:17 AM	-rw-r--r--
ajax-loader.gif	457	12/21/2009 1:17 AM	-rw-r--r--
background.gif	551	12/21/2009 1:17 AM	-rw-r--r--
closed.png	315	12/21/2009 1:17 AM	-rw-r--r--
default_header.jpg	1 KB	12/21/2009 1:17 AM	-rw-r--r--
item_back.gif	126	12/21/2009 1:17 AM	-rw-r--r--
replyto_arrow.gif	66	12/21/2009 1:17 AM	-rw-r--r--
sidebar_back.gif	160	12/21/2009 1:17 AM	-rw-r--r--
white-grad.png	115	12/21/2009 1:17 AM	-rw-r--r--

0 Folders, 11 Files, 11 Total (3 KB)

Figure 11-3:
The images
that exist in
the default
BuddyPress
child theme
folder.

Modifying Parent Template Files

I mention earlier in this chapter that modifying template files in the parent theme folder isn't recommended and isn't the best practice for modifying some of the functions that exist within those files. You might be wondering, then, how do you change any of the items within those files? Many WordPress and BuddyPress users really like to dig into their template files and customize them to add and subtract functions — it's all part of the fun of using BuddyPress software. For example, how can you add a link in your site's navigation menu when the navigation menu's file is one that I am telling you not to touch?

The BuddyPress parent/child theme framework already has a solution for you — and it's pretty easy! You can find the code for the navigation menu in the `header.php` file in the parent theme. To edit it, simply download a copy of the `header.php` file to your computer, make your changes, and then upload it into your child theme folder. The `header.php` file that exists within the child theme will override the one that exists within the parent theme. Basically, BuddyPress uses the template files from the parent theme by default — however, if a duplicate template file exists within your child theme, it will use that one instead.

You can apply this technique to any of the files and folders within the parent theme; you just have to remember that you have to re-create the very same folder and filenames in your child theme folder that exist within the parent theme folder.

For another example, say you want to change the way your Members Directory appears on your Web site. To do this, you would need to edit the files within the `/members/` folder. Because you shouldn't edit any of the files in the parent theme, you will need to re-create that file structure in your child theme. Create a folder called `/friends/` in the `/child-theme/` theme folder you created in the previous section of this chapter. Download a copy of the files from the version of that folder in the `/bp-default` parent theme, and then upload those files into the `/child-theme/members/` folder — at which point, you are free to edit and change the core template files to your heart's desire.

The beauty of the parent/child theme relationship, as it relates to editing core template files, is if you make a mistake in the coding of a core template file and don't know how to fix it, you can simply delete it from your child theme, and the copy of that same file within the parent theme takes over.

Using a WordPress Theme with BuddyPress

Users can download and use literally thousands of free WordPress themes on their WordPress-powered sites. The majority of those themes can be found in the official WordPress themes directory at `http://wordpress.org/extend/themes`.

Many WordPress users want to integrate BuddyPress features into their existing site, but want to continue using their favorite WordPress theme instead of switching to the BuddyPress Default theme. This is possible to accomplish with just a few steps:

1. **Make a backup copy of your existing WordPress theme.**

   Simply download a copy of your theme from your Web server to your local computer. It is always, always a good idea to make a backup of files before you do something that is going to affect them.

2. **Copy files from the BuddyPress parent theme.**

   Download all the folders and that exist within the `/bp-default` theme folder to your local computer. Just the folders, however; not the files that sit within the root of the `/bp-default` theme folder.

3. **Upload the BuddyPress parent theme folders to your WordPress theme folder.**

   Using your FTP program, upload the folders you copied in Step 2 into the WordPress theme folder that you are currently using on your site.

4. **Open the `style.css` file in your WordPress theme.**

   Using your FTP program, right-click the `style.css` file in your WordPress theme folder and choose Edit to open the file locally in a text editor, such as Notepad.

5. **Add the line to call in the `components.css` file from the parent theme.**

   Add the following line to your `style.css` file beneath the theme information comments:

   ```
   @import url( _inc/css/default.css );
   @import url( _inc/css/adminbar.css );
   ```

   This pulls in the component styling for BuddyPress components and applies it to your existing WordPress theme.

6. **Edit and adjust the CSS file, as needed.**

   You might need to do this to adjust the BuddyPress areas of your site for consistent styling with your WordPress theme. (See Chapter 12 for basic CSS information.)

Integrating BuddyPress into an existing WordPress theme is not an exact science, and there are no absolute steps to follow to create a perfect integration. The reason for this is simple — WordPress themes differ from one another in terms of style, function, and framework. You will probably need to play around with the CSS and styling of your WordPress themes to make the BuddyPress components fit in flawlessly; however, the previous steps get you started on your way to full and successful integration.

The development environment surrounding BuddyPress is pretty fast-paced, so the BuddyPress you know today is likely to be different than the BuddyPress you come to know in a year — or even six months — from now. It's good to be armed with a resource that can help you stay up-to-date on changing techniques and information. Bookmark the official BuddyPress Codex, which is a repository of documents and information on the use of BuddyPress, as well as what is new and changing: `http://codex.buddypress.org`.

Chapter 12

Tweaking the Default Theme with CSS

In This Chapter

▶ Styling with CSS

▶ Changing background colors

▶ Using your own logo

▶ Changing font style, sizes, and colors

▶ Finding CSS resources

*I*n Chapter 11 of this book, I provide information on how to create a new child theme using the BuddyPress Default parent theme as a framework, and you even dipped a little bit into editing the `style.css` file for your new child theme. However, I cannot tell you how many times people have asked me how they can customize a theme that they've found. They ask things to me like:

✔ I like this free theme I found, but I really want to change the header image — how do I do that?

✔ I found this great theme, but I really need to change the background color from black to pink — can I do that, or do I need to hire someone?

✔ This theme I have is perfect; although, I wish I could change the font from Times New Roman to Tahoma — can you tell me how to do that?

The practice of changing a few elements within an existing theme is *tweaking*, and thousands of Web site owners tweak their existing themes on a regular basis. This chapter provides you with information on some of the most common tweaks you can make to your theme, such as changing the header image, changing the color of the background or the text links in your theme, or changing font styles — and they are pretty easy, too! You'll be tweaking your own theme in no time!

Styling with CSS: The Basics

In every WordPress and BuddyPress theme you use in your blog, is a Cascading Style Sheet (CSS). The CSS provides style and design flair to the template tags in your templates. (See Chapter 11 for information about BuddyPress templates.) The CSS files (`.css`) for your theme are called into, and applied to, your site theme through the Header template (`header.php`) and is named `style.css`.

Have a look inside the `header.php` file of the parent BuddyPress theme. Remember, WordPress MU does not have a built-in theme editor, so you need to open the `header.php` file using your FTP program. Inside the header.php file is the following line of code, which pulls the CSS (`style.css`) into the page to provide the formatting of the elements of your site:

```
<link rel="stylesheet" href="<?php bloginfo('stylesheet_
        url'); ?>" type="text/css" media="screen" />
```

Do not tweak the line of code that calls in the `style.css` file; otherwise, the CSS won't work for your blog.

CSS selectors

With CSS, you can provide style (such as size, color, and placement) to the display of elements on your blog (by making changes to text links, header images, font size, font colors, paragraph margins, and line spacing). *CSS selectors* contain names, properties, and values to define which HTML elements in the templates you will style with CSS. Table 12-1 provides some examples of CSS selectors and their use.

Table 12-1		Basic CSS Selectors	
CSS Selector	*Description*	*HTML*	*CSS*
body	Sets the style for the overall body of the site, such as background color and default fonts	`<body>`	`body {background-color: white}` The background color on all pages is white.

CSS Selector	Description	HTML	CSS
p	Defines how paragraphs are formatted	`<p>This is a paragraph</p>`	`p {color:black}` The color of the fonts used in all paragraphs is black.
h1, h3, h3, h4	Provides bold headers for different sections of your site	`<h1>This is a site title </h1>`	`h1 {font-weight: bold;}` The fonts surrounded by the `<h1>..</h1>` HTML tags will be bold.
a	Defines how text links display in your site	`<a href= "http://wiley. com">Wiley Publishing</a>`	`a {color: red}` All text links appear in red.

Classes and IDs

Look at the `default.css` style sheet for the BuddyPress Default parent theme (see Figure 12-1). Everything in it might look foreign to you right now, but I want to bring your attention to two items:

✔ **#wp-admin-bar:** One type of CSS selector. The hash mark (#) indicates that it's a CSS *ID*.

✔ **.ajax-loader:** Another type of CSS selector. The period (.) indicates that it's a CSS *class*.

IDs and classes define styling properties for different sections of your WordPress theme. Table 12-2 shows examples of IDs from the `header.php` template in the BuddyPress parent theme. Armed with this information, you'll know where to look in the style sheet when you want to change the styling for a particular area of your theme.

Table 12-2	Connecting HTML with CSS Selectors	
HTML	**CSS Selector**	**Description**
`<div id= "header">`	`#header`	Styles the elements for the `header` ID in your template(s)

(continued)

Table 12-2 (continued)

HTML	CSS Selector	Description
`<h1 id="logo">`	`#logo`	Styles the elements for the `logo` ID in your template
`<ul id="nav">`	`ul#nav`	Styles the elements for the `nav` ID in your template(s)
`<div id="search-bar">`	`#search-bar`	Styles the elements for the search bar shown at the top of your site pages.
`<div id="container">`	`#container`	Styls the elements for the container ID in your template

If you find an element in the template code that says id (such as `div id=` or `p id=`), look for the hash symbol in the style sheet. If you find an element in the template code that says class (such as `div class=` or `p class=`), look for the period in the style sheet followed by the selector name.

```
default.css - Notepad
File  Edit  Format  View  Help
@import url( reset.css ); /* Reset browser defaults */

/* > Global Elements
-------------------------------------------------------------- */

body {
        background: #eaeaea url( ../images/background.gif ) top left repeat-x;
        font-size: 12px;
        font-family: Arial, Tahoma, Verdana, sans-serif;
        line-height: 160%;
        color: #555;
        width: 90%;
        min-width: 960px;
        max-width: 1250px;
        margin: 0 auto;
        padding-top: 0 !important; /* Remove the top padding space for the admin bar in this theme */
}
        body.activity-permalink {
                min-width: 500px;
                max-width: 760px;
        }

h2 {margin: 10px 0;font-size: 20px;}
h3 {font-size: 16px;margin: 15px 0;color: #888;}
h4 {font-size: 14px;margin: 10px 0;color: #888;}

a { color: #1fb3dd; }

.padder { padding: 15px; }
.clear { clear: left; }

p {      margin-bottom: 15px; }
p:last-child { margin-bottom: 0; }

img.avatar {
        float: left;
        border: 2px solid #eee;
}

/* > Admin Bar
-------------------------------------------------------------- */

#wp-admin-bar .padder {
        width: 90% !important; /* Line up the admin bar with the content body in this theme */
}
.ajax-loader {
        background: url( ../images/ajax-loader.gif ) center left no-repeat !important;
        padding: 8px;
        display: none;
}

span.activity, div#message p {
        display: inline-block;
}
```

Figure 12-1:
The BuddyPress default `.css` style sheet.

CSS properties and values

CSS properties are assigned to the CSS selector name. You also need to provide values for the CSS properties to define the style elements for the particular CSS selector you're working with.

In the BuddyPress Default parent theme, for example, one of the first pieces of markup in the Header template (header.php) is <div id="header">. This ID, with the name header, provides styling for the site page.

In the default.css of your child theme style sheet (found in /_inc/ css/), the CSS defined for the header ID, preceded by the hash mark (#), is as follows:

```
#header {
    overflow: auto;
    width: 100%;
}
```

Every CSS property needs to be followed by a colon (:), and each CSS value needs to be followed by a semicolon (;).

The CSS selector is #header, which has several properties; however, many users would like to change two:

- ✔ The CSS color property has the value #fff, which is white. You can edit that color to make it display whatever color you want just by removing #fff and replacing it with a different color value.

- ✔ The CSS background property has the value of url(../images/ default_header.jpg);. You can edit the background by changing the image file that is defined in the background value.

Table 12-3 provides some examples of commonly used CSS properties and values.

Table 12-3	Common CSS Properties and Values	
CSS Property	*CSS Value*	*Examples*
background-color	Defines the color of the background (such as red, black, or white)	**Markup:** <div id="header"> **CSS:** #header {background-color: black}

(continued)

Table 12-3 *(continued)*

CSS Property	CSS Value	Examples
`background`	Defines a background image	**Markup:** `<div id="header">` **CSS:** `#header {background: url(images/header.jpg) no-repeat;}`
`font-family*`	Defines the fonts used for the selector	**Markup:** `<body>` **CSS:** `body { font-family: 'Lucida Grande', Verdana, Arial, Sans-Serif;}`
`color`	Defines the color of the text	**Markup:** `<h1>Website Title </h1>` **CSS:** `h1 {color: blue}`
`font-size**`	Defines the size of the text	**Markup:** `<h1>Website Title </h1>` **CSS:** `h1 {font-size: 18px;}`
`text-align`	Defines the alignment of the text (left, center, right, or justified)	**Markup:** `<div id="header">` **CSS:** `#page {text-align: left;}`

* W3Schools has a good resource on the font-family property here: http://w3schools.com/CSS/pr_font_font-family.asp

Changing the Background Color

In this section, I show you how to tweak the `<body>` tag in the BuddyPress Default parent theme. The `<body>` tag is simple HTML markup. Every theme has this tag, which defines the overall default content for each page of your Web site — the site's *body*.

In the BuddyPress child theme that you create in Chapter 11, the `default. css` file (found in `/_inc/css/default.css`) has body styles defined like this:

```
body {
background: #eaeaea url( ../images/background.gif ) top
         left repeat-x;
font-size: 12px;
font-family: Arial, Tahoma, Verdana, sans-serif;
```

```
line-height: 160%;
color: #555555;
width: 90%;
min-width: 960px;
max-width: 1250px;
margin: 0 auto;
padding-top: 0 !important; /* Remove the top padding space
           for the admin bar in this theme */
}
```

The background for the <body> tag assigns a light gray color using the hex code #eaeaea (although an image is not assigned as a background element, you can assign one):

✔ **Color:** A hexadecimal (or *hex*) code represents a certain color. Hex codes always start with a hash symbol (#) and have six letters and/or numbers to represent a particular color — in this case, #eaeaea. Table 12-4 lists some common colors and the corresponding hex codes. (The W3Schools Web site has a great resource on hex codes at http://w3schools.com/HTML/html_colornames.asp.)

Image: You can easily use an image as a background for your site by uploading the image to the images folder in the BuddyPress child theme folder in /_inc/images/. That value would look like background: url(_inc/images/*yourimage*.jpg). (*Note:* The url portion of this code automatically pulls in the URL of your blog, so you don't have to change the url part to your URL.)

You can also use a combination of colors and images in your backgrounds.

Table 12-4	Common Colors and Hex Codes
Color	*Hex Code*
White	#FFFFFF
Black	#000000
Red	#FF0000
Orange	#FFA500
Yellow	#FFFF00
Green	#008000
Blue	#0000FF
Indigo	#4B0082
Violet	#EE82EE

In the case of some basic colors, you don't have to use the hex code. For colors such as white, black, red, blue, and silver, you can just use their names — `background-color: white`, for example. Additionally, CSS rules allow certain colors to use shortened hex codes down to three characters — these rules mainly apply to primary colors like white, which can be shortened to `#fff`, and black, which can be shortened to `#000`, for example.

To change the background color of your BuddyPress theme, add the following lines to the `default.css` file in the child theme (found in the `/_inc/css` folder) that you create in Chapter 11:

```
body {
background: #ffffff url( ../images/background.gif ) top
          left repeat-x;
font-size: 12px;
font-family: Arial, Tahoma, Verdana, sans-serif;
line-height: 160%;
color: #555555;
width: 90%;
min-width: 960px;
max-width: 1250px;
margin: 0 auto;
padding-top: 0 !important; /* Remove the top padding space
          for the admin bar in this theme */
}
```

Because this changes the `background` value from `#eaeaea` (light gray) to `#ffffff` (white), these lines change the color of the background of your BuddyPress site from gray to white.

Any styles you define in the `default.css` in the BuddyPress child theme folder overrules any styles that exist in any other style sheet within your theme. Adding CSS styling directives to the `default.css` causes those changes to occur on your site as soon as you edit and upload the file on your Web server.

Using Your Own Logo in the Header

In the BuddyPress Default theme, your site name appears as text, as shown in Figure 12-2. Although this is nice for some people, others might want to display a logo file or graphic in that area, instead of simple text.

To accomplish this, you need to have an image file that you are ready to use, and will need to add a few bits of CSS to your `default.css` file:

Figure 12-2:
The site
name dis-
played on
a Buddy
Press site
using the
BuddyPress
Default
theme.

1. **Upload your header graphic to your Web server.**

   Images used in the BuddyPress theme should be uploaded to the images folder in the child theme: `/_inc/images/` — this way, you always know where the image files are located. Using FTP, upload your chosen header graphic to your Web server.

2. **Open the `default.css` file from the BuddyPress child theme.**

   Using your FTP program, locate the `default.css` file in the `/_inc/css/` folder, right-click it, and then choose Edit.

3. **Add the CSS values to call in your header image.**

   For purposes of this section, let's say your header image has the file name: `header.jpg`. Because you want to use an image to replace the text, you also have to account for the CSS for this portion of the `header.php` file: `<h1 id="logo"><a href="`... The current CSS for the header is located in the `default.css` file in your child theme and looks like this:

   ```
   #header h1 {
   position: absolute;
   bottom: 12px;
   left: 15px;
   width: 44%;
   }
   #header h1 a {
   color: #fff;
   font-size: 26px;
   text-decoration: none;
   }
   ```

   In a recent project I did for a client, I used the following CSS in the `default.css` file to override the CSS code in the parent `default.css` file to use a logo for the header, instead of plain text:

```
#header h1 {
background: url(../images/logo.png) no-repeat;
width: 230px;
height: 60px;
position: absolute;
bottom: 0px;
left: 15px;
}

#header h1 a {
color: #fff;
font-size: 0px;
text-decoration: none;
}
```

You can see in the previous example that I included a header image file called logo.png and also added in a height and width property to the h1#logo selector and changed the font size to 0 so it displays only the image, not the text.

Your needs might vary when it comes to using an image file for the site name and top area of your Web site, depending on the type and size of the image you want to use. However, if you follow my previous example, it will point you toward making the necessary adjustments you need for your specific image, site design, and formatting.

Changing Font Styles, Colors, and Sizes

Fonts come in all shapes and sizes, and you can use CSS to define the font styles that display in your blog. Changing the font can change the look and feel of your blog dramatically, as well as improve your readers' experience by making the text easy on the eyes. Table 12-5 displays some of the most commonly used CSS properties and values for applying font styling to your style sheet.

Table 12-5	Common Font Styles in CSS
Font Properties	*Example Values*
font-family	Times New Roman
color	black or #000000
font-size	12px

The Web is actually kind of picky about how it displays fonts, as well as what kind of fonts you can use in the `font-family` property. Not all fonts display correctly on the Web. To be safe, here are some commonly used font families that display correctly in most browsers:

  ✔ **Serif fonts:** Times New Roman, Georgia, Garamond, Bookman Old Style

  ✔ **Sans-serif fonts:** Verdana, Arial, Tahoma, Trebuchet MS

Serif fonts have little tails, or curlicues, at the edges of letters. (This text is in a serif font.) Sans-serif fonts have straight edges and are devoid of any fancy styling. (Table 12-5 uses a sans-serif font.)

When you want to change a font family in your CSS, open the style sheet (`style.css`), search for `property: font-family`, change the values for that property, and then save your changes.

If, in your CSS file, the font is defined in the `<body>` tag like this:

```
font-family: 'Lucida Grande', Verdana, Arial, Sans-Serif;
```

You can change the family of the font by changing the font names to something like:

```
font-family: verdana, arial, Helvetica, sans-serif;
```

You can easily change the color of your font by changing the `color` property of the CSS selector you want to tweak. You can use hex codes (refer to Table 12-4) to define the colors.

If, in your CSS file, the font color is defined in the `<body>` tag like this:

```
color: #000000;
```

You can change the color by changing the value to something like:

```
color: #ffffff
```

You can tweak the size of your font by changing the `font-size` property of the CSS selector. Generally, units of measurement determine font sizes, as in these examples:

  ✔ **px:** Pixel measurement. Increasing or decreasing the number of pixels increases or decreases the font size (`12px` is larger than `10px`).

  ✔ **pt:** Point measurement. As with pixels, increasing or decreasing the number of points affects the font size accordingly (`12pt` is larger than `10pt`).

✔ **%:** Percentage measurement. Increasing or decreasing the percentage number affects the font size accordingly (50% is the equivalent to 7 pixels; 100% is the equivalent to 17 pixels).

Sometimes, the font size is defined in the body tag as a percentage, like this:

```
font-size: 62.5%;
```

Putting all three elements (font-family, color, and font-size) together in the <body> tag styles the font for the overall body of your site. Here's how they work together in the <body> tag of a CSS file:

```
body {
font-size: 62.5%;
font-family: 'Lucida Grande', Verdana, Arial, Sans-Serif;
color: #333;
}
```

Finding Additional CSS Resources

The following list offers some excellent CSS resources on the Web that you might find helpful for creating or editing a theme's style sheet. (Or you might want to pick up a copy of *CSS Web Design For Dummies,* by Richard Mansfield.)

✔ **Westciv:** http://westciv.com

A Web site with tools and resources for Web professionals.

✔ **Mezzoblue's CSS Crib Sheet:** http://mezzoblue.com/css/cribsheet

Web site run by renowned CSS expert and freelance designer, Dave Shea.

✔ **WebsiteTips.com's CSS page:** http://websitetips.com/css

An educational Web site on Web design and development.

✔ **Dave's CSS Guide:** http://davesite.com/webstation/css

A CSS (Cascading Style Sheet) tutorial for beginners.

✔ **W3Schools' CSS tutorial:** http://w3schools.com/css

The Internet authority on Web standards and CSS practices.

Part V
Extending
BuddyPress

The 5th Wave   By Rich Tennant

"I know it's a short profile, but I thought
'King of the Jungle' sort of said it all."

In this part . . .

Using community-developed plugins for BuddyPress, you can extend the functionality of your BuddyPress social community to fit your needs and the needs of your community members. This part explores where to find and download BuddyPress plugins and how to install and use them in your community. This part also explores the popularity of social networks and media Web sites, such as Facebook and Twitter, and shows you how to add their content to your community Web site.

Chapter 13

Getting Plugged In with Plugins

In This Chapter

▶ Understanding what plugins are

▶ Finding BuddyPress plugins

▶ Installing plugins

▶ Activating and using BuddyPress plugins

*F*or the WordPress platform, literally thousands of plugins are available that allow you to extend the features you can make available on your site. Actually, BuddyPress is a WordPress plugin — one that adds a social community component to your site. This chapter is about BuddyPress plugins — that is, it's about the plugins you can install into the WordPress plugin known as BuddyPress. It is a little confusing, I know. Think of it in a different way — the plugins you can install to extend the features of BuddyPress are actually WordPress plugins that work on a WordPress-powered site that has BuddyPress activated. If BuddyPress is not installed and activated, these plugins will not work. In short: BuddyPress is required.

This chapter takes you through the installation of a BuddyPress plugin, which then gives you the mechanics and knowledge you need to install any plugin using the same steps. In Chapter 14, I take you through the installation of plugins that integrate popular social network sites, such as Facebook and Twitter, into your BuddyPress community. Finally, Chapter 15 gives you a look at ten BuddyPress plugins that add some great features to your community Web site.

For this chapter, I assume that the WordPress MU software is successfully running along with the BuddyPress plugin on your Web server.

Understanding What Plugins Are

A *plugin* is a small script that interacts with an application to provide some additional functions and features. Plugins are not part of the core software files that you install when you upload the WordPress software to your Web server and they do not function as stand-alone programs. They require a host program (in this case, WordPress MU and BuddyPress) in order to function at all. If left by themselves, they do nothing, except maybe produce some unsightly PHP errors on your Web site.

Like WordPress and BuddyPress, most plugins are free. In fact, for WordPress, literally thousands of free plugins are available for users to download and install.

The plugins I talk about in this book are BuddyPress-related plugins; that is, these plugins will work only if you are running both WordPress MU and BuddyPress on your site.

Finding and Installing BuddyPress Plugins

There is no need to hunt and peck around the Internet to find useful plugins for BuddyPress. WordPress makes it easy to locate the plugins you want to try out — just use the handy plugin search feature on your WordPress MU dashboard (See Chapter 4 for information on where to find, and how to use the plugin search feature). To find the plugin you want, you choose Plugins➪Add New, which loads the Install Plugins page, as shown in Figure 13-1.

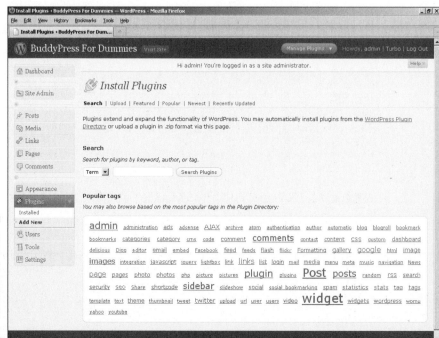

Figure 13-1: Find and install great plugins on the Install Plugins page.

The Install Plugins page gives you the ability to search, locate, install, and activate WordPress (and BuddyPress) plugins directly from your WordPress dashboard. This only works for plugins that are currently in the WordPress Plugin Directory, which you can find by browsing to `http://wordpress.org/extend/plugins`.

On the Install Plugins page, you can browse WordPress plugins with the filters provided at the top:

- ✔ **Featured:** Displays plugins currently featured in the WordPress Plugin Directory that WordPress wants to draw attention to, mostly due to their usefulness to WordPress users.

- ✔ **Popular:** Display the most popular plugins, determined by the number of user downloads.

- ✔ **Newest:** Displays the latest plugins added to the WordPress Plugin Directory.

- ✔ **Recently Updated:** Displays plugins recently updated within the WordPress Plugin Directory.

At the bottom of the Install Plugins page, you can also browse plugins in the Popular Tags section. This section provides you with a list of keywords that correspond to plugin topics. Click any of these keywords to find related plugins.

You have two methods of installing plugins on your WordPress site: use the automatic method with the built-in plugin installer in WordPress, or the manual method, which involves downloading the plugin and uploading it to your Web server. Both methods install the plugin on your site, and really, the only reason you would use the manual method is if the particular plugin you want to use is not in the Plugin Directory. Sometimes, plugin developers choose not to submit their plugins to the official directory, so you may find a plugin or two that you will have to download from the developer's site, and then upload it using FTP, to your Web server. I cover both installation methods in this chapter.

Installing plugins using the Install Plugins interface

Because you are setting up and running a BuddyPress social community site, you want to find plugins that help you extend the functionality of the BuddyPress features. One way to find them is by using the search feature found in the middle of the Install Plugins page. Just enter a keyword, author, or tag into the text box and then press the Search Plugins button. When you find what you're looking for, install the plugin. The following steps show you how to:

1. **Type** BuddyPress **into the search box.**

   Be sure Term is selected in the drop-down menu to the left of the search box; this tells the WordPress software that you want to search by a term or keyword. You also have the option to search by Author (the plugin author's name, if you know it) or Tag. When plugin developers add their plugin to the official directory, they can tag their plugins with defining keywords, and you can search the directory using these tags.

   In this case, you are searching for BuddyPress plugins, so type **BuddyPress** in the search box and then click the Search Plugins button; the Install Plugins page displays the plugins you can use with BuddyPress, as shown in Figure 13-2.

   Plugins appear in a table displaying several pieces of information for each plugin:

   - *Name:* The title of the plugin.

   - *Version:* The plugin version number.

   - *Rating:* The rating of the plugin, determined by community users and a star rating system in which five stars is the highest rating and one star is the lowest. The average number of stars the plugin has received displays in the Rating column.

   - *Description:* A description of the plugin features.

   - *Actions:* This column contains the link to click to install the plugin on your Web site.

2. **Install a BuddyPress plugin from the list.**

   The BuddyPress plugin I'm installing for this chapter is the Group Forum Subscription for BuddyPress plugin, which allows members to subscribe to individual forums and topics within the community so they receive notification when that particular forum or topic updates with new discussion.

   Find the Group Forum Subscription for BuddyPress plugin in the list and click the Install link in the Actions column. A small window appears and displays a description of the plugin, the version number, the author name, and an Install Now button, as shown in Figure 13-3.

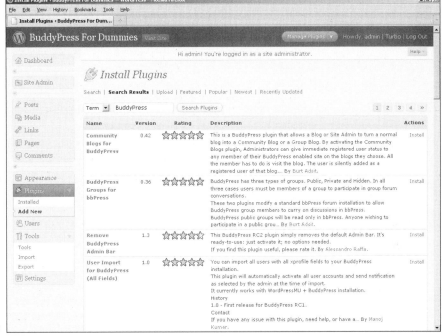

Figure 13-2:
A listing of BuddyPress plugins to choose from on the Install Plugins page.

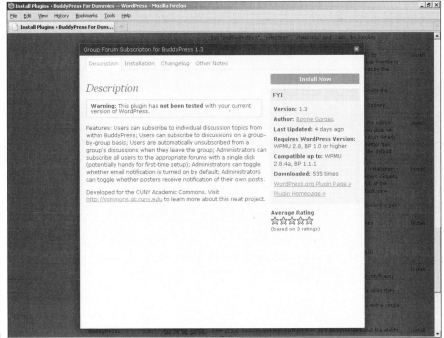

Figure 13-3:
The plugin installation window gives you the Install Now option.

3. **Click the Install Now button.**

   The Installing Plugin: Group Forum Subscription for BuddyPress page appears on your WordPress dashboard. A message confirms that the plugin has been downloaded, unpacked, and successfully stored in the correct directory on your Web server.

   Two links are shown beneath the confirmation message:

   - *Activate Plugin*: Click this link to activate the plugin you just installed on your site.

   - *Return to Plugins Page*: Click this link to go to the Manage Plugins page.

   Before you activate any BuddyPress-related plugins, you need to make sure that the BuddyPress plugin, itself, is activated. If BuddyPress is not activated, any BuddyPress-related plugins you try to activate will cause errors and the activation will fail.

4. **Click the Activate Plugin link.**

   This takes you to the Manage Plugins page, which displays a listing of plugins installed on your site. The new plugin you just installed is now listed with the active plugins. You should now have the Group Forum Subscription for BuddyPress plugin installed and activated on your site.

You can refer to the previous steps to install and activate any plugin on your site using the built-in plugin installer on your WordPress dashboard. Several plugins extend the features in your BuddyPress community, and I list some great ones in Chapter 15.

Installing plugins manually

In the previous section, I show you how to install plugins automatically using the WordPress dashboard. In this section, I show you how to find, upload, and install the Group Forum Subscription for BuddyPress plugin manually. This requires that you download, unpack, upload, and activate the plugin with your WordPress MU and BuddyPress community site.

The Group Forum Subscription for BuddyPress plugin allows members of your community to subscribe to individual forum discussion topics. After members subscribe to a forum or topic, they receive notifications via e-mail and via their BuddyPress accounts that a new discussion has been added. This feature encourages more discussions in your group forums because when people know that others are participating, it sparks more talk!

To install the Group Forum Subscription for BuddyPress on your site using the manual installation method, you must accomplish the following:

✔ Download and unpack the plugin files.

✔ Upload the plugin files to your Web server.

✔ Activate the plugin in your community.

The next sections discuss these tasks in detail.

Downloading the plugin files from the WordPress Plugin Directory

To download and unpack the Group Forum Subscription for BuddyPress using the manual installation method, follow these steps:

1. **Visit the WordPress Plugin Directory to find and install the plugin.**

   Type the URL for the plugin directory (`http://wordpress.org/extend/plugins`) in your browser address bar to go to the site.

2. **Search for the plugin by typing** Group Forum Subscription for BuddyPress **in the Search box and then click the Search Plugins button.**

   A page appears that lists the link to the plugin, as shown in Figure 13-4.

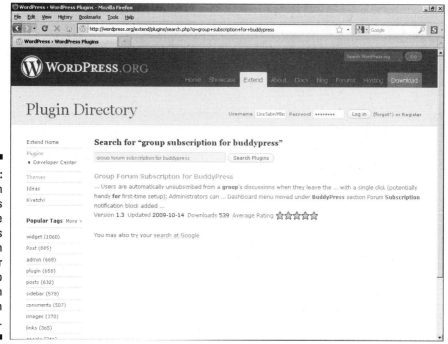

Figure 13-4:
Search results in the WordPress Plugin Directory for the Group Forum Subscription plugin.

3. **Click the Group Forum Subscription for BuddyPress link.**

   On the plugin page that appears, you find a description of the plugin, as well as other information about the plugin (see Figure 13-5). For example, take note of the following important information in the FYI box:

   - *Version*: The version number shown is the most recent version of the plugin.

   - *Other Versions*: This link takes you to a page that displays all the previous versions of the plugin. This is helpful if you have to revert to an older version of the plugin if the new version fails when you install it.

   - *Last Updated*: The date the plugin author last updated the plugin files in the directory.

   - *Requires WordPress Version*: This tells you the version of WordPress MU and BuddyPress that needs to be installed to run this plugin successfully on your site.

   - *Compatible Up to*: This tells you what version of the WordPress MU and BuddyPress software this plugin is compatible with. For example, if this section tells you that the plugin is compatible up to version 2.8, you cannot use the plugin with versions higher than 2.8.

   - *Author Homepage*: This link takes you to the plugin author's main Web site.

   - *Plugin Homepage*: This link takes you to the specific Web site address for the plugin. Often, this is a page within the plugin author's Web site.

4. **Download the Group Forum Subscription for BuddyPress plugin.**

   Click Download on the right of the Plugin Directory page; a dialog box opens and asks whether you want to open or save the file. Save the Zip file to your hard drive and remember where you save it.

5. **Locate the Zip file you just downloaded on your hard drive and open it with your preferred decompression program.**

   If you're unsure how to use a decompression program (such as WinZip or WinRar), refer to the documentation available with the program).

6. **Unpack the plugin file you downloaded for the Group Forum Subscription for BuddyPress plugin.**

   Using your preferred archiving program, such as WinZip, unpack the plugin files to a folder of your choice on your local computer.

Figure 13-5:
The Group
Forum
Subscription
for
BuddyPress
page in the
WordPress
Plugin
Directory.

Often, plugin authors include a helpful `readme.txt` file with their plugin files to give you some additional information about the use of the plugin. I strongly recommend opening that file and reading it, because more often than not, it contains information you should know. The Group Forum Subscription for BuddyPress plugin has a `readme.txt` file, as shown in the Plugins folder structure in Figure 13-6.

Figure 13-6:
The Group
Forum
Subscription
for
BuddyPress
plugin files.

Uploading the plugin files to your Web server

All plugin files, whether they are WordPress plugins, or BuddyPress-related plugins, are uploaded into a dedicated /wp-content/plugins folder in your WordPress installation directory on your Web server.

Using your preferred FTP (File Transfer Protocol) program, upload the plugin folder to the /wp-content/plugins/ folder within the WordPress installation on your Web server. If you need a quick review on how to use FTP to transfer files from your computer to your Web server, flip to Chapter 2.

Activating the plugin on your WordPress dashboard

After you upload the plugin files successfully to your Web server, open your browser, log in to your WordPress dashboard, and follow these steps to activate the Group Forum Subscription for BuddyPress plugin:

1. **Choose Plugins⇨Installed to visit the Manage Plugins page on your WordPress dashboard.**

2. **Locate the Group Forum Subscription for BuddyPress plugin.**

   Because you haven't activated this plugin, it's located in the Inactive Plugins section at the bottom of the Manage Plugins page.

3. **Click the Activate link.**

   The Activate link is directly beneath the plugin name; click it and the Manage Plugins page reloads. You now see the Group Forum Subscription for BuddyPress plugin listed in the Active Plugins section.

Before you activate any BuddyPress-related plugins, you need to make sure that the BuddyPress plugin is activated. If BuddyPress is not activated, any BuddyPress-related plugins you try to activate will cause errors and the activation will fail.

If you followed the steps in this section correctly, you now have the new plugin installed and activated on your site and ready to use — congratulations!

Managing Plugin Options

Many, but not all, WordPress/BuddyPress plugins provide an Options page that contains settings pertinent to the individual plugin. The settings on the plugin's Options page will vary from plugin to plugin, and generally contain settings that will assist you in individualizing the settings to suit your needs for your Web site. When the plugin is installed, the link to this page can usually be found on the Settings menu or the BuddyPress menu on your WordPress dashboard. In short, if the plugin you installed has an Options page, you just need to look in the menus on the WordPress dashboard to find the link to it.

In the case of the Group Forum Subscription for BuddyPress plugin you install in this chapter, the link to the Options page is labeled Group Forum Subscription on the BuddyPress menu. When you click it, the Group Forum Subscription Options page appears, as shown in Figure 13-7.

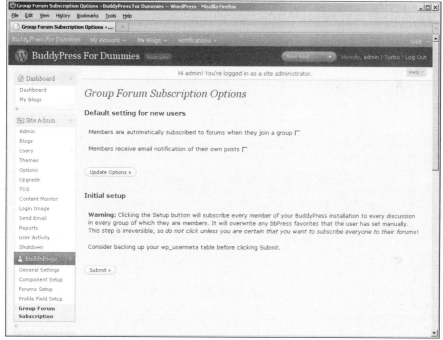

Figure 13-7:
The Group
Forum
Subscription
Options
page.

Uninstalling Plugins

After all this talk about installing and activating plugins, what happens when you decide you don't want to use a particular plugin anymore and want to un-install it? Don't worry — you aren't stuck forever with a plugin that you don't want. WordPress lets you be fickle and finicky about your plugin options.

To uninstall a plugin:

1. Choose Plugins➪Installed.

The Manage Plugins page appears.

2. Locate the plugin you wish to un-install.

3. Click the Deactivate link beneath the plugin's name.

The Manage Plugins page reloads and shows the plugin in the Inactive Plugin list.

4. Select the plugin.

Place a checkmark in the box to the left of the plugin name.

5. Select Delete and then click the Apply button.

The Delete Plugins(s) page opens and a confirmation message displays asking you whether you're sure that you want to delete this plugin.

When you delete a plugin, it's gone forever. Of course, you can follow the steps in this chapter to re-install the plugin if you really mess up or accidentally uninstall a plugin you didn't intend to.

6. Click the Yes Delete These Files button.

The Manage Plugins page reloads and the plugin you just deleted is gone from the list of plugins.

You're done with deleting the plugin — that's all it takes!

Don't forget to remove any bits of code that you added to your theme templates for that particular plugin; otherwise, they'll cause ugly error messages to display on your blog.

If you intend to de-activate the BuddyPress plugin, it is extremely important that you de-activate any BuddyPress-related plugins *before* you de-activate BuddyPress. If you do not, it will result in some pretty ugly errors on your site.

This chapter took you through finding BuddyPress plugins within the WordPress plugin interface; however, the following list shows you some places you can visit on the Web to find more about BuddyPress plugins, including where to find them and discussions related to their development.

- ✔ **BuddyPress Forums — Plugins** (`http://buddypress.org/forums/tags/plugins`): The section of the BuddyPress forums where users and developers discuss plugins.

- ✔ **BuddyPress Extend** (`http://buddypress.org/extend/plugins`): The page on the BuddyPress Web site that lists plugins.

- ✔ **WordPress Extend** (`http://wordpress.org/extend/plugins/search.php?q=BuddyPress`): The page in the WordPress Plugin Directory to find BuddyPress related plugins.

Understanding Open Source Concepts

The WordPress platforms and the BuddyPress suite of plugins are licensed by something called GPL, which stands for General Public License, and distributed as open source software. Simply put, software that is released as *open source* can be freely redistributed; does not require royalty, or any other associated, fees; the source code of the software is released to the general public; and any derivative work must adopt the very same license under which the original software was released. Plugins are considered derivative works, so you find that almost all the plugins out there are open source and free for you and I to use.

To find out more about the open source software, go to the Open Source Initiative Web site at `http://opensource.org`.

You might ask whether the Open Source/GPL concept even applies to you since you aren't a plugin developer. Yes, there are implications that you and I need to consider when using open source software and plugins, including:

- The software is free and that generally means that the developers who create WordPress, BuddyPress, and related plugins and themes are giving their development work away at no cost. For many developers, this is a way to boost their exposure in the community and pass on their work to a worthy cause, such as free and open software. This pretty much translates into zero overhead for you, me, and all other WordPress Web site owners, because the cost is exactly nothing. It's free.

  Because it's free, and because these developers are giving away their time and talents at no cost, the developer who created your favorite plugin is not obligated to continue development on it in the future. If the developer finds a new hobby, new job, or any other activity that takes him away from his development work, he can walk away from development work on your favorite plugin at any time. If no one picks up where he left off, and the plugin stops working with the latest version of your software, you can kiss that plugin goodbye.

- Developers of popular plugins are typically extremely good about updating the plugins when new versions of WordPress and BuddyPress are released, or when a security bug or flaw is discovered. Keep in mind, however, that no timetable exists for these developers. Many of these folks have day jobs, classes, or families that can keep them from devoting as much time to the project as you'd like them to.

- Beware of the pitfalls of falling in love with any particular plugin for BuddyPress because the world of plugin development is easy come, easy go. Try not to let your Web site become too dependent on any one plugin in particular, and don't be surprised if a plugin you love doesn't exist tomorrow. You can use the plugin for as long as it continues to work for you, but when it stops working (such as with a new WordPress or BuddyPress release, or a security exploit that makes it unusable), you have a decision to make. You can

- Stop using the plugin and try to find a suitable alternative.

- Hope that another developer takes over the project if the original developer discontinues his involvement.

- Try to find a consultant to hire and fix it for you (in which case, you'll more than likely have to pay his hourly fee for such services).

Understanding the dynamics in play with plugin development is very important and not all gloom and doom. However, I did want to make sure that you're aware of the potential problems you might encounter with the open source WordPress and BuddyPress technologies. Forewarned is forearmed; consider it food for thought as you continue building your online social community on the Web.

Chapter 14

Integrating Popular Social Media

- -

In This Chapter

▶ Exploring popular social media

▶ Connecting BuddyPress with Facebook

▶ Publishing Twitter feeds on member profiles

- -

Since 2007, Facebook.com, Twitter.com, MySpace.com, Youtube.com and Flickr.com have taken the Internet by storm. These Web sites all have one thing in common: They build social communities on the Web.

Running a social community on your Web site using BuddyPress presents you with a bit of a challenge: How does your community compete with all the other, much larger communities on the Web? The answer is easy: Your site doesn't compete; your site collaborates by inviting your members to connect their memberships in other social networks, like Facebook and Twitter, with their account on your site so they can use those tools together, rather than separately.

This chapter shows you how you can integrate some very popular social network services, like Facebook and Twitter, into your BuddyPress-powered social community to give your members features and tools that enable them to gather their content from other social communities and share them in your community.

Discovering Popular Social Networks

One great way to use the World Wide Web is to network with other people around the world by participating in social community Web sites. You can use these sites to share photos, videos, and music, or you can use them to have conversations with other people who share your interests. Social networks allow you to keep up with your friends, find old friends, and even make new ones. Social networks facilitate the sharing of content, and the content you find within them tends to be *user-generated* — meaning, the users create the content they share with others.

Social network sites and services are used by groups of people, such as small businesses or large corporations, and by individuals, such as your grocer down the street or your favorite big screen movie actor. Social network sites enable people to connect with other people from many different places in the world, which is something people normally wouldn't easily be able to do. Social media provides the population of the world with a thread of connection and helps people build new, and lasting, relationships through the sharing of information and conversation.

Table 14-1 displays four of the most popular social network sites on the Web, including their Web addresses and brief descriptions of their services. Later in this chapter, you discover how to connect these four social networks to your own BuddyPress social community, allowing your members to bring their shared content into your network.

Table 14-1	Four Popular Social Network Sites on the Web	
Social Network	*Web Address (URL)*	*Description*
Facebook	`http://facebook.com`	A free social networking Web site allowing its users to connect with one another, communicate, and share information.
Twitter	`http://twitter.com`	A free micro-blogging social network allowing its users to share updates and information in 140 characters or less.
Flickr	`http://flickr.com`	A free photo-sharing network that allows its users to share photographs and create and join groups.
YouTube	`http://youtube.com`	A free video-sharing network allowing its users to upload and share videos with other users.

Connecting BuddyPress and Facebook

People who are interested in joining your social community Web site are already likely to be members of some, if not all, of the social network sites I mention in this chapter. To encounter a savvy Web user today who doesn't have a Facebook account and profile set up is rare.

Using a simple plugin for BuddyPress, you can give your members the ability to log in to your community by using their Facebook credentials. Providing this option makes it more efficient for people who have a Facebook account to join your community because such users won't need to go through the entire new user sign up process I describe in Chapter 6. Here's how to add this plugin to your community:

1. **Download and install the BP-FB Connect (BuddyPress-Facebook Connect) plugin.**

   You can find the plugin in the WordPress Plugin Directory at `http://wordpress.org/extend/plugins/bp-fbconnect`. Download it and then manually install it on your site. (If you can't recall how to do this, refer to Chapter 13.) Or, you can choose the Plugins menu on your WordPress dashboard, search for the plugin, and then install it using the instructions in Chapter 13.

   Before you activate any BuddyPress-related plugins, you need to make sure that the BuddyPress plugin is activated. If BuddyPress is not activated, any BuddyPress-related plugins you try to activate will cause errors and the activation will fail.

2. **Activate the BP-FB Connect plugin.**

   Click the Activate link on the Manage Plugins page on your WordPress dashboard to activate the plugin on your site.

3. **Go to the Facebook Connect Plugin Options page.**

   When the plugin is active, you see a Facebook Connect link in the Settings menu — click that link to load the Facebook Connect Plugin Options page on your WordPress dashboard. (See Figure 14-1.)

4. **Read and follow the instructions on the Facebook Connect Plugin Options page.**

   Or do the following:

   a. Visit the Facebook application registration page by clicking that link on the Facebook Connect Plugin Options page.

      The Create Application page on the Facebook Web site appears at (`http://www.facebook.com/developers/createapp.php?version=new`).

   b. On this page, type the name of your new application — for simplicity's sake, type the name of your Web site.

   c. Indicate that you agree to Facebook's terms of service, by selecting the Agree option under Terms, and then click the Save Changes button. (See Figure 14-2.)

      When you click the Save Changes button, the Edit page for your new application appears.

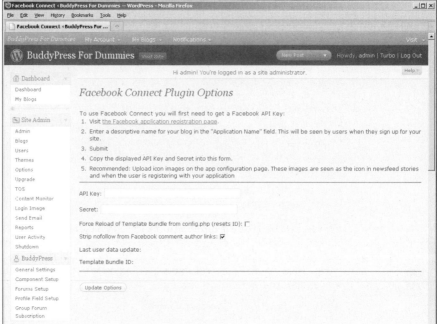

Figure 14-1:
The
Facebook
Connect
Plugin
Options
page.

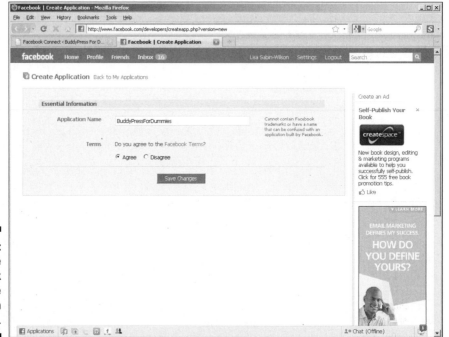

Figure 14-2:
The
Facebook
Create
Application
page.

5. Copy the API Key and the Secret for your application.

This information displays on the Edit page for your newly created application, shown in Figure 14-3.

Copy the API Key from the Facebook Edit application page and paste it into the API Key text box on the Facebook Connect Plugin Options page on your WordPress dashboard. (Refer to Figure 14-1).

6. Copy the Secret.

Copy the Secret from the Facebook Edit application page and paste it into the Secret text box on the Facebook Connect Plugin Options page on your WordPress dashboard (Refer to Figure 14-1).

7. (Optional) Upload an image to use as an icon and logo for your application on Facebook.

On the Facebook Edit application page, you can upload images to use as an icon or logo for your application that appears in and around the Facebook social network site. Click the Change Your Icon link to upload a new icon image; and click the Change Your Logo link to upload a new logo image.

8. Save Changes on your Facebook application.

On the Facebook Edit application page, click Save Changes at the bottom of the page to save your new application in your Facebook account.

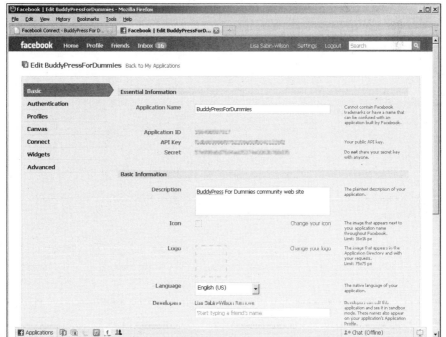

Figure 14-3:
The Facebook Edit application page.

9. Update the Facebook Connect Plugin Options.

At the bottom of the Facebook Connect Plugin Options page on your WordPress dashboard, click the Update Options button to save your settings, and you're done.

After you follow the steps to update the Facebook Connect Plugin options, it might take Facebook a few minutes to collect your information and activate it. Wait 5–10 minutes before trying the new Facebook Connect plugin feature on your site, just to be sure that you've given Facebook time to make the necessary changes for it to work.

With the BP-FB Connect plugin activated and set up, visitors to your site can easily register, log in, and begin using the features of your social community. Assuming you're using the BuddyPress Default theme, a new Facebook icon appears at the top-right of your site. When a visitor clicks the Facebook icon, a Facebook login window pops up (shown in Figure 14-4), allowing the user to enter her Facebook login information to log in to your community. Your site is now connected with Facebook!

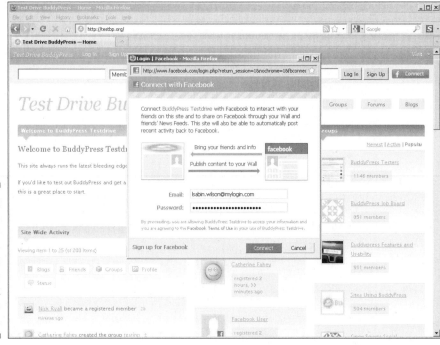

Figure 14-4: Logging into a BuddyPress-powered site using Facebook login credentials.

Integrating Twitter

Twitter (http:twitter.com) is a unique social community that allows users to communicate and connect with one another in messages of 140 characters or less. (This type of communication is often referred to as *micro-blogging*). Twitter members can send updates to the people following the member's Twitter account that can include anything from what you had for breakfast to the latest and greatest stock tips — any message at all, really, as long as it's at or under 140 characters in length.

Sending short updates to 100 of your closest friends on the Web might seem a little funny to people who have not used the service. However, individuals and businesses — from average people communicating with others to companies interacting with their client base to extend their reach — have discovered real value in the service. In June 2009, Twitter was on the cover of *TIME* magazine with the headline "How Will Twitter Change the Way We Live." The article revealed the depth of social interaction that the service has brought to millions of users.

The 140-character messages that Twitter users publish on the Twitter.com Web site are *Tweets,* or short updates. Soon after Twitter became popular, users wanted to see their Tweets show up in other areas of their social circle on the Web. You started seeing people publishing their latest Tweet on their blog and in their Facebook accounts, and through a bit of programming and code, developers began creating applications and scripts that made Tweets portable, allowing users to take their Tweets with them wherever they went on the Web.

In running a social community using WordPress and BuddyPress, it's natural to want to allow your community members to bring their Twitter updates into their profiles within your community. With an easy-to-install plugin called BuddyPress Group Twitter, developed by Andy Peatling, you have the ability to give your users that feature by following these easy steps:

1. **Navigate to the Plugins page in your WordPress Dashboard.**

   Click the Add New link in the Plugins menu in your WordPress Dashboard and search for the BuddyPress Group Twitter plugin in the search form provided.

2. **Install the BuddyPress Group Twitter plugin.**

   Click the Install link to the right of the BuddyPress Group Twitter plugin title and then click the Install Now link in the plugin installation pop-up window.

3. **Activate the BuddyPress Group Twitter plugin.**

   Click the Activate link displayed on the Installing Plugin: BuddyPress Group Twitter plugin page.

Now that the BuddyPress Group Twitter plugin is installed and functioning on your site, member Twitter accounts can be added to groups within the community by going to the Admin page of the group you're the administrator of and adding Twitter accounts for the members of your group.

The ultimate goal of building a social Web is allowing users to create content within their communities, share the content, and take it with them wherever they go. The plugins I've listed provide a means of reaching that goal in your own social community.

Additionally, future development of BuddyPress promises to bring in richer features and functions that will give you, and your users, numerous ways of sharing your content in and around the larger social Web. Have a peek at the Appendix in the back of this book for ways that you can keep up with BuddyPress developments, including using the bleeding edge, not-yet-released beta versions of BuddyPress.

Part VI
The Part of Tens

The 5th Wave   By Rich Tennant

"There's been a lot of interest shown in your
home, but no offers. I suggest we either lower
the price or start selling advertising space on
your virtual tour site."

In this part . . .

Welcome to The (infamous) Part of Tens! In this part, you discover ten stunning examples of real world applications of BuddyPress, ten useful BuddyPress plugins to help you extend your community, and ten really great BuddyPress themes to help you create a unique style for your BuddyPress community. All for the cost of exactly nothing!

Chapter 15

Ten Useful BuddyPress Plugins

In This Chapter

▶ BuddyPress Privacy Component

▶ Featured Members Widget

▶ Author Avatar List

▶ BuddyPress Events Calendar

▶ Invite Friends

▶ SEO (Search Engine Optimization) for BuddyPress

▶ BuddyPress/Facebook Connect

▶ Limit blogs per user

▶ Community blogs for BuddyPress

▶ BuddyPress Welcome Pack

*I*n Chapter 13, I provide you with information on where to find and download BuddyPress plugins, and show you why you would want to add plugins to your BuddyPress community to extend its default features to do some really cool things. That chapter also walks you through how to install, activate, and use plugins on your site.

This chapter introduces you to ten BuddyPress plugins that I've installed on various BuddyPress communities and have found to be exciting additions to any social community. I want to share these with you so you can provide your community members with additional features that will make your community so attractive that they'll never want to leave.

If these ten BuddyPress plugins aren't enough for you, at the end of this chapter I give you some great resources on where to find more plugins for your BuddyPress community.

This book is mainly about BuddyPress, not WordPress. Literally thousands of WordPress plugins can also add new functionality to your Web site. You can find WordPress plugins in the official WordPress Plugin Directory at `http://wordpress.org/extend/plugins`, or visit the Plugins page on your

WordPress Dashboard to search for and explore new WordPress plugins you can use. Many WordPress plugins exist that work well alongside BuddyPress and allow you to bring more social networking features to your site. When you search for plugins in the official WordPress Plugin Directory, use terms like *social*, *social media,* and *BuddyPress* to find new and interesting plugins for your social community site.

BuddyPress Privacy Component

Developer: Jeff Sayre

URL: `http://jeffsayre.com/2009/12/05/buddypress-privacy-component-released/`

Almost every single person using the internet today is concerned about privacy issues; specifically who has access to their information.

Being a member of a BuddyPress community is no different — users within a BuddyPress community may, or may not, want everyone to have access to the information they share on their profiles, in groups.

With the BuddyPress Privacy Component plugin, users are able to define and control who has access to certain pieces of data they share in their profiles, activity streams, friends' lists, blogs, private messaging, and more.

Featured Members Widget

Developer: Jeff Sayre

URL: `http://wordpress.org/extend/plugins/buddypress-featured-members-widget`

One of the advantages of being a member in any social community on the Web is the possibility that you'll gain just a bit more exposure on the Internet than you would have had you not joined a community Web site. Whether your community has a focus on business or any other topic, you have the ability to spotlight featured members in your community by adding the Featured Members Widget plugin to your BuddyPress-powered social community Web site.

After you install the Featured Members Widget, you can add it to your site on the Widgets page on the dashboard and start displaying featured community members immediately. Figure 15-1 illustrates how Tasty Kitchen (`http://tastykitchen.com`) uses the Featured Members Widget to spotlight an individual member of their social community.

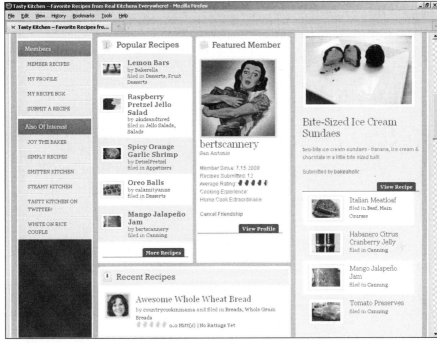

Figure 15-1:
Featured
Members
Widget as
used by
the Tasty
Kitchen
community.

Author Avatar List

Developers: Benedikt Forchhammer and Paul Bearne

URL: `http://wordpress.org/extend/plugins/author-avatars`

The Author Avatar List allows you to display a list of member avatars (or pictures) on your Web site. This plugin also allows you to display a member's avatar within a post or page, which is a great feature when you're posting about a member because you can insert the member's photo within the body of the post.

Using the Author Avatar List widget that comes with the plugin, you can display a configurable listing of user avatars on your community Web site. You can limit the number of avatars that display, adjust the size of the avatars, sort the list by name, display the list in random order, and change the avatar alignment to appear to the left, right, or center of the section you're displaying the avatar(s) in.

BuddyPress Events Calendar

Developer: Erwin Gerrits

URL: `http://wordpress.org/extend/plugins/bp-events`

The BuddyPress Events Calendar plugin adds an Events option to the user menu in each member's profile, which allows you and your community members to create events for other community members to view and join. This plugin also provides an Events item in the navigation menu of the main Web site so visitors to the site can see a full listing of events scheduled within your social community.

The BuddyPress Events Calendar plugin also provides you with a widget that gives you the option to display upcoming, newest, or active events within your community on your Web site.

This widget is very helpful within active communities that have scheduled events, conferences, Webinars, educational programming, or online chats.

BuddyPress Geo

Developer: Dale Mugford, Duane Storey

URL: `http://wordpress.org/extend/plugins/buddypress-geo`

Google's location feature, BuddyPress Geo, allows members of a BuddyPress social community to search for other members by geographical location. For example, say you live in Wisconsin and you want to find members within the community who live within a certain distance from you. You can search for members who live within 5, 10, 15, or 20 miles, or more, to connect with people who are local to your location.

You can search for, and install, this plugin by choosing Plugins⇨Add New on your WordPress dashboard. Here's a tip, however, do not activate it right away. Instead, after you install it with the built-in plugin installer, go to the Manage Plugins page by choosing Plugins⇨Installed, find the BuddyPress Geo plugin in the list, and then click the Activate BuddyPress Geo Site Wide link. This activates the plugin site wide, rather than per user blog. *Note:* The plugin will not work if you do not activate it site wide.

To find options for the BuddyPress Geo plugin, choose BuddyPress⇨ GeoSearch Setup on the WordPress dashboard. Figure 15-2 illustrates the Geo Search Setup page where you fill out the required information to complete the plugin's setup.

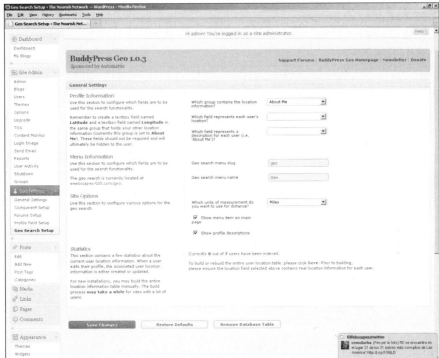

Figure 15-2:
The
BuddyPress
Geo Search
Setup page.

SEO (Search Engine Optimization) for BuddyPress

Developer: Sven Lehnert

URL: http://wordpress.org/extend/plugins/seo-for-buddypress

Search Engine Optimization (SEO) is something that every Web site owner should be concerned about. Search Engine Optimization helps make your Web site friendlier to the various search engines, such as Google, Yahoo!, or MSN. The easier the search engines can find and catalogue your content in their directories, the easier Internet surfers, like me, can find your site by searching with various keywords.

The SEO for BuddyPress plugin helps you improve the SEO of your BuddyPress community by giving you full control over the title, description, and keywords for each page within your BuddyPress community.

After you install and activate the plugin, the SEO for BuddyPress option appears on the BuddyPress menu. Click that link to go to the SEO for BuddyPress Options page where you fill the Title, Description, and Keyword fields with keywords and phrases that you think will best help the search engines find and include your content within their topical directories.

BuddyPress/Facebook Connect

Developer: Andy Peatling, Adam Hupp

URL: `http://wordpress.org/extend/plugins/bp-fbconnect`

This plugin adds the ability for your members, and potential or future members, to log in to your community with their Facebook account login. This is handy when someone who already has a Facebook account visits your community. They can use their Facebook login to log in to your community, as well, which prevents them from having to use your community's built-in registration and log in process. Basically, the BuddyPress/Facebook Connect plugin makes logging in and participating in your community quicker and easier.

If a visitor doesn't have a Facebook account, they can't take advantage of this feature and will need to go through the sign-up and login process built into your community.

BuddyPress-Kaltura Media Component

Developer: Kaltura.org

URL: `http://wordpress.org/extend/plugins/buddypress-kaltura-media-component`

Give your community members the opportunity to upload and share photos, videos, and audio files with other members. The Kaltura Media Component plugin adds a My Media menu to the users' profiles, as shown in Figure 15-3. In this menu, the user can choose to view and/or upload photos, videos, or audio files to their profile to share with the rest of the community.

This plugin not only allows users to upload media files from their own local computer, but also users can share media files from other social networks, such as Flickr, Photobucket, YouTube, and MySpace.

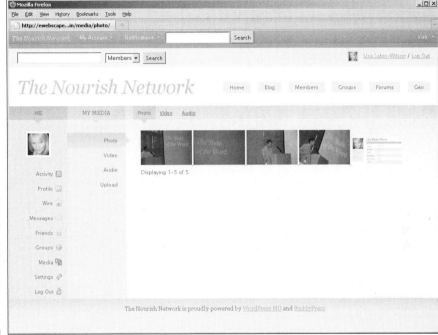

BuddyPress Stats

Developer: Jobjörn Folkesson

URL: `http://wordpress.org/extend/plugins/bp-community-blogs`

Every Web site owner is at least a little curious about his or her Web site's statistics. Knowing how many daily visitors a site has and where the traffic is coming from, at the very least, is interesting. In other cases, such as business sites and sites that offer advertising, Web site statistics can be very helpful in attracting new advertisers to your Web site, particularly when you can show that your Web site experiences high amounts of traffic.

The BuddyPress Stats plugin gives you stats on your BuddyPress community, including

✔ How many members, how many groups, and how much activity you have within your community.

✔ How many friends each member in your community has.

✔ Groups stats, including groups with the most active members.

✔ Activity stats, including which members have the most activity and what activity (blog posts, wire activity, and so on) is most prevalent in your community.

BuddyPress Welcome Pack

Developer: DJPaul

URL: `http://wordpress.org/extend/plugins/welcome-pack`

The Welcome Pack plugin gives the site administrator enhancements to add a customized welcome message for each new member of the BuddyPress community. Additionally, the plugin allows the site administrator to determine new member default items, such as

✔ A default friends list

✔ Membership in predetermined groups

Therefore, when new members join, they receive a friendly welcome message to your community, are members of active community groups, and have new friends to make them feel at home and help them get started.

Figure 15-4 shows you the administrative options for the BuddyPress Welcome Pack plugin.

If these ten BuddyPress plugins aren't enough for you, Table 15-1 provides great resources on where to find more plugins for your BuddyPress community.

Table 15-1	Where to Find More BuddyPress Plugins
Plugin Source	*Plugin URL*
Official BuddyPress Web Site	`http://buddypress.org/extend/plugins`
WordPress Themes Directory	`http://wordpress.org/extend/plugins/search.php?q=buddypress`
WPMU Dev	`http://wpmudev.org/buddypress`

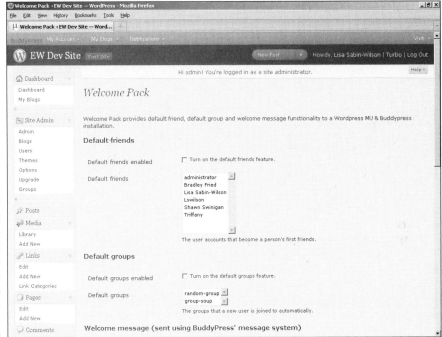

Figure 15-4:
The admin-
istrative
options
for the
BuddyPress
Welcome
Pack plugin.

Chapter 16

Ten Free BuddyPress Themes

In This Chapter

▶ Avenue K9

▶ BuddyPress Corporate

▶ Bruce

▶ BuddyPress Fun

▶ Shouty

▶ BuddyPress Community

▶ Purple & Black

▶ MuddyPress

▶ New Yorker

▶ BuddyPress Default

*B*ecause BuddyPress is relatively new to the scene, theme creation for it is just getting started. Soon, hundreds of BuddyPress themes will be available for you to download and use. BuddyPress development continues to make it easier for theme developers to design themes based on the parent/ child theme framework (which I discuss in Chapter 12), so new themes will be arriving all the time.

The listing of themes in this chapter is not exhaustive by any means, but does provide you with ten of the best themes that have already been created for you. In Part IV of this book, I discuss themes in depth and help you understand the ins and outs of the BuddyPress theme framework, including the best ways to customize the default BuddyPress themes to make your own unique look. In Chapter 10, especially, I show you how to install a theme after you download it from the developer's site.

Avenue K9

Theme designer: Michael Kuhlmann

URL: `www.avenuek9.com/2009/09/18/new-avek9-bp-1-1-theme`

The blues, greens, and yellows of this BuddyPress theme, built directly from the BuddyPress theme framework (see Chapter 12), make for a very cheery and bright color scheme. I installed and activated the Avenue K9 on my own BuddyPress community site, as shown in Figure 16-1.

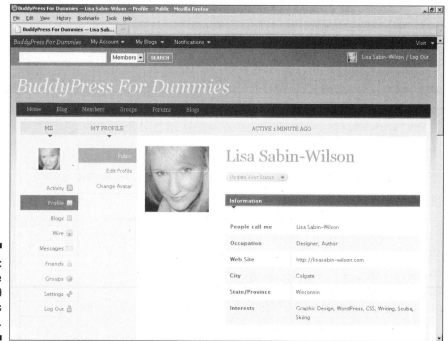

Figure 16-1:
The
Avenue K9
BuddyPress
theme.

BuddyPress Corporate

Theme designer: James Farmer

URL: `http://premium.wpmudev.org/project/buddypress-corporate-theme`

The BuddyPress Corporate theme is a sleek, professional looking theme that is suited perfectly for a small business Web site. In addition to its smooth design, the BuddyPress Corporate theme includes a menu that provides you with 12 color schemes to choose from. Figure 16-2 displays the default gray monochrome design of the BuddyPress Corporate theme.

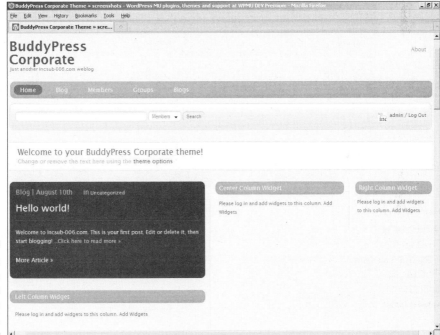

Figure 16-2:
The
BuddyPress
Corporate
theme.

Bruce

Theme designer: miloIIIVII

URL: http://wp2.3oneseven.com

The Bruce BuddyPress theme has a clean layout with a minimalistic, mono-chromatic color scheme. A clean, four-column layout enables you to display a lot of content on your Web site. The columns give the theme a magazine-like appearance, as shown in Figure 16-3.

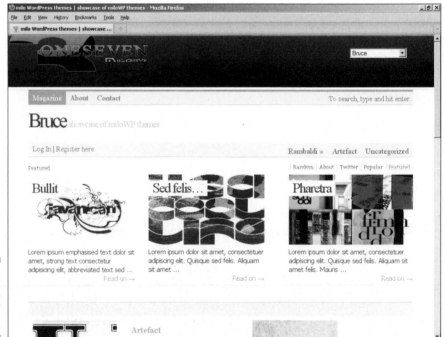

Figure 16-3:
The Bruce theme for BuddyPress.

Some of the highlights of the Bruce theme include

- ✔ A slider script that enables you to dynamically display a lot of content on the front page of your Web site without taking up a whole lot of room.

- ✔ Support for the various WordPress and BuddyPress widgets.

- ✔ An options menu in the WordPress dashboard that allows you to config-ure how you would like to feature a variety of content on the front page of your community Web site.

BuddyPress Fun

Theme designer: James Farmer

URL: `http://premium.wpmudev.org/project/buddypress-fun-theme`

The BuddyPress Fun theme is a fully customizable, light-hearted theme for your WordPress MU/BuddyPress-powered community site. This theme gives you the choice of a dark color scheme, as shown in Figure 16-4, or a light color scheme.

Other display options include

- ✔ The ability to change the background color.
- ✔ The ability to add a graphic to use for a background.
- ✔ The ability to change the font style used throughout the site.
- ✔ The ability to upload and crop a logo to use in the header of your site's pages.
- ✔ The ability to customize the CSS. (See Chapter 11 for information about editing CSS and basic CSS properties.)

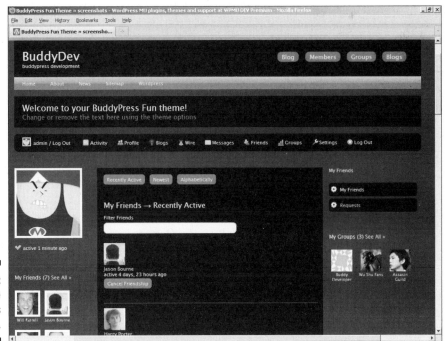

Figure 16-4: The BuddyPress Fun theme.

Shouty

Theme designer: BuddyDress

URL: http://buddydress.com

The Shouty theme has a fresh and clean look, with a vivid light blue, orange, and white color scheme in a comfortable two-column layout. This theme takes into consideration all the details within a BuddyPress community site and is a nicely designed theme for any community on the Web. The Shouty theme is one of many themes provided by the folks at BuddyDress.com, featured later in this chapter.

BuddyPress Community

Theme designer: James Farmer

URL: http://premium.wpmudev.org/project/buddypress-community-theme

The BuddyPress Community theme strives to make your BuddyPress-powered community Web site look and feel like Ning.com (http://ning.com), another popular social network.

The BuddyPress Community theme has a very sharp and clean look with a striking blue-and-white color scheme, making it a bright and cheery place for you and your community members.

As with James's other BuddyPress theme, the BuddyPress Fun theme, you can

✔ Change the background color.

✔ Add a graphic to use for a background.

✔ Change the font style used throughout the site.

✔ Upload and crop a logo to use in the header of your site's pages.

✔ Customize the CSS. (See Chapter 11 for information about editing CSS and basic CSS properties.)

This theme comes with two color options: blue and red. Figure 16-5 shows the blue option.

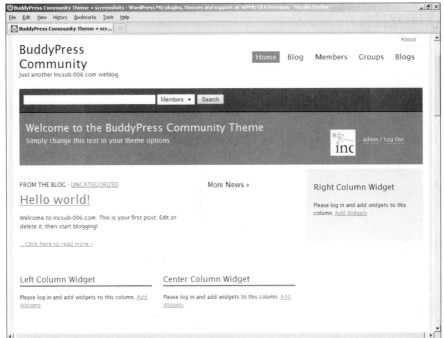

Figure 16-5:
The
BuddyPress
Community
theme.

Purple & Black

Theme designer: Christina Milburn

URL: `http://theeasybutton.com/blog/2009/06/01/buddypress-theme-purple-black`

This BuddyPress theme is exactly what the title states: purple and black! Christina, the designer, changed the BuddyPress Default theme's color scheme from orange and gray to present a striking color combination.

This theme, like the BuddyPress Default theme, is fully widgetized and compatible with all WordPress and BuddyPress widgets. Check out Chapter 9 to discover the wonder of widgets, including how you can use them to display different types of content and activities within your community.

MuddyPress

Theme Designer: Nagapress

URL: www.blogcastor.com/muddypress-theme

MuddyPress is a theme that plays off the BuddyPress Default theme with a few added options and differences, including

- ✔ Premium features that enable you to manage your theme's options (such as uploading and adding a new logo to your Web site) on your WordPress dashboard.
- ✔ Photoshop software by Adobe. The designer of this theme included the Photoshop files to help you easily create a new logo for your site.
- ✔ A clean, three-column design that gives you lots of room to display your Web site content and community activities.

New Yorker

Themes designer: miloIIIVII

URL: http://wp.3oneseven.com/

This is a theme created for a WordPress MU site with BuddyPress added for the social community layer. The theme is laid out in a magazine-style format with the content (articles, blog posts, and so on) taking center stage. Contents are arranged by category/topic rather than by the usual chronological arrangement. The design of the theme looks and feels very much like a magazine with large photos and striking typography. Figure 16-6 shows the front page of the New Yorker theme. By miloIIIVII.

BuddyPress Default Theme

No chapter on free BuddyPress themes would be complete without the mention of the BuddyPress Default theme and framework, provided for you within the BuddyPress suite of plugins. The Default theme, designed by Andy Peatling, the lead developer of the BuddyPress project, is provided for you to start running your BuddyPress-powered social community right out of the box, without having to worry about theme compatibility.

Figure 16-6:
The New
Yorker
BuddyPress
theme.

Because this theme works off the main theme framework, the BuddyPress Default theme is fully customizable. The parent theme framework contains all of the core code and programming that allow your BuddyPress theme to do its thing — the BuddyPress Default theme is just a Cascading Style Sheet (CSS) with some images to make everything look nice. I discuss parent/child themes in Chapter 12, so check that out if you require more information.

The advantage here is that you can now create an unlimited amount of themes by altering the CSS and changing the images, without having to be a certified code geek to make it happen. Chapter 11 takes you through some basic steps and CSS concepts that help you customize the BuddyPress Default theme. This setup makes customizing themes for BuddyPress really easy, without the complication of having to know the underlying PHP code. It's all done for you in the parent theme.

Brilliant!

The Future of BuddyPress Themes

BuddyPress recently released a major upgrade (September 2009) that introduced the parent/child theme framework, which makes the design process easier. This should mean that more and more designers will release themes for the BuddyPress community soon.

Keep your eye on the official BuddyPress Web site for announcements on new BuddyPress themes, specifically at `http://buddypress.org/extend/themes`.

Chapter 17

Ten Real World Examples of BuddyPress

In This Chapter

▶ BuddyPress.org

▶ Nourish Network

▶ WeEarth

▶ We Heart This

▶ GigaOM

▶ Flokka

▶ Unstructure

▶ Young People

▶ VW TankWars

▶ Tasty Kitchen

Since mid-2008, when BuddyPress hit the scene, some amazing examples of WordPress-powered sites with added BuddyPress social community components have launched on the Web. This chapter shows you ten shining examples of BuddyPress implementations in the wild so that you can see, from a visitor's standpoint, how BuddyPress social communities look and function. Feel free to visit any of these sites and sign up as a member to gain a community member's perspective!

BuddyPress

`http://buddypress.org`

The best example and implementation of the BuddyPress platform is the official BuddyPress site. BuddyPress.org is a Web property owned by Automattic, the company behind the very popular WordPress.com.

BuddyPress.org has developed a community of BuddyPress users where you can create member profiles, connect with other BuddyPress users, and participate in various BuddyPress user groups and forums. On BuddyPress.org, you will find a wealth of information and resources on the use and implementation of the BuddyPress platform and all of its features and options.

Also on the BuddyPress Web site is a BuddyPress demo (`http://testbgp.org`) where members can give BuddyPress a test drive. (See Figure 17-1.) You can create a membership, kick the tires a bit, and test all the features that your community members will have available to them after you add BuddyPress to your WordPress-powered Web site.

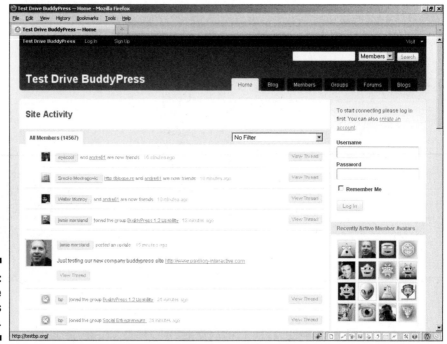

Figure 17-1:
The
BuddyPress
demo site.

Nourish Network

http://nourishnetwork.com

Nourish Network is a social community for people who love food, love to cook, and love to do it in an eco-friendly way. On the community's front page, the various articles (blog posts) appear within a handy tabbed box. The front page also pulls in a few BuddyPress components by displaying the site owner, site contributors, and status updates from profile pages — as well as the Group Forums in a box labeled "What's The Buzz?", which draws special attention to the conversations happening within Nourish Networks community.

Figure 17-2 displays the front page of Nourish Network, while Figure 17-3 shows you how the individual Member profile pages look.

Figure 17-2:
Nourish
Network is
an online
foodie
community.

Figure 17-3:
A Member
Profile page
on Nourish
Network.
com.

WeEarth

http://weearth.com

WeEarth is an online community of individuals who share their passion for "creativity, collaboration, and the urgent need for a sustainable society, with the ultimate goal to unveil the truth and reinvent what it means to be connected." (See Figure 17-4.)

I have to issue a small disclaimer and say that I was directly involved in the design and development of the WeEarth WordPress/BuddyPress project. To create the community, I built the foundation using the WordPress multiple blog option that allows WeEarth members to create individual member blogs within the community. I followed that with the implementation of a much-customized BuddyPress theme that encompasses Members, Blogs, and Groups directories, as well as individual member profiles, group pages, and activity streams.

Figure 17-4:
WeEarth.
com, a
community
focused
on envi-
ronmental
awareness.

The WeEarth community also has a Commerce section where they host a store and sell organic products. This was accomplished by adding the Shopp WordPress plugin and applying a fully customized design to the WeEarth shop.

WeEarth launched in July 2009 and has a very active membership of more than 485 members and counting.

We Heart This

http://wehearthis.com

They say it right on the top of their Web site: We Heart This is a community of chicks who love stuff. Built with the WordPress multiple blog option and BuddyPress to power the social community, We Heart This hosts a large network of mainly women who share ideas, deals, links, and passions on shopping, fashion, and beauty. (See Figure 17-5.)

Figure 17-5:
We Heart This, a community of chicks who love stuff.

I was involved in the design and development of this community. In July 2008, shortly after BuddyPress made a big splash on the Web, the We Heart This ladies asked me to help them develop a full-blown social community that had Facebook-like features. Since then, I've helped them upgrade the various plugins and platforms on their Web site to keep the software (WordPress MU and BuddyPress) and their various plugins that power their community up to date and running smoothly.

In addition to member blogs, profiles, and groups, We Heart This has a discussion forum that uses the bbPress software (`http://bbpress.org`).

GigaOM Pro

`http://pro.gigaom.com`

GigaOM Pro is a Web site that addresses "the gap that exists in real-time expert industry analysis on emerging technology markets." GigaOM Pro gives you expert insights and inside information on technology markets without the huge price tag that you'd usually expect for expert insider advice and analysis. (See Figure 17-6.)

GigaOM Pro offers memberships for $79.00. This is a great example of a Web site utilizing a combination of the WordPress and BuddyPress platforms to provide paid content and memberships. GigaOM Pro is an excellent example of how to accomplish this very popular business model with BuddyPress.

To give their site a dynamic feel, GigaOM Pro also integrates several popular WordPress features, such as:

✔ Featured content areas that spotlight content they feel is important to feature on the top of the front page.

✔ Multiple blogs that focus on topical information.

✔ Categorical display of content by topic rather than by date. This method of content delivery helps readers easily find the content they want to find because the content is sorted by topic.

✔ Easy subscription and online payment methods make it super easy for members to register for GigaOM Pro.

Figure 17-6:
GigaOM Pro, a community of technology industry insiders.

Flokka

`http://flokka.com`

Flokka.com uses WordPress and BuddyPress to deliver a social community focusing on women in the business world who use blogs to promote their products and services. Members of the Flokka community can add existing blogs, as well as create new blogs, on the Flokka Web site. Flokka showcases these blogs and members' business information as a membership benefit. (See Figure 17-7.)

Flokka uses their community to give individuals a platform to network and enter into conversations with other members about business-to-business services and products. Flokka also regularly features members and member blogs to promote them through the use of a Featured Members and Featured Blog widget that displays one member and blog at a time on their front page to put them center stage.

Figure 17-7: Flokka.com, a community of women in business.

Unstructure

http://unstructure.org

Unstructure brilliantly uses the WordPress and BuddyPress platforms to create a community for business professionals, bloggers, and thought leaders to "discuss and debate action ideas that would aid the evolution of business." (See Figure 17-8.)

The goal of Unstructure is to provide their community members a place to be heard, to teach, to learn, and to connect with one another. Unstructure provides these features to their members by using the BuddyPress platform.

The community members of Unstructure openly debate issues that face business professionals.

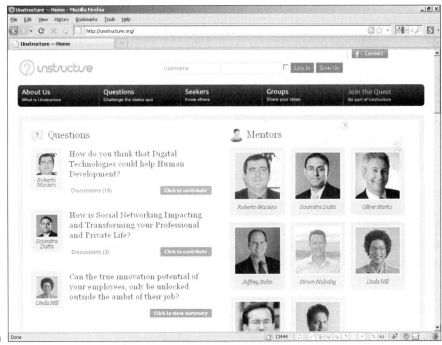

Figure 17-8:
Unstructure, a community of business professionals sharing ideas.

Young People

http://young-people.ch/home

Young People is a Web community for young people written in the German language, but even if you can't read German, the customized design and implementation of the WordPress and BuddyPress platform is so excellent I felt I had to include it here! (See Figure 17-9.)

Young People is a portal of information and community for youth on the Web. Their goal is to provide resources, media tips, and information, and to be a great place for young people to gather, share, and connect.

In addition to the usual community aspects of member profiles, groups, forums, and private mailings, Young People also provides their members the ability to create their own blogs and operate their own Web sites with the best free tools on the Web: WordPress and BuddyPress.

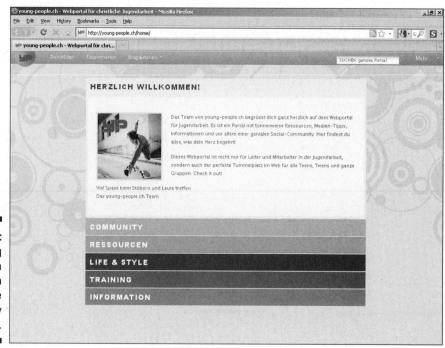

Figure 17-9:
Young People, a German language community for youths.

VW TankWars

http://tdi.vw.com

Want to know all there is to know about TDI clean diesel fuel? The Volkswagen car company thought you might, so they used the WordPress/BuddyPress platforms to put together a fabulous Web site and social community to discuss the truths, myths, and facts about TDI clean diesel fuel and TDI clean diesel vehicles. (See Figure 17-10.)

According to the VW Tank Wars site, the VW Jetta set a Guinness World Record for cleanest EPA ratings in 2009. VW is inviting you to join the site and share the miles per gallon of your TDI diesel vehicle as a challenge to their Web community to meet or beat the current Guinness World Record. This is a very effective way for a large corporation to use WordPress and BuddyPress to bring their customers together.

The VW Tank Wars Web site invites people to create a profile, using a BuddyPress plugin called Facebook Connect. (See Chapter 15.) This plugin allows people to log in to the VW Tank Wars site with their Facebook login rather than creating a new login. Once connected, members can create profiles and participate in the discussions on the site.

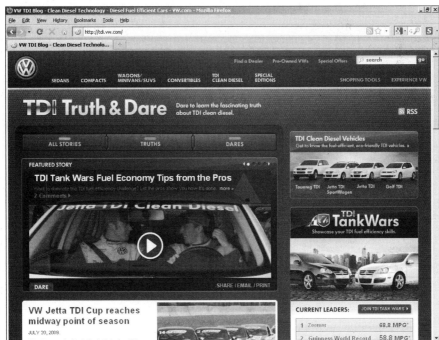

Figure 17-10: Volkswagen TDI TankWars Web site.

Tasty Kitchen

Tasty Kitchen is a well-designed implementation of WordPress and BuddyPress that invites its community members to connect with one another, share cooking tips, and search for recipes. Tasty Kitchen is a community of people who love food and love to cook. I have to admit, this is my kind of place! (See Figure 17-11.)

Tasty Kitchen happily invites you to "submit a recipe and join the fraternal order of the mitt!" Members can submit recipes to include on the main Tasty Kitchen site or just the Recipe Box section of their own member profile. Community members can rate other members' recipes, and members can search recipes by title, type, and rating. I just stick to searching for recipes. If I added any recipes of my own, I'm sure they'd be among the lowest rated — just ask my husband.

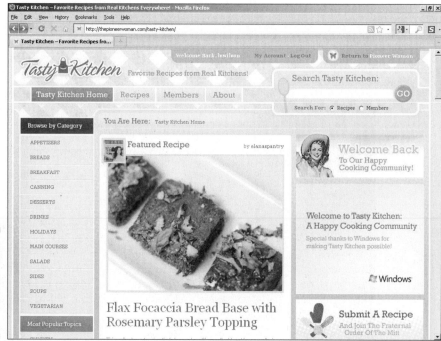

Figure 17-11: Tasty Kitchen, a community of foodies and cooks.

Appendix

Cutting Edge BuddyPress

In This Chapter

▶ Keeping up with the fast-paced development of BuddyPress

▶ Using BuddyPress Trac

▶ Creating a test environment

▶ Downloading and using nightly builds

▶ Upgrading your BuddyPress

*O*ne piece of advice that I give to BuddyPress users when they're starting out is this: Know what you're getting into. BuddyPress hit the scene in 2008 with a raw beta version of the software that was more conceptual than it was useful. This is what they call 'bleeding edge' in the software world — meaning, that version of BuddyPress wasn't stable at the time and was prone to bugs and flaws. In 2009, the stable version that we know and love today was released with much fanfare. Around that time, people began putting BuddyPress to good use, and the BuddyPress project began to grow by leaps and bounds.

BuddyPress, much like the WordPress project, is a living and breathing platform. Programmers and developers work every day to improve the existing programming and to add new features and components. Because BuddyPress is in constant development, the development team actually listens to its user base for new feature requests and bug reports. The one downside is that users sometimes find the development process arduous and difficult to keep up with. New developments come quickly, and sometimes it can feel like you're constantly upgrading to a new version of the software just to stay current.

In this chapter, you discover how to keep yourself up-to-date on the happenings within the BuddyPress development community. You also explore how to use and test the nightly builds, or beta versions, of the software in a test environment, and perhaps even participate in the bug-testing process. Lastly, I reveal important steps and tips on upgrading your existing BuddyPress installation.

Staying in the Know

Committing yourself, and your Web site, to the use of the BuddyPress platform to run your social community brings with it a certain responsibility to remain informed and updated on the latest BuddyPress features, flaws, bugs, and upgrade releases. I refer to this as a *responsibility* because after you decide to invite members to your site and use all the great BuddyPress features, those members will expect you to keep the site as up-to-date, safe, flaw-free, and feature-rich as you possibly can. With BuddyPress, you're not just running a Web site on your own; your site is a community effort. The content created by your members helps create the greatness of your Web site.

Staying up-to-date with the development of the BuddyPress platform might seem daunting, but this section de-mystifies it for you and shows that it's easy to take a few minutes out of your day to keep yourself informed.

Subscribe to BuddyPress.Org

The official Web site for the BuddyPress platform can be found at `http://buddypress.org`. There, on the official BuddyPress blog, you can find the latest announcements about new version releases of the BuddyPress software. Andy Peatling, the lead developer of the BuddyPress project, is extremely good about updating the BuddyPress blog when new upgrades become available. For the Twitter users out there, you can also subscribe to the official BuddyPress Twitter feed to stay updated (see Figure A-1) because BuddyPress also announce upgrade news on their Twitter account at `http://twitter.com/buddypressdev` (or @buddypressdev).

These upgrade announcements include:

- ✔ Highlights of the new upgrade
- ✔ Any new features introduced into the BuddyPress software
- ✔ Explanations of any bug fixes from previous versions
- ✔ Advice and tips on upgrading your current version of BuddyPress to the newest one available.

Using your favorite RSS feed reader, such as Google Reader or Bloglines, you can easily subscribe to the RSS feed at BuddyPress.Org so that you receive updates when BuddyPress update their blog with information you need to know.

In addition to subscribing to the BuddyPress site using your own, preferred RSS feed reader — RSS feed updates from the BuddyPress Web site also appear on your WordPress dashboard in the Other WordPress News box, as shown in Figure A-2.

Figure A-1: @Buddy PressDev on Twitter. com.

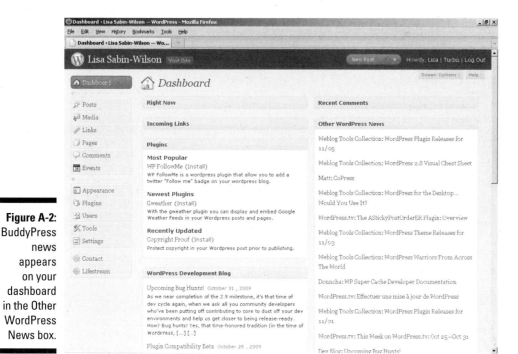

Figure A-2: BuddyPress news appears on your dashboard in the Other WordPress News box.

Browsing BuddyPress forums

Among the other helpful parts of the BuddyPress.Org Web site is the Forum Listing at `http://buddypress.org/forums` (shown in Figure A-3). Spend a bit of time browsing the discussions and posts within the Forum Listing and you'll find a wealth of information. Within the forums, you can find a wide array of users of the BuddyPress platform ranging from brand new (novice) users to the advanced-level, lead developers. Here people share their experiences, offer tips and advice, and try hard to help one another toward the mutual goal of using BuddyPress to grow their own social community on their Web site.

The discussion forums at BuddyPress.Org cover a variety of topics that you can search through to find helpful tips and information, including:

- **Installation:** Help for the initial steps of installing BuddyPress on your Web site.

- **Troubleshooting:** Tips and advice on troubleshooting any problems you experience after you install BuddyPress.

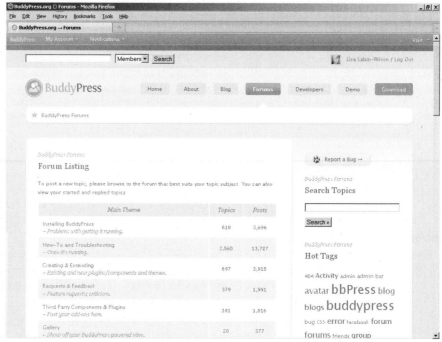

Figure A-3:
The discussion forums at
`http://buddypress.org/forums`.

✔ **Extending:** Information about new themes and plugins that you can use in tandem with BuddyPress to add new features to your Web site.

✔ **Requests:** Where you can give your great ideas for new features directly to the BuddyPress developers.

✔ **Third Party Plugins:** Where you can discover new plugins for BuddyPress, as well as read about, and participate in discussions relating to upcoming plugin development.

✔ **Gallery:** Where designers and developers show off the work they've done with BuddyPress on their, and others', Web sites. This area of the forum can give you some great inspiration!

✔ **General/Miscellaneous:** An area of the forum that doesn't quite fit into any of the categories and topics I've already mentioned.

Chances are, if you're experiencing problems with your BuddyPress installation, or have a question about it, someone else has already had the same problem or question. A good rule of thumb for using the forums on the BuddyPress Web site is to take full advantage of the search feature at the top of the forum section. Using keywords and phrases, the search feature allows you to search for topics already discussed about the particular issue you are having a problem with. You might be able to solve the problem, or answer your own question, by reading the experiences shared by other forum users.

A fantastic feature in the forums at the BuddyPress Web site is that each topic you find there has an RSS feed that you can subscribe to. This gives you the ability to follow a topic you're interested in and receive updates whenever someone adds to that topic. Figure A-4 shows the Help Installing BP topic in the BuddyPress forums. Notice the small, orange RSS icon to the right of the forum topic title. Click the icon to subscribe to the topic in your favorite RSS feed reader (like Google Reader or Bloglines).

When you use the forums at BuddyPress.Org to request support from users or developers, you should keep a few things in mind:

✔ Provide the user or developer the numbers of the WordPress MU and BuddyPress versions you are using. This information helps troubleshoot version-specific problems.

✔ Let the user or developer know if you are using WordPress MU with subdomains or subdirectories. (See Chapter 3 for information on subdomains versus subdirectories.) This information helps troubleshoot problems due to your WordPress MU configuration.

✔ Provide the user or developer a list of any plugins that you've installed on your site. This might clear up possible plugin compatibility issues or known conflicts that might be occurring.

Figure A-4:
An RSS feed
is available
for every
topic in the
BuddyPress
forums.

RSS Feed icon

✔ Give the user or developer information on the theme you're using on your BuddyPress-powered site. Are you using the BuddyPress Default theme with no alterations, a customized, modified version of the BuddyPress Default theme, or something else? This information can be vital in troubleshooting problems you might be experiencing.

✔ Provide the user or developer information on any other software or scripts that you're running on your Web site. Insight on this might help others assist you with your problem, but also its just good information to know.

✔ Be willing to answer more questions, provide additional information, and be patient. Not all problems with software like WordPress and BuddyPress are immediately apparent; sometimes, additional information is required to help pin down a possible solution for your particular problem.

You might not find answers or solutions for every problem you post to the BuddyPress forums. You might very well discover a new bug in the program. If that's the case, BuddyPress has a handy Report a Bug button in the forums that takes you to the BuddyPress Trac Web site (http://trac.buddy press.org), which I cover in the next section.

Browsing and using BuddyPress Trac

Several open source software programs, such as WordPress and BuddyPress, use an interface called Trac (`http://trac.edgewall.org`) to keep track of their software development. Trac provides many features to software developers that users don't need to be aware of. However, browsing and using the BuddyPress Trac at `http://trac.buddypress.org` (shown in Figure A-5) does offer advantages to non-developers:

- ✔ **Timeline:** Click the Timeline link to view a timeline of events that have occurred in the development of BuddyPress. This includes tickets, bug reports, and bug resolutions, and provides the identity of the developer responsible for resolving the reported problems and bugs.

- ✔ **Roadmap:** Click the Roadmap link to view items that are under development for future versions of BuddyPress. This is a great way to stay informed about upcoming features, including whether a bug is scheduled to be fixed, when, and in which version.

- ✔ **View Tickets:** Click the View Tickets link to browse every submitted or resolved ticket throughout the development of BuddyPress. This includes tickets with issues and problems that have not yet been resolved.

Figure A-5:
BuddyPress
Trac.

✔ **New Ticket:** Click the New Ticket link to submit your own ticket by providing an explanation of a bug that you experienced. To submit a ticket, you need to register on the BuddyPress Trac site, but registering has its benefits: It's a great way to contribute to the development of future versions of BuddyPress. You don't have to be a coding genius in order to contribute!

✔ **Browse Source:** Click the Browse Source link to view the source code of the files that make up the BuddyPress software. You can browse older versions, if you want to, but the good stuff is in the Trunk directory. The Trunk directory contains the absolute latest and greatest, cutting-edge version of the BuddyPress software. The files in the Trunk directory are the latest *nightly builds,* or beta versions. I describe using nightly builds and beta versions in a test environment in the upcoming "Downloading and Using Nightly Builds" section.

You can see there's a lot of browsing around, reading, and snooping to be done in the BuddyPress Trac so that you can stay informed and find out what's coming in future versions of BuddyPress. This information helps site owners plan the best ways to grow their communities. By knowing what new features are coming, you can build excitement and anticipation among your community members about upcoming features. By staying informed on the intended schedule of BuddyPress version releases, you can also plan your strategy for upgrading your site and keeping it fresh and new.

Setting Up a Test Environment

Something that helps me a great deal when I work with platforms that change as quickly as WordPress and BuddyPress is creating a test environment where I can install and run beta versions of the software. In a test environment, working with new features before they release to the public in an official version upgrade can be highly beneficial. The advantages of doing this include

✔ Becoming adept at using new features so that when you upgrade your site, you're informed enough to advise your users.

✔ The opportunity to install and test new plugins or themes before you commit to making those changes on your site.

✔ Testing early, beta versions of BuddyPress to help discover bugs and then using the BuddyPress Trac to report any problems. As I mention earlier, you don't have to be a programmer to contribute to the BuddyPress project; you can be a tester and help the developers and programmers fix issues for BuddyPress users worldwide.

There are several ways to create a test environment, and every one's mileage will vary on how they prefer to create one. The steps I take to create a test environment of my own are probably the easiest for you:

1. **Find out whether your hosting provider gives you the ability to create subdomains.**

   Generally, most hosting providers give you this option. I use the cPanel hosting account manager to create this subdomain, but your hosting account might offer you a different management tool, such as NetAdmin or Plesk.

   A *subdomain* is the second level of your current domain that can handle unique content separately than content in your main domain. Subdomains operate underneath your main domain, and can function as a wholly different section of your site, independent from your existing domain name.

   For an example of a subdomain on my domain, `ewebscapes.com`, see steps 3 and 4 where I create the subdomain `http://testing.ewebscapes.com`. The prefix `testing` in that Web address (or URL) is a subdomain that branches off `ewebscapes.com` that, when set up, handles completely different content than content currently installed on my main domain.

2. **Log in to your cPanel (or hosting account manager tool provided to you).**

3. **Locate and then click the Subdomains icon in the cPanel interface.**

   The Subdomains page within cPanel appears, as shown in Figure A-6.

Figure A-6:
The Subdomains page in cPanel where you can create a new subdomain.

4. **Type the name of your subdomain in the Subdomain text box.**

   For the purposes of making this straightforward and easy, type **testing** in the text box.

5. **On the drop-drop menu, choose the name of the domain on which you want to add the subdomain.**

   In Figure A-6, the drop-down menu shows the domain `ewebscapes.com`. I'm creating the subdomain on this domain, so my new subdomain is `http://testing.ewebscapes.com`.

   A unique folder name for your new subdomain appears in the Document/ Root text box. Don't alter this text because this tells your Web server where to install the necessary WordPress and BuddyPress files.

6. **Click the Create button.**

   It takes a few seconds, but the page refreshes and displays a message that the new subdomain has been created, as shown in Figure A-7.

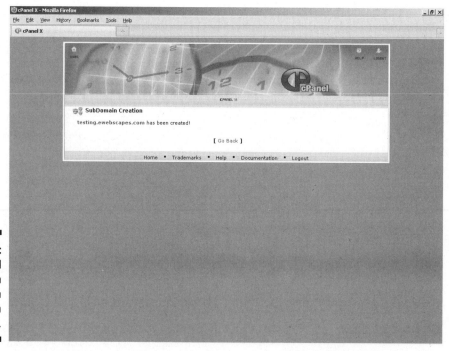

Figure A-7: Successful subdomain creation message in cPanel.

Now that you have a subdomain set up on your hosting account, you can install WordPress MU and BuddyPress into the folder that was created when you added the subdomain. For example, if you created a subdomain called testing, then the folder on your Web server you'll install into will be the /testing/ folder. For the steps to install WordPress MU and BuddyPress on your subdomain, refer to Chapters 2, 3, and 4.

Before going forward and installing WordPress MU and BuddyPress in your new test environment, read through the next section of this chapter to find out where to find the latest beta versions (or nightly builds) of the BuddyPress software because that is the version you want to install on your test environment so you can, well . . . test it!

Downloading and Using Nightly Builds

You can get your hands on the latest nightly build of the BuddyPress software several ways, but in this section, I'm going to give you the easiest way. It isn't the fastest way, but for non-techy types, it's the most sure-fire way to get the latest development version of the platform.

When I refer to *nightly builds,* what I am referring to is the latest development work that the BuddyPress developers have added to the source. Nightly builds are available only through the official BuddyPress site, and are not considered safe for public use. People use nightly builds for testing purposes and site development planning, not for use on live sites because these builds generally contain bugs or vulnerabilities that still need to be fleshed out and fixed before the next, official version of BuddyPress is released.

To find a Zip file of today's latest BuddyPress development version, follow these quick steps:

1. **Visit the BuddyPress Trac at http://trac.buddypress.org.**

2. **Click the Browse Source link in the navigation menu.**

   This opens the Root directory in the BuddyPress Trac.

3. **Click the Trunk directory.**

   The BuddyPress Trac displays a full listing of files available in this latest build of BuddyPress, as shown in Figure A-8.

4. **Click the Zip Archive link.**

   If you don't see this link, scroll all the way to the bottom of the page. Clicking Zip Archive opens a dialog box that allows you to save the Zip version of the BuddyPress files on your local computer.

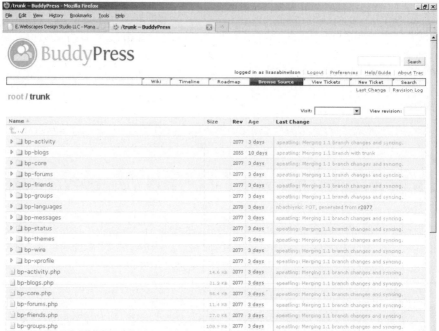

Figure A-8:
The Root/
Trunk direc-
tory in the
BuddyPress
Trac.

5. **Install WordPress MU on the subdomain you're using for your test environment.**

   If you need instructions on installing WordPress MU on your test environment subdomain, see Chapter 2.

6. **Install the BuddyPress nightly build that you downloaded from the BuddyPress Trac.**

   If you need instructions on manually installing BuddyPress, see Chapter 3.

7. **Finish setting up and configuring BuddyPress on your new test environment.**

   If you need the steps and configuration information to finish setting up BuddyPress on your test environment subdomain, see Chapter 4.

You now have WordPress MU and the latest nightly build of BuddyPress installed and setup on a test environment on a subdomain of your hosting account. With this environment, you are free to test new features or try out new plugins or themes before you make any changes to your main, public site. Having this environment also gives you the ability to test new development and provide BuddyPress developers feedback on their latest work.

You might have heard about another method of obtaining the nightly builds of the latest BuddyPress development called SVN, or Subversion. SVN is a higher-tech way of downloading and installing the BuddyPress files to your Web server and requires that you have access to a Subversion program, such as Tortoise SVN for the PC. Because the use of SVN is somewhat complex, I provide you only with the easiest way to obtain the files and do not cover SVN. However, if you feel brave and are curious about SVN, check out the informative article that appears in the WordPress Codex at `http://codex.wordpress.org/Using_Subversion`, which includes resources on using an SVN client and other helpful information for using SVN.

Having a test environment is not necessary, but I recommend it for site owners who are serious about maintaining a BuddyPress community on their own sites, for the various reasons I mention in this chapter.

Upgrading BuddyPress

When BuddyPress releases an official upgrade, you need to be armed with best practices for upgrading BuddyPress on your site. To keep you informed about newly released upgrades, your WordPress MU dashboard alerts you when a new version of BuddyPress is ready and waiting for you to download. So if you paid no attention to any of the resources that I provide in this chapter, you'll still stay informed about newly released upgrades. It's foolproof, really!

When a new version of BuddyPress or a plugin upgrade is available, you see a bright red circle in the Plugins menu on your WordPress dashboard. The number in the red circle gives you an indication of how many of your plugins have upgrades available. As shown in Figure A-9, the indicator tells me that I have 1 plugin upgrade available.

Click Plugins to go to the Manage Plugins page. There you see an alert directly beneath the BuddyPress plugin listing that a new version of BuddyPress is available. (See Figure A-10.)

Do not click the Upgrade Automatically link right way. Instead, follow these few steps to ensure a safe and smart upgrade to your BuddyPress plugin:

1. **Deactivate the current version of BuddyPress on your site.**

   Click the Deactivate link beneath the BuddyPress plugin title to deactivate the BuddyPress plugin. The Manage Plugins page reloads, indicating that the BuddyPress plugin is deactivated.

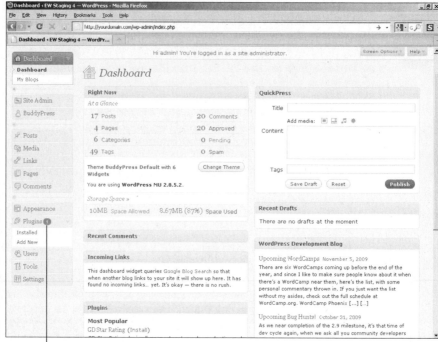

Figure A-9:
A bright
red circle
indicates
plugin
upgrades
are
available.

A plugin upgrade indicator

2. **Deactivate any additional plugins that require BuddyPress.**

   Any other plugins you might have installed that require BuddyPress also need to be deactivated at this time.

3. **Upgrade BuddyPress.**

   Click the Upgrade Automatically link beneath the BuddyPress plugin title on the Manage Plugins page. This loads the Upgrade Plugin page where you see a series of messages alerting you that the newest version of BuddyPress is being downloaded, unpacked, installed, and upgraded.

4. **Reactivate BuddyPress.**

   Click the Activate Plugin link on the Upgrade Plugin page, as shown in Figure A-11. This takes you to the Manage Plugins page where BuddyPress is showing as an activated plugin.

Your BuddyPress installation is the latest version, and you're ready to share all the new features and fixes in this latest version with your entire member community. Congratulations!

Figure A-10:
The
BuddyPress
upgrade
alert on the
WordPress
dashboard.

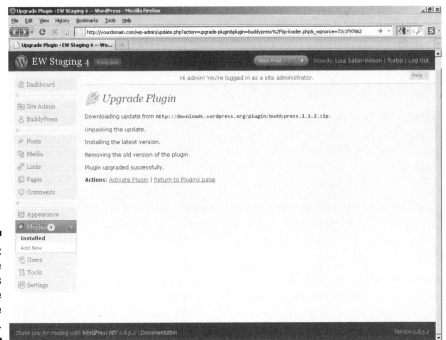

Figure A-11:
Activate
BuddyPress
on the
Upgrade
Plugin page.

Index

• *Numerics* •

3oneseven Web site, 187
403: Forbidden Access message, 44
404: Page Not Found message, 44
500: Internal Server Error message, 44

• *A* •

a CSS selector, 205
Account Activate page, 111–112
account administration interface,
    Web hosting, 33–35
Actions field, Install Plugins page, 220
Activate link, Manage Themes page, 190
Activate Plugin link
  Upgrade Plugin page, 286
  WordPress, 69
activating
  BP-FB Connect plugin, 233
  BuddyPress, 72–73
  BuddyPress Geo plugin, 244
  plugins, 222, 226
  themes, 190–191
Active option
  Groups widget, 157, 178
  Members widget, 176
activity folder, 194
Activity item, My Account menu, 114
Activity page
  navigating, 116–118
  overview, 116
  status updates, 118–120
  user blog activity, 149
activity stream
  blog activity in, 148–149
  BuddyPress Settings page, 84

defined, 2, 18
group activity in, 155
group front page, 160
overview, 86–87
activity wire, 18
Add Blog section, Blogs page, 50,
    146–147
Add Field page, 99–100
Add Friend button
  Member Directory, 136
  Profile page, 120
Add Group button, Add Group page, 102
Add Group page, 102
Add New Field link, Profile Field Setup
    page, 99
Add New Group link, Profile Field Setup
    page, 102
Add New option
  Links menu, 58
  Media menu, 58
  Pages menu, 58
  Plugins menu, 60, 67, 237
  Posts menu, 57
  Users menu, 60
Add New Post page, 151–152
Add New Themes option, Appearance
    menu, 59, 190
Add New User text box, cPanel, 35
Add user section,
    WordPress Users page, 51
Add Users to Database section,
    cPanel, 35
address, e-mail. *See* e-mail
address, Web
  blog, 50
  login page, 44
  running WordPress install script, 39
  subdirectory, 38

address, Web *(continued)*
  subdomain, 38
  test account blog, 109
  WordPress login page, 45–46
admin bar, 73–74, 83, 113–115
Admin Email text box, Blogs page,
    50, 147
Admin Notice Feed text box,
    Site Options page, 56
Admin option
  Groups subnavigation menu, 131–132
  Site Admin menu, 48–49
Admin page, 48–49
adminbar.css file, 199
administration panel, WordPress, 42
administrative access, WordPress
    dashboard, 56
administrator
  group, 130–133, 159
  site, 48
Administrator role, blog user, 54
.ajax-loader CSS selector, 205
alert, notification, 126
All option, Inbox page Select drop-down
    menu, 123
All Privileges check box, cPanel, 35
Allow New Registrations options, Site
    Options page, 53, 143
Alphabetical option
  Groups Directory, 156
  My Groups page, 128
Apache, configuration of, 37
API Key, Facebook, 235
Appearance menu, WordPress, 59,
    170, 190
Archive option, Blogs page, 146
Archives widget, 171, 182
ASCII transfer mode, FTP, 36
Author Avatar List plugin, 243
Author Homepage field, Group Forum
    Subscription for BuddyPress plugin
    page, 224
Author role, blog user, 54
Authors & Users option, Users menu, 60
Auto Renew service, domain name, 25

automatic installation, BuddyPress,
    66–70
avatar
  Author Avatar List, 243
  BuddyPress Settings page, 83–85
  changing, 110–111, 122
  defined, 2, 18
  group, 130, 156, 159
  Recently Active Member Avatars
    widget, 182
  Who's Online Avatars widget, 182
Avenue K9 theme, 252

• *B* •

Backend option, Blogs page, 145
background color, changing, 208–210
background CSS property, 207–208
background-color CSS property, 207
backup copy, WordPress theme, 201
bandwidth, 29–31
Banned Names text box,
    Site Options page, 54
banning member, 131
Base Profile Group Name setting,
    BuddyPress Settings page, 83
bb-config.php file, 95–96
bbPress, 79, 154–155
bbPress forums
  enabling with Groups feature, 154–155
  existing installation, using, 96–97
  new installation, setting up, 95–96
  overview, 88–89, 93–94
beta version, 280, 283–285
binary transfer mode, FTP, 36
blog
  overview, 2
  post, on Activity page, 116
  privacy options, 110
  storage space for uploads, 55
  test account, 109–110
  user
    adding, 146–148
    deleting multiple, 146

enabling user blog creation, 142–144
individual, 145–146
managing, 144–148
overview, 53–54, 141–142
publishing posts, 151–152
Search feature, 144–145
tracking activity, 148–150
Web hosting
account administration interface,
33–35
bandwidth, 29–31
disk space, 29–30
by domain registrars, 26
MySQL, 28
overview, 27–28
PHP, 28
root directory, 35–36
specialized, 28–29
support services, 28–29
Blog Activity Only option,
Groups page, 133
Blog Address text box, Blogs page,
50, 146
Blog Addresses section, WordPress, 40
Blog Domain item, Blogs page, 50
Blog Domain text box,
Create a Blog page, 143
blog network, 17
Blog Title text box
Blogs page, 50, 147
Create a Blog page, 143
Sign Up page, 110
blog tracking, 2, 19, 87–89, 148–150
Blog URL text box, Sign Up page, 109
BLOG_URL variable, Site Options
page, 55
BLOG_URLwp-login.php variable, Site
Options page, 55
blog-related widgets, 182–183
blog-roll, 58
Blogs Directory, 137–138, 149–150
blogs folder, 194
Blogs item
My Account menu, 114
Search feature, 139

Site Admin menu, 49–50
Users page, 51
Blogs page, 49–50, 122, 144–148
body CSS selector, 204
<body> tag, 208–210, 214
bp-default theme folder, 194–195, 201
BP-FB Connect plugin, 233–236, 246
bp-snparent-theme folder, 194–195
brand, domain name as, 26
Brazell, Aaron, 4–5
Browse button, 110
Browse Source link, BuddyPress Trac,
280, 283
Bruce theme, 253–254
BuddyPress
ease of use, 18
extended capabilities, 19–21
flexibility, 18–19
overview, 1–8, 15–16
WordPress platform, 16–18
BuddyPress Classic theme, 21, 107,
168–169, 172–175
BuddyPress Codex, 66, 202
BuddyPress Community theme, 256–257
BuddyPress Component Setup page, 79,
85–86, 148, 154
BuddyPress Corporate theme, 252–253
BuddyPress Default theme
activating, 76–77
for blogs, 147–148
child theme folder, creating, 196–197
versus Classic, 107
general discussion, 167–169, 258–259
overview, 20, 107
as parent theme, 194
widgets, 170
BuddyPress Events Calendar plugin, 244
BuddyPress Extend page, 228
\buddypress folder, 71
BuddyPress Forums, Plugins page, 228
BuddyPress Fun theme, 254–255
BuddyPress Geo plugin, 244–245
BuddyPress Group Twitter plugin,
237–238
BuddyPress menu, WordPress, 78–80, 82,
85, 93, 148, 154

BuddyPress Privacy Component plugin, 242
BuddyPress Settings page, 79, 82–85, 115
BuddyPress Social Network Parent Theme, 168
BuddyPress Stats plugin, 247–248
BuddyPress Trac, 279–280, 283–284
BuddyPress Web site
  downloading files from, 71
  as example of platform, 262
  forums on, 276–278
  overview, 22
  plugins, 248
  subscribing to, 274–275
  themes directory, 186
BuddyPress/Facebook Connect plugin, 246
bugs, 278–280
business social communities, 14
buying domain name, 24, 26

• C •

Calendar widget, 171
Cancel Friendship button, Member Directory, 136
Cascading Style Sheet (CSS)
  custom files, using in child theme folder, 199
  styling themes with
    additional resources, 214
    background color, changing, 208–210
    classes, 205–206
    fonts, changing, 212–214
    IDs, 205–206
    overview, 203–204
    personal logo, using in header, 210–212
    properties, 207–208
    selectors, 204
    values, 207–208
Categories option, Posts menu, 58
Categories page, 58
Categories widget, 171, 182

Change Avatar item, Profile page subnavigation menu, 120, 122
Change Your Icon link, Facebook Edit application page, 235
Change Your Logo link, Facebook Edit application page, 235
Checkboxes option, Field Type drop-down menu, 100
child/parent theme relationship
  child theme, 195–196
  child theme folder, creating, 196–199
  custom CSS file, using in child theme, 199
  images, using in child theme, 199–200
  overview, 74, 188–189, 193–194
  parent template files, modifying, 200–201
  parent theme, 194–195
Choose a Password field, Sign Up page, 109
City field, Profile Field Setup page, 99
class, CSS, 205–206
Classic theme, 21, 107, 168–169, 172–175
client, FTP, 31–32
Close button, Inbox page, 123
Codex
  BuddyPress, 66, 202
  WordPress, 285
color, font, 212–214
`color` CSS property, 207–208, 212–214
comment, blog, in activity stream, 148
Comment link, Activity page, 118
Comments menu, WordPress, 59
community, BuddyPress
  admin bar, navigating, 113–115
  blogs
    adding, 146–148
    deleting multiple, 146
    enabling user blog creation, 142–144
    individual, 145–146
    managing, 144–148
    overview, 2, 53–54, 141–142
    post, on Activity page, 116
    privacy options, 110

publishing posts, 151–152
Search feature, 144–145
storage space for uploads, 55
test account, 109–110
tracking activity, 148–150
Web hosting, 27–36
building, 11–14
directories, 134–139
forums
  on BuddyPress.Org Web site, 276–278
  enabling with Groups feature, 154–155
  existing installation, using, 96–97
  group, 160–162
  new installation, setting up, 95–96
  overview, 2, 19, 88, 93–94
  support, 22
Groups feature
  Activity page, 116
  enabling, 154–155
  forums, 160–162
  front page items, 158–160
  Groups Directory, 155–156
  Groups menu, 163
  Groups widget, 157
  joining, 160
  managing groups, 130–133
  My Groups list, 128
  new groups, creating, 128–130
  overview, 18, 90, 127–128, 153
  Site Activity, 157–158
overview, 1–2, 107
participating in, 21–22
profiles
  Activity feature, 116–120
  blog, creating from, 143–144
  blog activity in, 149–150
  Blogs feature, 122
  Extended Profiles component, 2, 18,
    91–93, 103–104
  Friends feature, 126–127
  Groups feature, 127–133
  Messages feature, 123–126
  overview, 115–116

Profile feature, 120–122
Settings feature, 133–134
updates, on Activity page, 116
WordPress, 60
searches, 134–139
sign up process
  activating account, 111–113
  overview, 108
  registration, 108–111
Site Activity stream, 134–139
Community theme, 255–256
community-related widgets, 182–183
Compatible Up to field, Group Forum
    Subscription for BuddyPress plugin
    page, 224
Complete Installation button
  Forums Setup, Existing bbPress
    Installation page, 97
  Forums Setup, New bbPress
    Installation page, 95
Complete Sign Up button,
    Sign Up page, 110
Component Setup link, BuddyPress
    menu, 79, 148, 154
components, BuddyPress
  activity streams
    blog activity in, 148–149
    BuddyPress Settings page, 84
    defined, 2, 18
    group activity in, 155
    group front page, 160
    overview, 86–87
  bbPress forums
    enabling with Groups feature, 154–155
    existing installation, using, 96–97
    new installation, setting up, 95–96
    overview, 88–89, 93–94
  blog tracking, 2, 19, 87–89, 148–150
  Extended Profiles, 2, 18, 91–93, 103–104
  Friends
    Activity page, 116
    My Friends list, 126–127
    overview, 2, 88–89

components, BuddyPress *(continued)*
  Groups
    Activity page, 116
    enabling, 154–155
    forums, 160–162
    Groups menu, 163
    managing groups, 130–133
    My Groups list, 128
    new groups, creating, 128–130
    overview, 18, 90, 127–128, 153
    participating in, 155–160
  overview, 85–86
  Private Messaging, 2, 90–91
components.css file, 202
Compose page, 125
compressed WordPress software, 33
configuration, BuddyPress
  bbPress forums, setting up
    existing installation, 96–97
    new installation, 95–96
    overview, 93–94
  components
    activity streams, 86–87
    bbPress forums, 88
    Blog Tracking, 87–88
    Extended Profiles, 91–93
    Friends, 88–89
    Groups, 90
    overview, 85–86
    Private Messaging, 90–91
  general settings, 81–85
  overview, 81
  profile fields, adding, 98–101
  profile groups, creating, 101–104
content
  defined, 28
  user-generated, 231
Content text box
  Post a New Topic form, 161
  Welcome widget, 180
Contributor role, blog user, 54
cookie, WordPress, 46
Corporate theme, 252–253
cPanel, 33–35, 281–282
Create a Blog item, My Blogs menu, 114

Create a Blog page, 143–144
Create a Configuration File button,
    WordPress, 39
Create a Group, Avatar page, 130
Create a Group, Group Invites
    page, 130
Create a Group page, 128–129
Create a Group, Settings page, 130
Create a New Blog link, Admin page, 49
Create a New User link, Admin page, 49
Create and Continue button, Create a
    Group page, 129
Create Application page, Facebook,
    233–234
Create Database button, cPanel, 35
Create User button, cPanel, 35
cropping tool, 111
CSS (Cascading Style Sheet)
  custom files, using in child theme
    folder, 199
  styling themes with
    additional resources, 214
    background color, changing, 208–210
    classes, 205–206
    fonts, changing, 212–214
    IDs, 205–206
    overview, 203–204
    personal logo, using in header,
      210–212
    properties, 207–208
    selectors, 204
    values, 207–208
css folder, 189
Currently Active Site Wide Plugins
    heading, Manage Plugins page, 73
customizing child theme, 198

dashboard, WordPress
  activating plugins, 226
  administrator management
    of user's, 145
  Appearance menu, 59
  blog tracking, enabling, 148

Comments menu, 59
forum options, enabling, 154
general site options, 57–62
groups, enabling, 154
Links menu, 58
logging into, 45–46
Media menu, 58
navigating, 47–48
Other WordPress News box, 274–275
overview, 45
Pages menu, 58
plugins, finding and installing, 218–222
Plugins menu, 59–60
Posts menu, 57–58
publishing blog posts, 151
Settings menu, 61–62
Site Admin menu
  Admin option, 48–49
  Blogs option, 49–50
  Options option, 52–56
  overview, 48
  Themes option, 52
  Upgrade option, 56
  Users option, 50–51
theme, activating new, 189–191
Tools menu, 60–61
user blog creation, enabling, 142
Users menu, 60
widgets, 170
dashboard blog, 53–54
database, MySQL, 33–35
Database drop-down menu, cPanel, 35
Database Host text box, WordPress
    installation page, 41
Database Name text box, WordPress
    installation page, 40–41
Date Selector option, Field Type
    drop-down menu, 100
Dave's CSS Guide, 214
Deactivate option
  Blogs page, 145–146
  Manage Plugins page, 228, 285

decompressing
  BuddyPress plugin files, 71
  WordPress software, 33
Default theme
  activating, 76–77
  for blogs, 147–148
  child theme folder, creating, 196–197
  versus Classic, 107
  general discussion, 167–169, 258–259
  overview, 20, 107
  as parent theme, 194
  widgets, 170
Default User Avatar setting, BuddyPress
    Settings page, 84–85
default.css file
  background color, changing, 208–210
  CSS classes, 205–206
  CSS IDs, 205–206
  CSS properties, 207
  CSS values, 207
  custom CSS file in child theme, 199
  logo, adding to header, 210–212
Delete Group option, Admin menu, 132
Delete option
  Blogs page, 146
  Manage Themes page, 190
Delete Plugins(s) page, 228
Delete Selected option, Inbox page, 124
deleting multiple blogs, 146
demo site, BuddyPress, 262
Description field, Install Plugins
    page, 220
developers community, BuddyPress, 22
development, BuddyPress
  keeping informed about
    BuddyPress forums, browsing,
      276–278
    BuddyPress Trac, browsing and using,
      279–280
    BuddyPress Web site, 274–275
    overview, 274
  nightly builds, downloading and using,
    283–285
  overview, 273

development, BuddyPress *(continued)*
  test environment, setting up, 280–283
  upgrading BuddyPress, 285–287
development tools, Web site
  domain name extensions, 25
  domain name fees, 25
  domain name registration, 26
  overview, 24
directories
  Blogs Directory, 137, 138, 149–150
  Forums Directory, 136
  Global Forums Directory, 84
  Groups Directory, 90, 91, 136, 155–156
  Member Directory, 133, 136–137, 201
  root, 35–36
  searchable, 19
  Trunk, 280, 283–284
  WordPress Plugin Directory, 70, 219,
    223–225, 241
  WordPress Themes Directory, 190, 248
Disable Activity Stream commenting
    on blog and forum posts? setting,
    BuddyPress Settings page, 84
Disable Avatar Uploads? setting,
    BuddyPress Settings page, 83
Disable BuddyPress to WordPress
    Profile Syncing? setting, BuddyPress
    Settings page, 83
Disable Global Forum Directory? setting,
    BuddyPress Settings page, 84
Disable User Account Deletion? setting,
    BuddyPress Settings page, 84
Disabled option, Site Options page,
    53, 143
Disabled radio button, BuddyPress
    Component Setup page, 86
disallowed user name, WordPress, 54
discussion forums
  bbPress
    enabling with Groups feature, 154–155
    existing installation, using, 96–97
    new installation, setting up, 95–96
    overview, 88, 93–94
  on BuddyPress.Org Web site, 276–278
  group, 160–162
  overview, 2, 19
  support, 22

Discussion option, WordPress Settings
    menu, 62
discussion thread, 162
disk space, 29–30
`<div id="header">` ID, 207
DNS (domain name server), 38
Domain item, Blogs page, 145
domain name
  defined, 24
  extensions, 25
  registration fees, 25
  registration of, through Web host, 29
  registration process, 26
  WordPress installation page,
    entering on, 41
domain name server (DNS), 38
Download BuddyPress page, 71
Download button, Group Forum
    Subscription for BuddyPress plugin
    page, 224
Download option, BuddyPress
    Web site, 71
downloading
  BuddyPress files, 71
  nightly builds, 283–285
  plugin files from WordPress Plugin
    Directory, 223–225
  themes, 187–189
drag-and-drop method, FTP, 32
Drop-Down Select Box option, Field Type
    drop-down menu, 100

• E •

Edit Blog page, 145
Edit Comments page, 59
Edit Details option, Admin menu, 131
Edit link, Users page, 51
Edit option
  Blogs page, 145
  Links menu, 58
  Pages menu, 58
  Posts menu, 57
Edit page, Facebook, 233, 235
Edit Posts page, 151

Edit Profile item, Profile page subnavigation menu, 120–121
Edit Profile page, 101, 103
Edit Themes page, 59
Editing page, 121
editing profile, 121–122
Editor option
  Appearance menu, 59
  Plugins menu, 60
Editor role, blog user, 54
e-mail
  BuddyPress member addresses, 91
  group notifications by, 133–134
  site administration, 53
  WordPress registration, limiting to certain addresses, 54
Email Address field, Sign Up page, 108
Email text box
  Users page, 51
  WordPress installation page, 42
Enable Discussion Forum checkbox, Create a Group, Settings page, 130
Enabled. Blogs and User Accounts Can Be Created option, Site Options page, 53, 143
Enabled option, BuddyPress Component Setup page, 86, 148
Error Connecting to the Database message, 44
error message
  PHP, 38
  WordPress, 44
Events Calendar plugin, 244
expiration, domain name, 24
Export option, Tools menu, 61
Extended Profiles component, 2, 18, 91–93, 103–104
extending, forums covering, 277

● *F* ●

Facebook, 11–13, 232–236, 246
Facebook Connect Plugin Options page, 233–236
Featured filter, Install Plugins page, 219
Featured Members Widget plugin, 242–243

Field Description text box, Add Field page, 100
Field Title text box, Add Field page, 99
Field Type drop-down menu, Add Field page, 100
file permissions, 36, 44
file size, blog upload, 56
File Transfer Protocol (FTP)
  BuddyPress files, uploading, 71–72
  child theme folder, 198
  logo, adding to header, 211
  plugin files, uploading, 226
  theme files, uploading, 188
  theme folders, moving with, 75
  transferring files with, 31–32
  WordPress files, uploading, 35–36
  WordPress theme, using with BuddyPress, 201–202
file type, blog upload, 55–56
files
  BuddyPress
    downloading, 71
    uploading to host, 71–72
  downloading from WordPress Plugin Directory, 223–225
  transfers, 31–32
  uploading plugins to Web server, 226
  uploading to WordPress host, 35–36
FileZilla, 32
filtering, Blogs page, 122
First Post text box, Site Options page, 55
First-Section sidebar, Widgets page, 172–173
500: Internal Server Error message, 44
Flickr, 232
Flokka Web site, 268
font, 212–214
`font-family` CSS property, 208, 212–214
`font-size` CSS property, 208, 212–214
Forum link, Groups subnavigation menu, 132
Forum Listing, 276
Forum option, Groups menu, 163
Forum page, 161–162
forum topic, 160, 162

forums
  bbPress
    enabling with Groups feature, 154–155
    existing installation, using, 96–97
    new installation, setting up, 95–96
    overview, 88, 93–94
  on BuddyPress.Org Web site, 276–278
  group, 160–162
  overview, 2, 19
  support, 22
Forums Directory, 136
forums folder, 194
Forums option, Search feature, 139
Forums Setup: Existing bbPress
    Installation page, 96–97
Forums Setup link, BuddyPress menu,
    79, 93
Forums Setup: New bbPress Installation
    page, 95
Forums Setup page, 93–97
403: Forbidden Access message, 44
404: Page Not Found message, 44
Free BuddyPress Themes Web site, 187
free themes
  Avenue K9, 252
  Bruce, 253–254
  BuddyPress Community, 256–257
  BuddyPress Corporate, 252–253
  BuddyPress Default Theme, 258–259
  BuddyPress Fun, 254–255
  finding, 185–187
  future of BuddyPress themes, 259
  MuddyPress, 258
  New Yorker, 258
  overview, 251
  Purple & Black, 257
  Shouty, 255–256
Friends feature
  Activity page, 116
  My Friends list, 126–127
  overview, 2, 88–89
Friends item, My Account menu, 114
front page, Group feature, 158–160
FTP (File Transfer Protocol)
  BuddyPress files, uploading, 71–72
  child theme folder, 198
  logo, adding to header, 211
  plugin files, uploading, 226

theme files, uploading, 188
theme folders, moving with, 75
transferring files with, 31–32
WordPress files, uploading, 35–36
WordPress theme, using with
    BuddyPress, 201–202
Full Name Field Name setting,
    BuddyPress Settings page, 83
Fun theme, 254–255
FYI box, Group Forum Subscription for
    BuddyPress plugin page, 224

• G •

Gallery forums, 277
General item, Settings page
    subnavigation menu, 133
General option, Settings menu, 61–62
General Public License (GPL), 229
General Settings link, BuddyPress menu,
    79, 82
General/Miscellaneous forums, 277
Geo plugin, 244–245
Geo Search Setup page, 244–245
GigaOM Pro Web site, 14, 266–267
Global Forums Directory, 84
global variables, PHP, 39
GPL (General Public License), 229
Group Avatar option, Admin menu, 131
Group Description field, Create a Group
    page, 129
group forum, 160–162
Group Forum Activity Only option,
    Groups page, 133
Group Forum Subscription for
    BuddyPress plugin
  automatic installation of, 220–222
  manual installation of, 222–226
  Options page, 227
Group Name field, Create a Group
    page, 129
Group Settings option, Admin menu, 131
Groups Directory, 90–91, 136, 155–156
Groups feature
  Activity page, 116
  enabling, 154–155
  forums, 160–162
  Groups menu, 163

managing groups, 130–133
My Groups list, 128
new groups, creating, 128–130
overview, 18, 90, 127–128, 153
participating in
  front page items, 158–160
  Groups Directory, 155–156
  Groups widget, 157
  joining, 160
  overview, 155
  Site Activity, 157–158
groups folder, 194
Groups item, My Account menu, 114
Groups menu, 163
Groups option, Search feature, 139
Groups widget, 157, 171, 177–179

• *H* •

h1 CSS selector, 205
header ID, 207
header.php file, 200, 204, 207
Headers Already Sent Error Messages
    message, 44
hexadecimal (hex) code, 209–210
hidden group, 130, 155
Hide Admin Bar for Logged Out Users?
    option, BuddyPress Settings page,
    83, 115
Home option, Groups menu, 131, 163
hosting, Web
  account administration interface, 33–35
  bandwidth, 29–31
  disk space, 29–30
  by domain registrars, 26
  MySQL, 28
  overview, 27–28
  PHP, 28
  root directory, 35–36
  specialized, 28–29
  support services, 28–29
hostname record, 38
.htaccess file, 39
HTML, connecting with CSS selectors,
    205–206
httpd.conf file, 37–38
hyperlink, 122

• *I* •

ICANN (Internet Corporation for
    Assigned Names and Numbers), 26
icons used in book, 7–8
ID
  blog, 50, 145
  CSS, 205–206
image
  for background, 209
  in child theme folder, 199–200
  Facebook application, 235
images folder, 189
@import command, 199
Import option, Tools menu, 61
Inbox page, 123–124
_inc folder, 189, 194, 196
/_inc/css/ folder, 199
_inc/images folder, 199–200, 211
index.php home page, 44
Install Now button, BuddyPress pop-up
    window, 69
Install Plugins page, 60, 67–68, 218–222
install script, running WordPress, 39–44
Install Themes page, 59
installation
  bbPress forum, 95–97
  BuddyPress
    admin bar, 73–74
    automatic method, 66–70
    BuddyPress menu, 78–80
    manual method, 71–73
    overview, 65–66
  common problems with, 44
  forums covering, 276
  plugins
    manual method, 222–226
    overview, 218–219
    using Install Plugins interface, 219–222
  themes, 187–189
"Installation Finished!" page, WordPress,
    42–43
Installed option, Plugins menu, 60
Installing Plugin: BuddyPress page, 69

Installing Plugin: Group Forum
  Subscription for BuddyPress
  page, 222
integration, 96
Interests field, Profile Field
  Setup page, 99
Internet Corporation for Assigned Names
  and Numbers (ICANN), 26
IP address, FTP, 31
Is This Field Required? drop-down menu,
  Add Field page, 100

• *J* •

Join Group button
  group front page, 159, 160
  Groups Directory, 136, 156
joining group, 160

• *K* •

Kaltura Media Component plugin,
  246–247
keyword, search, 139

• *L* •

Last Active option
  Groups Directory, 155
  My Groups page, 128
Last Updated item
  Blogs page, 50, 145
  Group Forum Subscription for
    BuddyPress plugin page, 224
Leave Group option
  group front page, 159, 160
  Groups Directory, 136, 156
  Groups menu, 163
  Groups subnavigation menu, 133
Library option, Media menu, 58
Link Categories option, Links menu, 58
Links menu, WordPress, 58
Links widget, 171

Load More link, Activity page, 116
localhost, WordPress installation
  page, 41
Log In button
  "Installation Finished!" page, 43
  WordPress login page, 46
Log Out link
  My Account menu, 114
  WordPress, 108
login area, Web site, 112
login information, WordPress, 42–43
login page, WordPress, 43, 45–46
logo
  Facebook application, 235
  in header, 210–212

• *M* •

mail. *See* e-mail
Make Changes button, cPanel, 35
Manage Members option, Admin menu,
  131–132
Manage Plugins page, 60, 70, 73, 222,
  226–228, 285–287
Manage Themes page, 59, 77, 190–191
manual installation
  BuddyPress
    activating BuddyPress after, 72–73
    downloading BuddyPress files, 71
    overview, 66, 71
    uploading BuddyPress files, 71–72
  plugin
    activating on WordPress
      dashboard, 226
    downloading files from WordPress
      Plugin Directory, 223–225
    overview, 222–223
    uploading files to Web server, 226
Mark as Read option, Inbox page, 123
Mark as Unread option, Inbox page, 123
Max Groups to Show option, Groups
  widget, 178

Max Items to Show option, Site Wide Activity widget, 173

Max Members to Show option, Members widget, 175

media, social. *See* social media, integrating

Media Library page, 58

Media menu, WordPress, 58

Media option, Settings menu, 62

media plugin, 246–247

media upload buttons, Site Options page, 55

Member Directory, 133, 136, 137, 201

members
  avatars
    Author Avatar List, 243
    BuddyPress Settings page, 83–85
    changing, 110–111, 122
    defined, 2, 18
    group, 130, 156, 159
    Recently Active Member Avatars widget, 182
    Who's Online Avatars widget, 182
  banning, 131
  forums
    on BuddyPress.Org Web site, 276–278
    enabling with Groups feature, 154–155
    existing installation, using, 96–97
    group, 160–162
    new installation, setting up, 95–96
    overview, 2, 19, 88, 93–94
    support, 22
  on group front page, 160
  profiles
    Activity feature, 116–120
    blog, creating from, 143–144
    blog activity in, 149–150
    Blogs feature, 122
    Extended Profiles component, 2, 18, 91–93, 103–104
    Friends feature, 126–127
    Groups feature, 127–133
    Messages feature, 123–126
    overview, 115–116

Profile page, 120–122

Settings feature, 133–134

updates, on Activity page, 116

WordPress, 60

promoting, 132

sign up process
  activating account, 111–113
  overview, 108
  registration, 108–111

status updates, 19, 116, 118–120

members folder, 195

Members option
  Groups menu, 133, 163
  Search feature, 139

Members widget, 171, 175–177

membership, social community, 14

memory limit, PHP, 39

Menus section, Site Options page, 56

message, private, 2, 90–91

message board, 88

Message text box, Compose page, 125

Messages item, My Account menu, 114

Messages page
  composing messages, 125
  Inbox, managing, 123–124
  notifications, 126
  overview, 123
  sent messages, viewing, 124–125

Meta widget, 171

Mezzoblue CSS Crib Sheet, 214

microblogging, 237

Miscellaneous option, Settings menu, 62

mod re_write module, 37

Moderator, 132

Most Members option
  Groups Directory, 155
  My Groups page, 128

MuddyPress theme, 258

Multi Select Box option, Field Type drop-down menu, 100

Multi User option, WordPress, 17

Multi-Line Text Box option, Field Type drop-down menu, 100

My Account menu
  Activity item, 116–120
  Blogs item, 122
  Friends item, 126–127
  Groups item, 127–133
  Messages item, 123–126
  overview, 114, 115–116
  Profile item, 120–122
  Settings item, 133–134
My Activity stream, 116–117
My Blogs item, Site Admin menu, 143
My Blogs menu, 114
My Friends list, 126–127
My Friends page, 126–127
My Groups page, 127–128
My Media menu, 246–247
MySQL
  database, setting up, 33–35
  in WordPress platform, 28
MySQL Databases icon, cPanel, 34

• *N* •

name, MySQL database, 34–35
Name field
  cPanel, 34
  Install Plugins page, 220
  Sign Up page, 110
  Users page, 51
navigation bar, 115
navigation menu
  BuddyPress
    Activity item, 116–120
    Blogs item, 122
    Friends item, 126–127
    Groups item, 127–133
    Messages item, 123–126
    overview, 115–116
    Profile item, 120–122
    Settings item, 133–134
  WordPress dashboard, 48
network, blog, 17
network, social. *See* social media,
    integrating

New Blog Comments Only option,
    Activity page, 117
New Blog Posts Only option, Activity
    page, 117
New Friendships Only option, Activity
    page, 118
New Group Forum Replies Only option,
    Activity page, 118
New Group Forum Topics Only option,
    Activity page, 117
New Ticket link, BuddyPress Trac, 280
New Yorker theme, 258, 259
Newest filter, Install Plugins page, 219
Newest option
  Groups widget, 157, 178
  Members widget, 176
Newly Created option
  Groups Directory, 156
  My Groups page, 128
News section, group front page, 160
niche communities, 1–2
nightly build, 280, 283–285
Ning.com social network, 255
No Filter option, Activity page, 117
Notices page, 126
Notifications item, Settings page
    subnavigation menu, 133–134
Notifications menu, 114
Nourish Network Web site, 263–264
Number of Items per Page option, Site
    Wide Activity widget, 173

• *O* •

Obama, Barack, 14
Occupation field, Profile Field
    Setup page, 98
Only Logged In Users Can Create New
    Blogs option, Site Options page, 53, 143
Only User Accounts Can Be Created
    option, Site Options page, 53, 143
Open Source Initiative Web site, 229
open source software, 229–230
Options option, Site Admin menu, 52–56
Options page, plugin, 226–227

Other Versions field, Group Forum Subscription for BuddyPress plugin page, 224
Other WordPress News box, dashboard, 274–275
owner, blog, 50

• *P* •

p CSS selector, 205
Pages menu, WordPress, 58
Pages widget, 171
parent/child theme relationship
  child theme, 195–196
  child theme folder, creating, 196–199
  custom CSS file, using in child theme, 199
  images, using in child theme, 199–200
  overview, 74, 193–194
  parent template files, modifying, 200–201
  parent theme, 194–195
password
  changing, 133
  MySQL database, 35
  test account, 109
Password text box
  WordPress installation page, 41
  WordPress login page, 46
PASSWORD variable, Site Options page, 55
People Call Me (Core) field, Profile Field Setup page, 98
% unit of measure, 214
Permalinks option, Settings menu, 62
permissions, file, 36, 44
PHP (PHP Hypertext Preprocessor)
  configuration of, 38–39
  file permissions, 36, 44
  MySQL database, 33
  in WordPress platform, 27–31
php.ini file, 38–39
Plugin Directory, WordPress, 70, 219, 223–225, 241
Plugin Editor page, 60

Plugin Homepage field, Group Forum Subscription for BuddyPress plugin page, 224
plugins
  Author Avatar List, 243
  BP-FB Connect, 233–236, 246
  BuddyPress Events Calendar, 244
  BuddyPress Geo, 244–245
  BuddyPress Group Twitter, 237–238
  BuddyPress Privacy Component, 242
  BuddyPress Stats, 247–248
  Featured Members Widget, 242–243
  forums covering, 277
  Group Forum Subscription for BuddyPress
    automatic installation of, 220–222
    manual installation of, 222–226
    Options page, 227
  installing
    manually, 222–226
    overview, 218–219
    using Install Plugins interface, 219–222
  Kaltura Media Component, 246–247
  open source software, 229–230
  Options page, 226–227
  overview, 19–20, 217–218, 241–242
  SEO for BuddyPress, 245–246
  uninstalling, 227–228
  Welcome Pack, 248–249
Plugins check box, Site Options page, 56
Plugins menu, 59–60, 67, 70, 237, 285
Plugins page, 241–242
political social communities, 14
Popular filter, Install Plugins page, 219
Popular option
  Groups widget, 157, 178
  Members widget, 176
Popular Tags section, Install Plugins page, 219
post, blog
  on Activity page, 116
  in activity stream, 148
  publishing, 151–152
Post a New Topic form, Forum page, 161–162
Post Tags option, Posts menu, 58

Post Update button, Activity page, 120
Posts menu, WordPress, 57–58, 151
Press This application, 61
Preview link, Manage Themes page, 77, 190
Privacy Component plugin, 242
Privacy option, Settings menu, 62
Privacy options, Create a Blog page, 143
private blog, 110, 143, 149
private group, 130, 160
Private Messaging component, 2, 90–91
profile
  Activity feature
    navigating, 116–118
    overview, 116
    status updates, 118–120
  blog, creating from, 143–144
  blog activity in, 149–150
  Blogs feature, 122
  Extended Profiles component, 2, 18, 91–93, 103–104
  Friends feature
    My Friends list, 126–127
    overview, 126
  Groups feature
    creating new groups, 128–130
    managing groups, 130–133
    My Groups list, 128
    overview, 127–128
  Messages feature
    composing messages, 125
    managing Inbox, 123–124
    notifications, 126
    overview, 123
    viewing sent messages, 124–125
  overview, 115–116
  Profile page
    changing avatar, 122
    editing, 121–122
    overview, 120
  Settings feature, 133–134
  updates, on Activity page, 116
  WordPress, 60
profile field, 98–101
Profile Field Setup link, BuddyPress menu, 79

Profile Field Setup page, 98–99, 102
profile group, 83, 98, 101–104
Profile Group Name text box, WordPress, 102
Profile item, My Account menu, 114
Profile page
  changing avatar, 122
  editing, 121–122
  overview, 120
properties, CSS, 207–208
`pt` unit of measure, 213
public blog, 110
public group, 130
Public item, Profile page subnavigation menu, 120
publisher, site, 48
publishing posts, 151–152
purchasing domain name, 24, 26
Purple & Black theme, 257
`px` unit of measure, 213

• R •

Radio Buttons option, Field Type drop-down menu, 100
Random Blog item, Visit menu, 114
Random Group item, Visit menu, 114
Random Member item, Visit menu, 114
Rating field, Install Plugins page, 220
RDBMS (relational database management system), 28
Read option, Inbox page Select drop-down menu, 123
Reading option, Settings menu, 62
`readme.txt` file, plugin, 225
Recent Comments widget, 171
Recent News field, Create a Group page, 129
Recent Posts widget, 171, 182
Recently Active Member Avatars widget, 171, 182
Recently Updated filter, Install Plugins page, 219
Registered item
  Blogs page, 50, 145
  Users page, 51

registrar, domain name, 25–26
registration
  domain name
    cost of, 25
    general discussion, 24
    by Web host, 29
  WordPress user, 53, 54
registration folder, 195
registration page, user, 143, 144
relational database management system
    (RDBMS), 28
Remember Me check box, WordPress
    login page, 46
Report a Bug button, 278
Request Membership button, group front
    page, 160
requests, forums covering, 277
Requires WordPress Version field, Group
    Forum Subscription for BuddyPress
    plugin page, 224
Roadmap, BuddyPress Trac, 279
root directory, 35–36
RSS feed
  BuddyPress.org, 274–275
  forum, 277–278
RSS widget, 171
running WordPress install script, 39–44

• **S** •

Sabin-Wilson, Lisa, 4
safe mode, 36
Sans-serif fonts, 213
Save button
  Add Field page, 100
  Groups widget, 178
  Members widget, 175
  Site Wide Activity widget, 173
  Welcome widget, 180
Save Changes button
  Editing page, 121
  Facebook Edit application page, 235
Save Settings button
  BuddyPress Component Setup
    page, 148
  BuddyPress Settings page, 85

screenshot, child theme, 189
screenshot.png file, 189, 196
Search Blogs feature, WordPress, 49
Search Engine Optimization (SEO) for
    BuddyPress plugin, 245–246
Search feature
  Blogs page, 49, 144–145
  Forum Listing, 277
  Install Plugins page, 219–220
  navigating community with, 137–139
  overview, 19
Search Plugins button, Install Plugins
    page, 67–68
Search Users feature, WordPress, 49
Search widget, 171
Secret, Facebook, 235
Select drop-down menu, Inbox page, 123
selectors, CSS, 204
Send Invites link, Groups menu, 133, 163
Send Message button
  Compose page, 125
  Profile page, 120
Send To field, Compose page, 125
Sent Messages page, 124–125
SEO (Search Engine Optimization) for
    BuddyPress plugin, 245–246
Serif fonts, 213
server, Web
  configurations, for WordPress MU
    Apache, 37
    DNS, 38
    mod re_write module, 37
    overview, 37
    PHP, 38–39
    Virtual Host, 37–38
  uploading plugin files to, 226
Server Address text box, WordPress
    installation page, 41
Set Up a New bbPress Installation option,
    Forums Setup page, 93, 95
Settings item, My Account menu, 114
Settings menu, WordPress, 61–62
Settings page, 133–134
Shouty theme, 255–256
Sign Up link, Site Admin menu, 108
Sign Up page, 101, 102, 108–110

sign up process
  activating account, 111–113
  overview, 108
  registration, 108–111
Site Activity stream, 134–139, 149, 157–158
Site Admin Email text box, Site Options
    page, 53
Site Admin menu, WordPress
  Admin option, 48–49
  blog, creating from member profile, 143
  Blogs option, 49–50
  new member registration, 108
  Options option, 52–56
  overview, 48
  themes, enabling in, 189
  Themes option, 52
  Upgrade option, 56
  Users option, 50–51
site administrator, 48
Site Name text box, Site Options page, 53
Site Options page, 52–56, 142–143
site publisher, 48
Site Themes page, 52, 76, 190
Site Title text box, WordPress
    installation page, 42
Site Upgrade page, 56
Site Wide Activity widget, 149, 157, 160,
    172–175
SITE_NAME variable, Site Options page, 55
SITE_URL variable, Site Options page, 55
sites
  activating theme on, 190–191
  BuddyPress
    downloading files from, 71
    as example of platform, 262
    forums on, 276–278
    overview, 22
    plugins, 248
    subscribing to, 274–275
    themes directory, 186
  BuddyPress implementations on
    BuddyPress, 262
    Flokka, 268

GigaOM Pro, 266–267
    Nourish Network, 263–264
    overview, 261
    Tasty Kitchen, 272
    Unstructure, 269
    VW TankWars, 271
    We Heart This, 265–266
    WeEarth, 264–265
    Young People, 270
  BuddyPress resources, 80
  development tools
    domain name extensions, 25
    domain name fees, 25
    domain name registration, 26
    overview, 24
  social communities on, 13–14
  themes, activating, 75–77
  WordPress MU resources, 80
social community, BuddyPress
  admin bar, navigating, 113–115
  blogs
    adding, 146–148
    deleting multiple, 146
    enabling user blog creation, 142–144
    individual, 145–146
    managing, 144–148
    overview, 2, 53–54, 141–142
    post, on Activity page, 116
    privacy options, 110
    publishing posts, 151–152
    Search feature, 144–145
    storage space for uploads, 55
    test account, 109–110
    tracking activity, 148–150
    Web hosting, 27–36
  building, 11–14
  directories, 134–139
  forums
    on BuddyPress.Org Web site, 276–278
    enabling with Groups feature, 154–155
    existing installation, using, 96–97
    group, 160–162
    new installation, setting up, 95–96

overview, 2, 19, 88, 93–94
support, 22
Groups feature
　Activity page, 116
　enabling, 154–155
　forums, 160–162
　front page items, 158–160
　Groups Directory, 155–156
　Groups menu, 163
　Groups widget, 157
　joining, 160
　managing groups, 130–133
　My Groups list, 128
　new groups, creating, 128–130
　overview, 18, 90, 127–128, 153
　Site Activity, 157–158
overview, 1–2, 107
participating in, 21–22
profiles
　Activity feature, 116–120
　blog, creating from, 143–144
　blog activity in, 149–150
　Blogs feature, 122
　Extended Profiles component, 2, 18,
　　91–93, 103–104
　Friends feature, 126–127
　Groups feature, 127–133
　Messages feature, 123–126
　overview, 115–116
　Profile feature, 120–122
　Settings feature, 133–134
　updates, on Activity page, 116
　WordPress, 60
searches, 134–139
sign up process
　activating account, 111–113
　overview, 108
　registration, 108–111
Site Activity stream, 134–139
social media, integrating
　Facebook, 232–236
　overview, 231
　popular social networks, 231–232
　Twitter, 237–238

source code, 280
South by Southwest Interactive, 13
Spam option, Blogs page, 146
SQL (Structured Query Language), 28
State/Province field, Profile Field Setup
　page, 99
statistics, WordPress, 48
Stats plugin, 247–248
status update, 19, 116, 118–120
storage space, blog upload, 55
stream, activity. *See* activity stream
Structured Query Language (SQL), 28
style sheet, child theme, 189
style.css file, 189, 196, 197–199, 202, 213
styling theme, with CSS
　additional resources, 214
　background color, changing, 208–210
　classes, 205–206
　font style, color, and size, changing,
　　212–214
　IDs, 205–206
　overview, 203–204
　personal logo, using in header, 210–212
　properties, 207–208
　selectors, 204–205
　values, 207–208
subdirectory, 38, 40, 142
subdomain, 38, 40, 142, 281–283
Subject field, Compose page, 125
Submit button, WordPress installation
　page, 42
subnavigation menu
　Groups, 130–133
　Messages page
　　Compose item, 125
　　Inbox item, 123
　　Notices item, 126
　　Sent Messages item, 124
　of profile navigation menu, 116
　Profile page, 120–122
　Settings page, 133–134
Subscriber role, blog user, 54
support forums, 22, 276–278
SVN (Subversion), 285

• T •

tag, theme, 198
Tag Cloud widget, 171
Tags page, 58
Tags text box, Post a New Topic form, 161–162
TankWars Web site, 14, 271
Tasty Kitchen Web site, 14, 242–243, 272
TDI clean diesel fuel, 271
template files, modifying parent, 200–201
test environment, setting up, 280–283
Text Box option, Field Type drop-down menu, 100
Text widget, 171
text-align CSS property, 208
themes
  activating, 75–78, 190–191
  BuddyPress Classic, 21, 107, 168–169, 172–175
  BuddyPress Default
    activating, 76–77
    for blogs, 147–148
    child theme folder, creating, 196–197
    versus Classic, 107
    general discussion, 167–169, 258–259
    overview, 20, 107
    as parent theme, 194
    widgets, 170
  downloading, 187–189
  enabling in WordPress MU, 189–190
  extending capabilities through, 20–21
  folders, moving, 74–75
  free
    Avenue K9, 252
    Bruce, 253–254
    BuddyPress Community, 256–257
    BuddyPress Corporate, 252–253
    BuddyPress Default Theme, 258–259
    BuddyPress Fun, 254–255
    finding, 185–187
    future of, 259
    MuddyPress, 258
    New Yorker, 258
    overview, 251
    Purple & Black, 257
    Shouty, 255–256
  installing, 187–189
  overview, 74, 185, 193
  parent template files, modifying, 200–201
  parent/child relationships
    child theme, 195–196
    child theme folder, creating, 196–199
    custom CSS file, using in child theme, 199
    images, using in child theme, 199–200
    overview, 193–194
    parent theme, 194–195
  styling with CSS
    additional resources, 214
    background color, changing, 208–210
    classes, 205–206
    font style, color, and size, changing, 212–214
    IDs, 205–206
    overview, 203–204
    personal logo, using in header, 210–212
    properties, 207–208
    selectors, 204–205
    values, 207–208
  WordPress, using with BuddyPress, 201–202
Themes Directory, WordPress, 190, 248
Themes option
  Appearance menu, 59
  Site Admin menu, 52, 189–190
third party plugin, forums covering, 277
third-party application, 27
This Is a Hidden Group option, Create a Group — Settings page, 130
This Is a Notice to All Users checkbox, Compose page, 125
This Is a Private Group option, Create a Group — Settings page, 130
This Is a Public Group option, Create a Group — Settings page, 130

3oneseven Web site, 187
tickets, 279–280
Timeline, BuddyPress Trac, 279
title
  blog, 50
  group, 159
  test account blog, 110
  Web site, 42
Title text box
  Post a New Topic form, 161
  Welcome widget, 180
Tools menu, WordPress, 60–61
Tools option, Tools menu, 61
topic, forum, 160, 162
top-level domain extension, 25
Trac, 279–280, 283–284
tracking, blog, 2, 19, 87–89, 148–150
transfer mode, FTP, 36
troubleshooting, forums covering, 276
Trunk directory, 280, 283–284
tweaking theme, with CSS
  additional resources, 214
  background color, changing, 208–210
  classes, 205–206
  font style, color, and size, changing,
    212–214
  IDs, 205–206
  overview, 203–204
  personal logo, using in header, 210–212
  properties, 207–208
  selectors, 204–205
  values, 207–208
Tweets, 237
Twitter, 22, 118, 232, 237–238, 274–275

• U •

Uniform Resource Locator (URL)
  blog, 50
  login page, 44
  running WordPress install script, 39
  subdirectory, 38
  subdomain, 38
  test account blog, 109
  WordPress login page, 45–46
uninstalling plugin, 227–228

Unread option, Inbox page Select drop-
    down menu, 123
Unstructure Web site, 269
update
  profile, 116
  status, 19, 116, 118–120
Update Options button
  Facebook Connect Plugin
    Options page, 236
  Site Options page, 143
  Site Themes page, 56, 190
Update Themes button, Site
    Themes page, 76
Updates Only option
  Activity page, 117
  Groups page, 133
upgrade, BuddyPress, 274, 285–287
Upgrade Automatically link, Manage
    Plugins page, 286
Upgrade option
  Site Admin menu, 56
  Tools menu, 61
Upgrade Plugin page, 286–287
Upload Image button, 110
Upload New Media page, 58
uploading
  BuddyPress files to host, 71–72
  defined, 31
  files to WordPress host, 35–36
  plugin files to Web server, 226
  WordPress software, 33
uploads, blog, 55
URL (Uniform Resource Locator)
  blog, 50
  login page, 44
  running WordPress install script, 39
  subdirectory, 38
  subdomain, 38
  test account blog, 109
  WordPress login page, 45–46
Use an Existing bbPress Installation
    option, Forums Setup page, 93, 96
user. *See also* community, BuddyPress;
    members
  account deletion settings, 84
  adding new, on Users page, 51

user blog
  enabling creation of, 142–144
  managing
    adding blogs, 146–148
    deleting multiple blogs, 146
    individual blogs, 145–146
    overview, 144
    Search feature, 144–145
  overview, 53–54, 141–142
  publishing posts, 151–152
  tracking activity, 148–150
User drop-down menu, cPanel, 35
User Name text box, WordPress
    installation page, 41
user registration page, 143, 144
user-generated content, 231
username
  disallowed, on WordPress, 54
  logging into site with, 112
  MySQL database, 35
  with WordPress dashboard
    administrative access, 56
Username field
  Sign Up page, 108
  Users page, 51
  WordPress login page, 46
USERNAME variable, Site Options
    page, 55
Users item, Blogs page, 50, 145
Users menu, WordPress, 60
Users option, Site Admin menu, 50–51
Users page, 50–51, 60

● **V** ●

value, CSS property, 207–208
Version field
  Group Forum Subscription for
    BuddyPress plugin page, 224
  Install Plugins page, 220
View option, FTP program, 198

View Tickets link, BuddyPress Trac, 279
<VirtualHost> section, httpd.conf
    file, 37–38
Visit Blog button, Blogs Directory, 137
Visit menu, 114
Visit option, Blogs page, 146
VW TankWars Web site, 14, 271

● **W** ●

W3Schools' CSS tutorial, 214
We Heart This Web site, 265–266
Web address
  blog, 50
  login page, 44
  running WordPress install script, 39
  subdirectory, 38
  subdomain, 38
  test account blog, 109
  WordPress login page, 45–46
Web hosting
  account administration interface, 33–35
  bandwidth, 29–31
  disk space, 29–30
  by domain registrars, 26
  MySQL, 28
  overview, 27–28
  PHP, 28
  root directory, 35–36
  specialized, 28–29
  support services, 28–29
Web server
  configurations, for WordPress MU
    Apache, 37
    DNS, 38
    mod re_write module, 37
    overview, 37
    PHP, 38–39
    Virtual Host, 37–38
  uploading plugin files to, 226

Web Site field, Profile Field Setup
    page, 98
Web sites
  activating theme on, 190–191
  BuddyPress
    downloading files from, 71
    as example of platform, 262
    forums on, 276–278
    overview, 22
    plugins, 248
    subscribing to, 274–275
    themes directory, 186
  BuddyPress implementations on
    BuddyPress, 262
    Flokka, 268
    GigaOM Pro, 266–267
    Nourish Network, 263–264
    overview, 261
    Tasty Kitchen, 272
    Unstructure, 269
    VW TankWars, 271
    We Heart This, 265–266
    WeEarth, 264–265
    Young People, 270
  BuddyPress resources, 80
  development tools
    domain name extensions, 25
    domain name fees, 25
    domain name registration, 26
    overview, 24
  social communities on, 13–14
  themes, activating, 75–77
  WordPress MU resources, 80
WebsiteTips.com CSS page, 214
WeEarth Web site, 87, 264–265
Welcome Email text box,
    Site Options page, 55
Welcome Pack plugin, 248–249
Welcome to WordPress MU message, 39
Welcome widget, 171, 180–182
Westciv Web site, 214
What Do I Need? section, WordPress, 39
What's New? text box, Activity page, 120

Who's Online Avatars widget, 171, 182
widgets
  Archives, 171, 182
  blog versus community, 182–183
  Calendar, 171
  Categories, 171, 182
  Groups, 157, 171, 177–179
  Links, 171
  Members, 171, 175–177
  Meta, 171
  overview, 169–172
  Pages, 171
  Recent Comments, 171
  Recent Posts, 171, 182
  Recently Active Member Avatars,
    171, 182
  RSS, 171
  Search, 171
  Site Wide Activity, 149, 157, 160, 172–175
  Tag Cloud, 171
  Text, 171
  Welcome, 171, 180–182
  Who's Online Avatars, 171, 182
Widgets option, Appearance menu, 59
Widgets page
  adding widgets, 170
  Groups widget, 178
  Members widget, 175
  Site Wide Activity widget, 172–173
  Welcome widget, 180
wildcard record, 38
wire, activity, 18
Wire item, My Account menu, 114
WordPress Bible (Brazell), 4–5
WordPress Codex, 285
WordPress community support
    forum, 94
WordPress Extend page, 228
WordPress For Dummies
    (Sabin-Wilson), 4
WordPress MU platform
  activating BuddyPress, 72–73
  as advantage of BuddyPress, 15

WordPress MU platform *(continued)*
  automatic installation of
    BuddyPress, 67
  bbPress forums, setting up, 93–97
  blog tracking, enabling, 148
  BuddyPress components
    activity streams, 86–87
    bbPress forums, 88, 89
    Blog Tracking, 87–88, 89
    Extended Profiles, 91–93
    Friends, 88
    Groups, 90, 91
    overview, 85–86
    Private Messaging, 90–91
  BuddyPress menu, 78–79
  BuddyPress settings, configuring
    general, 81–85
  dashboard
    administrator management
      of user's, 145
    Appearance menu, 59
    blog tracking, enabling, 148
    Comments menu, 59
    forum options, enabling, 154
    general site options, 57–62
    groups, enabling, 154
    Links menu, 58
    Media menu, 58
    navigating, 47–48
    Other WordPress News box, 274–275
    overview, 45
    Pages menu, 58
    plugins, activating, 226
    plugins, finding and installing, 218–222
    Plugins menu, 59–60
    Posts menu, 57–58
    publishing blog posts, 151
    Settings menu, 61–62
    Site Admin menu, 48–56
    theme, activating new, 189–191
    Tools menu, 60–61
    user blog creation, enabling, 142
    Users menu, 60
    widgets, 170

  domain names for site
    extensions, 25
    fees, 25
    overview, 24
    registration, 26
  forum options, enabling, 154
  as foundation for BuddyPress, 16–18
  FTP, 31–32
  general discussion, 1–3, 23–24
  groups, enabling, 154
  install script, running, 39–44
  installation page, 40–42
  logging into, 45–46
  MySQL database, setting up, 33–35
  overview, 23–24
  planned upgrade for, 75, 168
  as platform for BuddyPress, 16–18
  plugins, 218–222, 241–242
  profile groups and fields, building,
    98–104
  publishing blog posts, 151
  resources, 4–5
  themes
    activating BuddyPress, 75–76
    enabling in, 189–190
    using with BuddyPress, 201–202
  as third party application, 27
  uploading files to host, 35–36
  user blog creation, enabling, 142
  Web hosting
    bandwidth, 29–31
    disk space, 29–30
    MySQL, 28
    overview, 27–28
    PHP, 28
    specialized, 28–29
  Web server configurations for
    Apache, 37
    DNS, 38
    `mod re_write` module, 37
    overview, 37
    PHP, 38–39
    `Virtual Host`, 37–38
  widgets, 170–171, 182–183

WordPress Plugin Directory, 70, 219,
    223–225, 241
WordPress Themes Directory, 190, 248
WordPress.com, 16–17
/wordpress-mu folder, 35–36
WordPress.org, 16–17, 24, 27
#wp-admin-bar CSS selector, 205
wp-config.php file, 43, 44
/wp-content/plugins folder, 71, 226
/wp-content/plugins/buddypress/
    bp-themes folder, 74–75
/wp-content/themes folder, 75,
    188, 194
WPMU Dev Web site, 187, 248
Writing option, Settings menu, 62

• Y •

Young People Web site, 270
Your Profile option, Users menu, 60
YouTube, 232

• Z •

Zip Archive link, Trunk directory, 283
Zip file
  BuddyPress development version, 283
  Group Forum Subscription for
    BuddyPress plugin, 224
  theme, 187
  WordPress software, 33

Internet

Blogging For Dummies,
2nd Edition
978-0-470-23017-6

eBay For Dummies,
6th Edition
978-0-470-49741-8

Facebook For Dummies
978-0-470-26273-3

Google Blogger
For Dummies
978-0-470-40742-4

Web Marketing
For Dummies,
2nd Edition
978-0-470-37181-7

WordPress For Dummies,
2nd Edition
978-0-470-40296-2

Language & Foreign Language

French For Dummies
978-0-7645-5193-2

Italian Phrases
For Dummies
978-0-7645-7203-6

Spanish For Dummies
978-0-7645-5194-9

Spanish For Dummies,
Audio Set
978-0-470-09585-0

Macintosh

Mac OS X Snow Leopard
For Dummies
978-0-470-43543-4

Math & Science

Algebra I For Dummies
978-0-7645-5325-7

Biology For Dummies
978-0-7645-5326-4

Calculus For Dummies
978-0-7645-2498-1

Chemistry For Dummies
978-0-7645-5430-8

Microsoft Office

Excel 2007 For Dummies
978-0-470-03737-9

Office 2007 All-in-One
Desk Reference
For Dummies
978-0-471-78279-7

Music

Guitar For Dummies,
2nd Edition
978-0-7645-9904-0

iPod & iTunes
For Dummies,
6th Edition
978-0-470-39062-7

Piano Exercises
For Dummies
978-0-470-38765-8

Parenting & Education

Parenting For Dummies,
2nd Edition
978-0-7645-5418-6

Type 1 Diabetes
For Dummies
978-0-470-17811-9

Pets

Cats For Dummies,
2nd Edition
978-0-7645-5275-5

Dog Training For Dummies,
2nd Edition
978-0-7645-8418-3

Puppies For Dummies,
2nd Edition
978-0-470-03717-1

Religion & Inspiration

The Bible For Dummies
978-0-7645-5296-0

Catholicism For Dummies
978-0-7645-5391-2

Women in the Bible
For Dummies
978-0-7645-8475-6

Self-Help & Relationship

Anger Management
For Dummies
978-0-470-03715-7

Overcoming Anxiety
For Dummies
978-0-7645-5447-6

Sports

Baseball For Dummies,
3rd Edition
978-0-7645-7537-2

Basketball For Dummies,
2nd Edition
978-0-7645-5248-9

Golf For Dummies,
3rd Edition
978-0-471-76871-5

Web Development

Web Design All-in-One
For Dummies
978-0-470-41796-6

Windows Vista

Windows Vista
For Dummies
978-0-471-75421-3

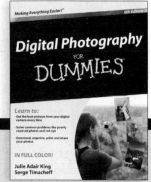

Business/Accounting & Bookkeeping

Bookkeeping For Dummies
978-0-7645-9848-7

eBay Business
All-in-One For Dummies,
2nd Edition
978-0-470-38536-4

Job Interviews
For Dummies,
3rd Edition
978-0-470-17748-8

Resumes For Dummies,
5th Edition
978-0-470-08037-5

Stock Investing
For Dummies,
3rd Edition
978-0-470-40114-9

Successful Time
Management
For Dummies
978-0-470-29034-7

Computer Hardware

BlackBerry For Dummies,
3rd Edition
978-0-470-45762-7

Computers For Seniors
For Dummies
978-0-470-24055-7

iPhone For Dummies,
2nd Edition
978-0-470-42342-4

Laptops For Dummies,
3rd Edition
978-0-470-27759-1

Macs For Dummies,
10th Edition
978-0-470-27817-8

Cooking & Entertaining

Cooking Basics
For Dummies,
3rd Edition
978-0-7645-7206-7

Wine For Dummies,
4th Edition
978-0-470-04579-4

Diet & Nutrition

Dieting For Dummies,
2nd Edition
978-0-7645-4149-0

Nutrition For Dummies,
4th Edition
978-0-471-79868-2

Weight Training
For Dummies,
3rd Edition
978-0-471-76845-6

Digital Photography

Digital Photography
For Dummies,
6th Edition
978-0-470-25074-7

Photoshop Elements 7
For Dummies
978-0-470-39700-8

Gardening

Gardening Basics
For Dummies
978-0-470-03749-2

Organic Gardening
For Dummies,
2nd Edition
978-0-470-43067-5

Green/Sustainable

Green Building
& Remodeling
For Dummies
978-0-470-17559-0

Green Cleaning
For Dummies
978-0-470-39106-8

Green IT For Dummies
978-0-470-38688-0

Health

Diabetes For Dummies,
3rd Edition
978-0-470-27086-8

Food Allergies
For Dummies
978-0-470-09584-3

Living Gluten-Free
For Dummies
978-0-471-77383-2

Hobbies/General

Chess For Dummies,
2nd Edition
978-0-7645-8404-6

Drawing For Dummies
978-0-7645-5476-6

Knitting For Dummies,
2nd Edition
978-0-470-28747-7

Organizing For Dummies
978-0-7645-5300-4

SuDoku For Dummies
978-0-470-01892-7

Home Improvement

Energy Efficient Homes
For Dummies
978-0-470-37602-7

Home Theater
For Dummies,
3rd Edition
978-0-470-41189-6

Living the Country Lifestyle
All-in-One For Dummies
978-0-470-43061-3

Solar Power Your Home
For Dummies
978-0-470-17569-9

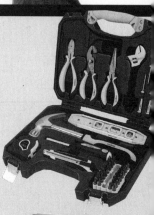